ANCHORED GRACE
PUBLISHING

My Graceful Transition
A Daily Devotional for
Newly Retired Women

365 DAILY INSPIRATIONS AND PRAYERS FOR FINDING PURPOSE, FAITH, AND JOY

A Gift for You

Thank you for choosing this devotional.

To support your journey of faith, we created a special gift bundle for our readers.

Inside the Anchored Grace Reader Gift Bundle, you will receive:

READER GIFT BUNDLE

- A free digital devotional

- Printable prayer journal pages

- Scripture reflection cards

- Bonus devotionals for different seasons of life

- Daily encouragement from Anchored Grace

Simply scan the QR code below or visit the link to receive your free bundle.

devo.anchoredgraces.com/retiredgift

Scan the QR code with your phone camera or type the link into your browser.

We pray these resources continue to encourage your heart each day.

NEW BEGINNINGS WITH GOD

"See, I am doing a new thing! Now it springs up; do you not perceive it? I am making a way in the wilderness and streams in the wasteland." **Isaiah 43:19**

DEVOTIONAL

After retiring from a long career, Betty found herself standing at the threshold of a new chapter. Initially, she felt lost without her routine, as if the vibrant colors of life had dulled. But one sunny afternoon, while gardening, she noticed a tiny sprout pushing its way through the soil. In that moment, she realized just as that little plant was beginning anew, so could she. She joined a painting class, met new friends, and discovered the joy of creating beauty for the first time. Each day became a delightful adventure, filled with new possibilities and laughter.

Life teaches us that every ending has the potential to be a beautiful new beginning with God's gentle guidance.

DAILY REFLECTION

What new beginnings is God inviting you to embrace in this season of your life? How can you open your heart to the possibilities that await?

PRAYER

Dear God, thank You for the gift of new beginnings. Help me to trust in Your plans and embrace each day with hope and joy. Amen.

"Every sunrise brings a new opportunity to start afresh with God's grace."

TRUSTING GOD'S TIMING

"For I know the plans I have for you, declares the Lord, plans to prosper you and not to harm you, plans to give you hope and a future." **Jeremiah 29:11**

DEVOTIONAL

In her garden, Margaret toiled each spring, eagerly planting seeds for blooms she hoped to see right away. Yet, each year was a lesson in patience as she watched those seedlings push through the soil at their own pace. One sunny afternoon, as she sat sipping tea, she noticed the vibrant roses finally bursting forth after weeks of waiting—each petal a testament to the beauty of trusting the process. It dawned on her that just as flowers take time to flourish, so too does God's plan for her life, unfolding with each passing day.

Trusting in God's timing not only nurtures our patience but reveals the beauty of His perfect plans for our lives.

DAILY REFLECTION

What areas of your life do you find it hardest to trust God's timing, and how might surrendering those to Him bring you peace?

PRAYER

Dear God, thank You for the gift of time and the promise of Your perfect plan. Help me to rest in Your timing and to find joy in each moment You provide.

"God's timing is not just about waiting; it's about growing and discovering His purpose in the waiting."

EMBRACING GRACE, NOT PERFECTION

"Being confident of this, that he who began a good work in you will carry it on to completion until the day of Christ Jesus." **Philippians 1:6**

DEVOTIONAL

Once upon a time, there was a lovely retired woman named Margaret who had spent countless hours perfecting her knitting skills. Every stitch had to be flawless, or she'd unravel it and start over. One sunny afternoon, while chatting with her friend at a garden tea party, she noticed her friend proudly wearing a scarf made from "mistakes". "It adds character," her friend said with a warm smile. Inspired, Margaret decided to embrace her own tiny imperfections, letting those little quirks in her work reflect her journey. The next project she took up was filled with colors and slight mismatches, and she found joy in the vibrant uniqueness of her creation.

Embrace every beautifully imperfect part of your life, for it is a testament to the grace you've received and a reminder that you are a work in progress.

DAILY REFLECTION

What does embracing grace, rather than seeking perfection, look like in your everyday life? How can you extend grace to yourself when you face challenges or setbacks?

PRAYER

Dear Lord, thank You for the gift of grace. Help me to see my value in every moment, to let go of perfection, and to embrace the beautiful journey You've set before me.

"Grace is not about being flawless; it's about being free."

FINDING PEACE IN GOD'S PRESENCE

"Be still, and know that I am God."
Psalm 46:10

DEVOTIONAL

Mabel, a vibrant 65-year-old, often found herself overwhelmed by the mixed feelings that came with retirement. One sunny afternoon, she decided to take a stroll in her garden, where daisies danced in the breeze. As she crouched down to admire their delicate petals, she realized how easy it was to get lost in the to-do lists that plagued her mind. In that moment, she chose to breathe deeply and focus on the simple beauty surrounding her. Instantly, she felt God's peace envelop her like a warm hug, reminding her that she didn't have to accomplish anything to be loved.

Life becomes much more delightful when we acknowledge that God's presence is a source of peace—a refuge in every season of life.

DAILY REFLECTION

What does it mean for you to truly rest in God's presence, even in the quiet moments of your day? How can you invite His peace into your heart as you reflect on the blessings of your journey?

PRAYER

Dear Lord, thank You for being a constant presence in our lives. Help me to seek You daily and find peace in Your loving embrace, resting in the knowledge that You are always near. Amen.

"True peace comes from being fully present with God, where worries dissipate and joy fills the soul."

YOUR IDENTITY IN CHRIST

"Do not fear, for I have redeemed you; I have summoned you by name; you are mine."
Isaiah 43:1

DEVOTIONAL

Once, a retired teacher found herself feeling lost after leaving the classroom. With days stretching ahead, she felt a void, as if her identity had been tied solely to her profession. One sunny afternoon, while sipping tea and watching her granddaughter practice ballet, she felt a stirring in her heart. This little girl, twirling and giggling, reminded her that her value was not just in teaching lessons but in nurturing joy and love in her family. She realized her true identity in Christ was alive and flourishing in the beautiful relationships she now cherished.

You are more than your past; your identity in Christ is a beautiful tapestry woven with love, joy, and purpose in this new chapter of life.

DAILY REFLECTION

What does it mean to you to be a beloved daughter of the King? Can you identify moments in your life when you've felt His presence guiding you and affirming your identity in Him?

PRAYER

Dear Lord, thank You for the gift of my identity as Your child. Help me to embrace the truth that I am loved, valued, and cherished by You, today and every day.

"You are not defined by your past, but by the love of Christ that surrounds you each moment."

GOD'S FAITHFULNESS THROUGH THE YEARS

"The righteous will flourish like a palm tree, they will grow like a cedar of Lebanon; planted in the house of the Lord, they will flourish in the courts of our God. They will still bear fruit in old age, they will stay fresh and green." **Psalm 92:12-14**

DEVOTIONAL

Evelyn sat on her porch, sipping iced tea as she watched the birds flit between the trees—a scene she had taken in countless times over the years. Reflecting on her life, she smiled at the ups and downs: the joy of her children growing, the pain of loss, and the beauty of friendships woven through the fabric of time. One chilly evening, she remembered this promise of faithfulness as a light flickered in her heart during challenging seasons. Each event, whether delightful or difficult, revealed God's unwavering hand leading her gently forward. Standing in her garden, she marveled at how each flower had once been a seed, nurtured by the sun and rain, blossoming beautifully over time.

With every season of life, trust that God's faithfulness will continue to nurture your spirit and help you blossom anew.

DAILY REFLECTION

What moments in your life can you recall where God's faithfulness has been evident, even when times were tough or uncertain?

PRAYER

Dear God, thank you for your unwavering faithfulness throughout the seasons of our lives. Help us to recognize your presence and trust in your plans as we continue our journey.

"Through every chapter of our lives, God has been the constant thread of grace and love."

STRENGTH FOR THE JOURNEY

*"But those who hope in the Lord will renew their strength. They will soar on wings like eagles; they will run and not grow weary, they will walk and not be faint." **Isaiah 40:31***

DEVOTIONAL

Last summer, Doris took up gardening for the first time. Initially, her hands were sore, and the weeds seemed to outnumber her flowers. Frustrated but determined, she kept showing up in her backyard, watering daily and talking to her plants. Slowly but surely, not only did her garden bloom, but she also discovered a new passion that filled her heart with joy and contentment. Just as the flowers flourished with care, Doris realized that nurturing herself and her interests could lead to beautiful new beginnings.

Every day holds the potential for new growth and unexpected joy, so let your heart remain open to the adventures yet to come.

DAILY REFLECTION

What journey are you currently navigating in your life, and how can you seek strength in your faith to guide you through the twists and turns ahead?

PRAYER

Dear Lord, as I walk this phase of my journey, grant me the strength and wisdom to embrace each day with grace. Help me to find delight in the little moments and courage in the challenges ahead.

"Strength grows from the quiet resolve to keep moving forward, even when the path feels uncertain."

A QUIET HEART IN A NOISY WORLD

"In repentance and rest is your salvation, in quietness and trust is your strength."
Isaiah 30:15

DEVOTIONAL

Once upon a time in a charming little town, there lived a retired woman named Eleanor. Every day, she would sit on her porch with a cup of tea, listening to the chatter of the neighborhood children and the distant sounds of bustling cars. One sunny afternoon, Eleanor noticed a few friends were gathered at the park, their laughter echoing through the air. While she enjoyed the merriment, she also craved a moment to breathe deeply and appreciate the gentle rustle of leaves. So, she decided to take a short walk. As she embraced the peacefulness of nature, Eleanor realized that even in a noisy world, a quiet heart can be found when she seeks it in small moments.

In the midst of life's chaos, a few moments of stillness can nourish your spirit and rejuvenate your heart.

DAILY REFLECTION

What are some sacred spaces or moments in your day where you can cultivate a sense of quiet and peace amidst the busyness around you?

PRAYER

Dear God, help me to find stillness in the chaos of my life. May I seek your gentle presence each day and embrace the tranquility that comes from you.

"Amidst the clamor of life, a quiet heart draws closer to the whisper of God."

One Week Together

You've just completed your first week of devotionals.

If these reflections have brought peace or encouragement into your day, would you consider sharing a short Amazon review?

devo.anchoredgraces.com/retired

Your words help other women discover devotionals that may support them on their own faith journey.

Thank you for spending these moments in reflection.

COURAGE TO LET GO

"Forget the former things; do not dwell on the past. See, I am doing a new thing! Now it springs up; do you not perceive it?" **Isaiah 43:18-19**

DEVOTIONAL

Mabel stared out her window at the garden she had tended for years, now filled with daisies and fading roses. After much thought, she decided it was time to clear out some of the overgrown foliage that no longer bloomed with joy. With each clump she tore away, she felt a little lighter. She remembered the vibrant times of her youth as well as the cherished memories of family gatherings, yet realized that new blooms waited to take their place. Her heart danced with excitement as she imagined planting fresh seeds for a new chapter, where vibrant colors could splash across her patio again.

Sometimes, letting go of the past makes space for the beautiful new experiences that await us.

DAILY REFLECTION

What are the things in your life that you've held onto for too long, and how might your world change if you chose to let them go? Reflect on what emotional weight you're carrying and how freedom awaits you if you release it.

PRAYER

Dear Lord, help me find the courage to let go of what no longer serves me. Grant me peace as I release my burdens and embrace the new opportunities You have for me. Fill my heart with hope and joy in this journey of transition.

"Letting go allows for new beginnings to take root in the fertile soil of our hearts."

COURAGE TO LET GO

"But I trust in you, Lord; I say, 'You are my God.' My times are in your hands."
Psalm 31:14-15

DEVOTIONAL

Once upon a time in a quaint little town, there lived a vibrant woman named Mabel. After decades of nurturing her family, Mabel found herself in a house that felt too big and filled with memories that tugged at her heart. One day, while sipping tea on her porch, she watched a young couple struggling to carry a heavy sofa into their new home. Inspired, she realized that just as the couple had to let go of their comfort zones to embrace fresh beginnings, so too could she. Mabel chose to donate some of her cherished possessions, transforming both her space and her spirit, making room for new adventures and connections in her community.

Letting go can be daunting, but it often leads to beautiful new beginnings that enrich our lives.

DAILY REFLECTION

What are the things you've held onto that might be weighing you down, and how could letting go bring you closer to a new chapter in your life?

PRAYER

Dear Lord, grant me the courage to release what no longer serves me, and fill my heart with peace as I embrace the new beginnings you have in store.

"Sometimes, letting go is the greatest act of bravery."

WHEN YOU FEEL OVERLOOKED

*"Since you are precious and honored in my sight, and because I love you, I will give people in exchange for you, nations in exchange for your life." **Isaiah 43:4***

DEVOTIONAL

Margaret sat on her porch, sipping tea and watching the world go by. She felt a twinge of sadness as she noticed how her friends seemed to forget her invitations and often included their newer, fresher friends in their plans. Yet, on one sunny afternoon while reminiscing, she received an unexpected call from her granddaughter who just wanted to hear her voice. "Grandma, you're the best! Can we make cookies together?" In that moment, Margaret realized that even when she felt overlooked, she held a special place in someone's heart—a role that was uniquely her own.

You may feel unnoticed at times, but remember, you are cherished and loved by those who truly matter, often in ways you might not see right away.

DAILY REFLECTION

What are some ways you can remind yourself of your worth and value when you feel overlooked by those around you? How can you seek those moments of connection that truly matter?

PRAYER

Dear Lord, help me to find comfort in Your presence when I feel unseen. Remind me that I am treasured and valued, no matter the circumstances surrounding me. Thank You for Your never-ending love.

"Even in the quietest moments, you are woven into the fabric of God's plan."

RESTING IN HIS PROMISES

*"He says, 'Be still, and know that I am God; I will be exalted among the nations, I will be exalted in the earth.'" **Psalm 46:10***

DEVOTIONAL

Mabel, at 65, found herself tangled in a web of to-do lists and worries, even in retirement. She'd been busy knitting blankets for every grandchild, planning her garden, and volunteering at the community center. One sunny afternoon, while sipping tea on her porch, Mabel noticed how the flowers were blooming without her interference. It dawned on her that just like those flowers, she didn't need to rush to do everything. With a newfound sense of peace, she decided to take it easy, resting in the knowledge that God had everything under control.

The greatest joy in retirement can come from resting in God's promises rather than striving to do it all on our own.

DAILY REFLECTION

What promises of God bring you the deepest comfort in this season of life, and how can you remind yourself of these truths daily?

PRAYER

Dear Lord, thank You for Your faithful promises that soothe and guide our hearts. Help us to rest in Your goodness and find peace in the plans You have for us. Amen.

"Rest is not a destination; it is the embrace of His unwavering love."

BEAUTY FROM BROKENNESS

"and provide for those who grieve in Zion—to bestow on them a crown of beauty instead of ashes, the oil of joy instead of mourning, and a garment of praise instead of a spirit of despair. They will be called oaks of righteousness, a planting of the Lord for the display of his splendor." **Isaiah 61:3**

DEVOTIONAL

Once, there was a woman named Eleanor who had devoted her life to raising her children and nurturing her family. After they grew up and moved away, she found herself feeling lost and a bit broken. One day, she decided to attend a pottery class to fill her time. To her surprise, she discovered the art of kintsugi, where broken pottery is mended with gold. Each piece, once shattered, became a beautiful work of art, unique in its imperfections. Inspired, Eleanor began to embrace the lessons of her own life's bumps and bruises, realizing that her experiences had added depth and strength to her character, much like the gold in the pottery.

Every tear and challenge adds a special sparkle to our story; embrace the cracks, for they make us beautifully whole.

DAILY REFLECTION

What broken pieces in your life have the potential to reveal new beauty and purpose? How might embracing those moments help you grow?

PRAYER

Dear God, thank You for being with us through each season of life. Help us to see Your hand in our brokenness and to embrace the beauty that emerges from it.

"In every crack, there is a chance for light to shine through."

THE POWER OF PRAYER

"Do not be anxious about anything, but in every situation, by prayer and petition, with thanksgiving, present your requests to God. And the peace of God, which transcends all understanding, will guard your hearts and your minds in Christ Jesus." **Philippians 4:6-7**

DEVOTIONAL

Margaret, a lively 65-year-old, found herself feeling restless in retirement. With the days stretching out before her, she sometimes felt a bit lost. One day, she decided to try an old habit: prayer. She began to pray not only for herself but also for others—her family, her friends, and even that sweet neighbor down the street who seemed a bit lonely. As she lifted her heart in gratitude and concern, Margaret felt a renewed sense of purpose, as if she had tapped into an endless well of love and connection. The more she prayed, the more vibrant her days became, paving the way for unexpected friendships and opportunities.

The true power of prayer lies in how it transforms our hearts and our perspectives, reminding us that even in our golden years, we are never alone.

DAILY REFLECTION

What moments in your life have shown you the true power of prayer? How have those experiences shaped your relationship with God and those around you?

PRAYER

Dear Heavenly Father, thank You for the gift of prayer and for hearing our hearts. Help us to trust in Your presence and guidance as we lift our thoughts and worries to You today.

"Prayer is not just a routine; it's a comforting embrace from our Creator."

JOY IN THE ORDINARY

"Rejoice in the Lord always. I will say it again: Rejoice!"
Philippians 4:4

DEVOTIONAL

Mabel woke up one sunny Monday morning, her cozy slippers hugging her feet as she shuffled to the kitchen. While brewing her favorite chamomile tea, she caught sight of her garden through the window—a riot of colors bursting with life. She smiled at the little hummingbird darting to and fro and immediately felt that tingle of joy that comes from nature's simple pleasures. Each flower reminded her that even the ordinary days could bloom with happiness. After sipping her tea, she decided to spend the day tending to her garden, turning the mundane into a joyful celebration of life.

Finding joy in the little things, like a morning cup of tea or a blooming flower, can enrich your everyday routines with happiness and gratitude.

DAILY REFLECTION

What small moments in your daily routine bring you unexpected joy, and how might you be more present to them today?

PRAYER

Dear God, thank you for the gift of each day and the simple joys it brings. Help me to see your hand in the ordinary and to savor the beauty in each moment.

"Joy often hides in the little things, waiting for us to take notice."

GOD'S WISDOM FOR TODAY

"For the Lord gives wisdom; from His mouth come knowledge and understanding."
Proverbs 2:6

DEVOTIONAL

Once, there was a sweet grandmother named Mabel who took it upon herself to bake the most delicious cookies for the church bake sale. As she measured and mixed ingredients, she overheard a group of women whispering about all the things they wished they had done differently in their lives. Mabel paused, flour dust clouding the air, and decided to share her secret: it wasn't so much about how many grand adventures she had experienced, but rather the little, wise choices made each day that filled her heart with joy. By the time the cookies were ready, the laughter and warmth in the kitchen had brewed up a beautiful bond, reminding everyone that wisdom doesn't always come from big experiences, but often from the simple moments of connection.

Even in retirement, seek out the small moments of joy and let God's wisdom guide your everyday choices.

DAILY REFLECTION

What is one area in your life where you feel uncertain, and how can you invite God's wisdom into that situation today?

PRAYER

Dear God, thank you for your unending wisdom and guidance. Help me to seek your truth in every decision I make and to trust that you are leading me on the right path.

"Embracing God's wisdom opens the door to peace in our hearts and clarity in our minds."

FREEDOM FROM FEAR

*But now this is what the Lord says— he who created you, Jacob, he who formed you, Israel: "Do not fear, for I have redeemed you; I have summoned you by name; you are mine. **Isaiah 43:1***

DEVOTIONAL

Once, there was a spirited grandmother named Edna who had always dreamed of soaring in a hot air balloon. With a heart full of excitement but a whisper of fear fluttering in her mind, she stepped into the basket. As the balloon rose high above the ground, she looked down at the world and felt the wind around her. Suddenly, the fear that had almost kept her grounded turned into exhilaration. She laughed with delight, realizing that sometimes, freedom resides just beyond our fears waiting for us to take that first leap.

Embrace new experiences without fear; they might just set your spirit soaring!

DAILY REFLECTION

What fears do you find yourself holding onto, and how might lifting them to God free you to embrace this new season of life?

PRAYER

Dear Lord, thank You for the gift of this day and the new opportunities it brings. Help me to release my fears and embrace the freedom that comes from trusting in Your plan for my life.

"Fear often masquerades as a protective shadow, but in truth, God's light offers us the freedom to step boldly into our future."

RETIRED WOMAN

As for me, I will always have hope; I will praise you more and more.
Psalm 71:14

DEVOTIONAL

Once upon a time, in a cozy little town, there lived a vibrant woman named Martha who had just retired after decades of teaching. She loved her garden, where blooming flowers seemed to dance with joy on sunny days. One afternoon, Martha found herself sitting on her porch, sipping herbal tea while watching the clouds drift lazily by. As she reflected on her life, a thought struck her: just like the flowers she nurtured, she too needed daily care, especially in matters of the heart. Rolling up her sleeves, she decided to plant an array of hope—small goals, joyful gatherings with friends, and new hobbies that excited her. With every little seed she sowed, her heart grew fuller and more anchored in hope.

In this season of life, it's the simple acts of nurturing hope that can anchor our hearts and fill our days with joy.

DAILY REFLECTION

What does hope mean to you in this season of life, and how can you nurture it within your heart each day?

PRAYER

Heavenly Father, thank You for the gift of hope that anchors our souls. Help me to embrace each day with trust in Your promises and a heart open to the joy You bring.

"Hope is the gentle whisper of tomorrow's possibilities, inviting us to embrace each day with renewed faith."

LIVING WITH ETERNAL PURPOSE

*"Even to your old age and gray hairs I am he, I am he who will sustain you. I have made you and I will carry you; I will sustain you and I will rescue you." **Isaiah 46:4***

DEVOTIONAL

Once, a retired woman named Grace found herself pondering her place in the world after leaving her teaching career. One sunny afternoon, while enjoying tea with friends, she shared that she felt a bit adrift. Her friend Martha, a volunteer at a local shelter, invited her to join in. There, Grace discovered her love for mentoring young women, guiding them through struggles she once faced. Suddenly, her days were filled with laughter, purpose, and continuous learning—not just for her mentees, but for herself, too.

Even in this wonderfully seasoned chapter of life, there's always room for new adventures and making an impact.

DAILY REFLECTION

What does it mean for you to live with a sense of eternal purpose in this season of your life? How can you embrace opportunities to serve and grow in faith each day?

PRAYER

Dear Lord, thank you for the gift of this season in my life. Help me to see the beauty of my purpose as I seek to live it out with joy and grace.

"Every moment given in service is an investment in eternity."

TRUSTING GOD WITH FAMILY

*"Trust in the Lord with all your heart and lean not on your own understanding; in all your ways submit to Him, and He will make your paths straight." **Proverbs 3:5-6***

DEVOTIONAL

Once, a grandmother named Edna found herself fretting over her children and grandchildren. They were all grown, pursuing their own dreams — some living far away. While she baked her famous cookies, she reminisced about the days of family dinners and laughter. One afternoon, she decided instead of worrying, she would pray for each child. With a cookie in one hand and her phone in the other, she reached out to one loved one at a time, offering her thoughts, prayers, and encouragement. By the evening, the warmth in her heart from connecting with each family member transformed her worries into peace, reminding her that every family's journey is in God's capable hands.

Letting go of worry and replacing it with prayer can bring peace, knowing God is in control of every family chapter.

DAILY REFLECTION

What does trusting God with your family's journey mean for you today? How can you release your worries into His care and embrace His peace?

PRAYER

Dear God, thank you for the gift of family. Help me to trust You fully with their lives, knowing You hold each one in Your loving embrace.

"Let go of the need to control, and watch how beautifully God works in your family's life."

WHEN YOU NEED STRENGTH

"I can do all things through Christ who strengthens me."
Philippians 4:13

DEVOTIONAL

One sunny afternoon, Sarah sat in her garden, the one she had lovingly tended for years. As her fingers brushed against the petals of blooming roses, she felt a wave of fatigue wash over her; the vigor of younger days had slipped away. Yet, as she watched a small bird struggle to lift a twig for its nest, she remembered life's trials often come with God-given strength. Inspired, she rose with renewed purpose, knowing that both her cherished blooms and the spirit within her required patience and care, even in moments of weakness.

Embrace the truth that God's strength is a constant companion, even when you feel weary, helping you rise and bloom anew.

DAILY REFLECTION

What moments in your life have challenged you to seek strength beyond your own? How have you turned to your faith during those times?

PRAYER

Dear Lord, as I face the challenges of this season, grant me the strength I need. Help me to remember that you are always by my side, ready to lift me up with your unwavering love.

"Strength is not just in enduring the storm, but in finding the peace and shelter that comes from faith."

LISTENING FOR GOD'S WHISPER

"Whether you turn to the right or to the left, your ears will hear a voice behind you, saying, 'This is the way; walk in it.'" **Isaiah 30:21**

DEVOTIONAL

After years of nurturing her family, Martha found herself in a quieter home, with the hustle and bustle of daily life giving way to peaceful moments. One afternoon, while tending to her small garden, she noticed how the gentle breeze seemed to carry whispers through the leaves, almost urging her to pause and listen. In that serene moment, she closed her eyes and became aware of her surroundings—the birds singing, the rustling of nature, and the soft call of God urging her to look inward. As thoughts bubbled to the surface, she felt a deep sense of purpose rekindling in her heart, reminding her that even in the quiet, God was guiding her steps.

Sometimes, it takes the gentle nudging of silence for us to hear the profound truths God wants to share, reminding us of our ongoing journey and purpose, even in retirement.

DAILY REFLECTION

In your quiet moments, trust that God is always speaking; find joy in listening for His gentle guidance.

PRAYER

Dear God, thank You for the gift of hope that anchors our hearts. May we cling to the promises You have for us, especially in moments of uncertainty. Fill our spirits with Your peace and joy today.

"Hope is the gentle whisper that assures us each new day carries the possibility of grace."

Three Weeks of Reflection

You've now spent several weeks walking through these devotionals.

If this book has encouraged your heart, a brief Amazon review helps other women find the same encouragement.

devo.anchoredgraces.com/retired

Your experience may guide someone else toward the hope they are searching for.

Thank you for being here.

BECOMING A WOMAN OF THE WORD

"Your word is a lamp to my feet and a light for my path."
Psalm 119:105

DEVOTIONAL

After years of working hard, raising children, and juggling life's many demands, Martha found herself with unexpected free time. One rainy afternoon, she pulled out a dusty Bible from her shelf, determined to fill her days with something meaningful. As she read, the stories began to illuminate her heart, guiding her through memories and challenges she'd faced over the years. Each verse became a gentle reminder of God's love and promises, and she felt a renewed sense of purpose flood her spirit.

In this season of life, immersing yourself in God's Word can illuminate your path and provide comfort and guidance.

DAILY REFLECTION

What does it truly mean for you to be a woman of the Word in this season of your life? How can you deepen your relationship with Scripture and let it guide your days?

PRAYER

Dear Heavenly Father, thank You for the gift of Your Word. As I seek to know You more, help me to find joy and understanding in Scripture each day.

"God's Word is a treasure chest, waiting to be opened and explored."

HEALING THROUGH SCRIPTURE

"He heals the brokenhearted and binds up their wounds."
Psalm 147:3

DEVOTIONAL

Once upon a time in a cozy little town, there lived a retired teacher named Mrs. Jenkins. After dedicating her life to nurturing young minds, she found herself feeling a bit lost and lonely. One day, she discovered a lovely garden in her neighborhood, overgrown but bursting with potential. Inspired, she began tending to the flowers, gently pulling weeds and watering the thirsty blooms. As she nurtured each petal, she realized that the garden mirrored her own heart — in need of a little care and healing, just like the words of her favorite Scriptures promised.

Embrace this new season of your life, for just as you can heal a garden, you can heal your heart through the stories woven in Scripture.

DAILY REFLECTION

What parts of your life need healing, and how might the comforting words of scripture guide you through this process?

PRAYER

Dear Lord, thank you for the healing promises found in your Word. May I find peace and restoration as I seek your guidance and comfort today.

"God's whispers often bring the loudest healing."

WHEN LIFE FEELS HEAVY

"So do not fear, for I am with you; do not be dismayed, for I am your God; I will strengthen you and help you; I will uphold you with my righteous right hand." **Isaiah 41:10**

DEVOTIONAL

There was once a sweet retired teacher named Marjorie who always carried a heavy purse, filled not just with her essentials, but also the weight of unfulfilled dreams and worries about the future. One sunny afternoon, while visiting the park, she spotted a little girl struggling to lift her oversized backpack. Marjorie chuckled and walked over, helping the girl remove items until the pack was light enough for her. In that moment, Marjorie realized that just like the little girl, she too needed to let go of some burdens, finding joy in simplifying her own life. Laughing at her own silliness, she went home that day, determined to simplify her purse and, metaphorically, her worries too.

Sometimes, it's okay to lighten your load and let go of what's weighing heavily on your heart, because joy is often found in a simpler life.

DAILY REFLECTION

What burdens are you carrying today that weigh heavily on your heart, and how might you invite God's lightness into those moments?

PRAYER

Dear Lord, as the days unfold, help me lean into Your strength when the heaviness of life feels overwhelming. Grant me the grace to find joy in my journey and to trust in Your loving presence.

"Even in our heaviest moments, God invites us to exchange our burdens for His peace."

GOD'S GRACE FOR PAST MISTAKES

"As far as the east is from the west, so far has he removed our transgressions from us."
Psalm 103:12

DEVOTIONAL

Once upon a time, there was a lovely retiree named Clara who loved to bake. She cherished the joy of making sweet treats for her friends and family, but she had a tendency to burn the cookies. Every time the smoke alarm went off, she would giggle and say, "Well, it's just a little crispy!" One day, reflecting on her baking blunders, she realized that just like those burned cookies, her past mistakes didn't define her. With a heart filled with grace, she decided to embrace her imperfections and share her stories, all while creating laughter and delicious new recipes.

Just as Clara learned to laugh at her baking mishaps, remember that God's grace allows you to savor every moment, reminding you that your past doesn't hold power over you.

DAILY REFLECTION

What past mistakes are you holding onto that God's grace wants to heal and transform in your life today?

PRAYER

Dear Lord, thank you for your endless grace that covers our shortcomings. Help me to release my past mistakes into your loving hands, trusting in your forgiveness and new beginnings.

"God's grace is the gentle reminder that our past does not define our future."

LIVING LOVED

For I am convinced that neither death nor life, neither angels nor demons, neither the present nor the future, nor any powers, neither height nor depth, nor anything else in all creation, will be able to separate us from the love of God that is in Christ Jesus our Lord.
Romans 8:38-39

DEVOTIONAL

Once upon a time in a cozy little neighborhood, there lived a retired woman named Marge. Every morning, she brewed her favorite cup of tea and sat on her porch, savoring the birds chirping and the flowers blooming. One day, as she watched her neighbor struggle to carry heavy groceries, Marge hopped into action, helping her friend with a warm smile and a kind word. Afterward, the neighbor expressed her gratitude, saying, "You truly make my day brighter!" Marge realized in that moment that her kindness was a reflection of the love she'd received throughout her life. Like a ripple, love spreads, making everyone feel cherished.

You are deeply loved, and sharing that love with others brings joy not only to them but also fills your heart with warmth and purpose.

DAILY REFLECTION

What does it mean for you to embrace the love that surrounds you each day, and how can you express that love back to the world around you?

PRAYER

Dear God, help me to recognize and embrace the love that flows in my life. Let Your peace fill my heart, reminding me that I am cherished and never alone. Amen.

"You are loved deeply, and your worth is immeasurable."

DECLUTTERING THE SOUL

"Come to me, all you who are weary and burdened, and I will give you rest."
Matthew 11:28

DEVOTIONAL

Once there was a woman named Grace who spent years caring for her family and home, always nurturing others before herself. After retiring, she realized that her closet was crammed with clothes and memories that no longer served her. One day, with a cup of tea in hand, she decided to take a gentle approach to decluttering not just her closet, but her heart as well. As she sorted through old items, she found joy in remembering what each piece represented, but she also felt a lightness as she let go of things that no longer fit her life. That afternoon, she felt renewed, as if she had made space not just in her home, but in her soul for new adventures.

As you cherish the memories of your past, remember to clear out what holds you back and make room for the blessings of today.

DAILY REFLECTION

What emotional baggage or negative thoughts might you be holding onto that weigh down your spirit and clutter your joy? How can you begin to release them and allow space for peace and fulfillment in your life?

PRAYER

Dear God, thank you for the gift of this new season in life. Help me to gently release what no longer serves me and to fill my heart with your love and light.

"Decluttering the soul opens the door to a heart full of grace."

ROOTED AND GROUNDED IN LOVE

"So that Christ may dwell in your hearts through faith—that you, being rooted and grounded in love, may have strength to comprehend with all the saints what is the breadth and length and height and depth of the love of Christ, and to know the love of Christ that surpasses knowledge, that you may be filled with all the fullness of God."
Ephesians 3:17-19

DEVOTIONAL

Once, a grandmother named Martha decided to start a garden in her retirement. With each seed she planted, she remembered the nurturing love she had received throughout her life—from her mother's gentle encouragement to her children's loving hugs. As time passed, the flowers bloomed incredibly vibrant and cheerful, just like the love she had woven into her family stories. Neighbors often stopped by to admire her garden, and marveled at how it inspired their own patches of earth. Each blossom served as a lovely reminder that love, like a garden, grows stronger the more it is shared and tended.

Love is the foundation that keeps our lives colorful and flourishing, so plant it generously wherever you go.

DAILY REFLECTION

What does it mean for you to feel truly rooted and grounded in love at this stage of your life? How can you deepen that love in your relationships and in your community?

PRAYER

Dear Lord, thank you for the gift of love that surrounds us. Help us to nurture and cultivate that love in our hearts, so we may share it freely with others.

"Love is the soil from which our joy and purpose blossom."

GUARDING YOUR HEART

"Above all else, guard your heart, for everything you do flows from it." **Proverbs 4:23**

DEVOTIONAL

Once upon a time, there was a lovely retired woman named June who loved to bake. One day, while sorting through her family recipes, she stumbled upon an old note that simply read, "You are loved." It filled her heart with warmth, but it also made her realize how easily life's distractions could lead her to forget that precious truth. So, she decided to start each day with gratitude and a little reminder of the love that surrounded her, whether through friends, family, or the beauty of nature. Little by little, her simple practice helped guard her heart, filling it with joy more than ever!

Life teaches us that guarding our hearts with love and gratitude is the sweetest recipe for a joyful retirement.

DAILY REFLECTION

What are the things you allow to influence your heart and spirit these days, and how can you intentionally focus on safeguarding your emotional well-being?

PRAYER

Dear God, thank You for being a constant source of love and comfort. Help me to guard my heart, filling it with peace, joy, and wisdom as I navigate this season of my life.

"Guarding your heart is a daily choice, one that opens the door to true peace and fulfillment."

A FAITH THAT ENDURES

"They will still bear fruit in old age, they will stay fresh and green."
Psalm 92:14

DEVOTIONAL

Once upon a time in a cozy little town, there lived a sweet lady named Mabel who, at 65, had just celebrated her retirement. Instead of slowing down, Mabel started a community garden, inviting her neighbors to grow their own vegetables and flowers. With every seed she planted, Mabel shared stories of her faith journey, showing how life's trials only made her trust in God stronger. As the garden flourished, so did the bonds between neighbors, proving that with faith, both friendships and hopes can blossom beautifully—even in the golden years.

Even in retirement, your faith can bear fruit, nurturing both yourself and those around you.

DAILY REFLECTION

What challenges have you faced in your journey of faith, and how have they shaped your relationship with God?

PRAYER

Dear Lord, thank you for guiding us through the seasons of our lives. Help us to find strength in our faith, no matter what trials we may face. Fill our hearts with your peace as we trust in your everlasting love.

"Endurance in faith is the quiet whisper of hope that carries us through life's storms."

STEPPING INTO THE NEW WITH BOLDNESS

"Brothers and sisters, I do not consider myself yet to have taken hold of it. But one thing I do: Forgetting what is behind and straining toward what is ahead, I press on toward the goal to win the prize for which God has called me heavenward in Christ Jesus."
Philippians 3:13-14

DEVOTIONAL

Margaret, at 65, found herself in a new season of life after retiring from a job she had devoted thirty years to. Initially, she felt lost, as though her purpose had vanished along with her daily routine. One afternoon, while sorting through old photographs, she stumbled upon pictures of her college days, vibrant with dreams of travel and art. Inspired, she enrolled in a local painting class and began creating again, rediscovering passions she had shelved away. Each brushstroke reminded her that life still had new adventures waiting, and she was capable of stepping boldly into them.

In this new chapter, remember that your experiences have built an incredible foundation for the vibrant and fulfilling adventures that still lie ahead.

DAILY REFLECTION

What new opportunities are you feeling called to explore in this season of your life, and how can you embrace them with courage?

PRAYER

Dear Lord, thank you for this new chapter filled with possibilities. Help her to step forward boldly, trusting in Your guidance and love as she embraces her unique journey ahead.

"With each new dawn, there lies an invitation to redefine our path and walk it confidently."

CHOOSING FAITH OVER FEELINGS

"Now faith is confidence in what we hope for and assurance about what we do not see."
Hebrews 11:1

DEVOTIONAL

Once, there was a woman named Clara who found herself feeling lost after retiring. She often felt lonely and restless, missing the daily interactions of her work life. One day, she decided to start volunteering at a local shelter. To her surprise, as she poured her heart into helping others, her feelings of loneliness began to fade. Each day, her faith in the goodness of connection and purpose grew stronger, reminding her that even when her feelings were low, she could choose to act in faith and find joy.

In times when emotions feel overwhelming, choose to act in faith, allowing it to lead you toward purpose and connection.

DAILY REFLECTION

What feelings have you been wrestling with lately that may be clouding your faith? How can you gently remind yourself of the promises God has for you during this season of your life?

PRAYER

Dear Lord, thank You for being a constant source of strength and comfort. Help me to lean on You when my feelings seem overwhelming, and guide me to choose faith in every circumstance.

"Faith is the quiet assurance that God is working, even when my heart feels unsure."

THE GOD WHO SEES YOU

"She gave this name to the Lord who spoke to her: 'You are the God who sees me,' for she said, 'I have now seen the One who sees me.'" **Genesis 16:13**

DEVOTIONAL

As a retired woman, you may find yourself spending quiet afternoons sipping tea, reminiscing over life's little treasures. Think of Hagar, who felt abandoned and alone in the wilderness, yet encountered a God who saw her—truly saw her—in her pain and despair. Just like Hagar, you might have moments when you feel unnoticed or unappreciated. But remember, in those still moments, the Lord sees you. He understands your struggles, your joys, and all that makes up your beautiful life tapestry.

No matter where life's journey takes you, the essence of being seen is comforting, like a warm hug on a cool day. Embrace these times with confidence, trusting that while the world may be busy, there's a divine presence always watching out for you, wishing to walk alongside you.

DAILY REFLECTION

You are never invisible; the God who sees you is always present in your life, cherishing every moment you live.

PRAYER

Dear God, thank you for always being present and for seeing me in times of joy and sorrow. Help me to trust in your love and guidance as I navigate my days.

God's gaze does not miss a single moment of our lives; He is with us in every joy and sorrow.

LOVING OTHERS FROM A FULL HEART

"Above all, love each other deeply, because love covers over a multitude of sins." 1 **Peter 4:8**

DEVOTIONAL

At the local coffee shop, a 65-year-old woman named Ruth would often sit by the window, enjoying her favorite scone while observing the world outside. One morning, she noticed a young mother struggling to manage two little ones, a toddler tugging on her leg while an infant cried for attention. With a warm heart and a smile, Ruth invited them to join her at her table, offering a reassuring presence and sharing her cookies. That simple act of kindness not only brightened the young mother's day but also filled Ruth's heart with warmth and joy as they chatted and laughed together.

When you love others from a full heart, you create new connections that enrich not only their lives but your own as well.

DAILY REFLECTION

What does it mean for you to love others when your heart feels full? How can you share that love with the people around you each day? Reflect on the simple ways you might express that love to family, friends, or even strangers.

PRAYER

Dear God, thank You for filling our hearts with love. Help us to share that love with others in meaningful ways, allowing us to be a blessing in their lives. Amen.

"From a heart overflowing with love, even the smallest acts become powerful gestures."

WAITING WELL WITH GOD

"Wait for the Lord; be strong and take heart and wait for the Lord." **Psalm 27:14**

DEVOTIONAL

When Ruth retired from her job of over 40 years, she envisioned an exciting new chapter filled with travel and leisurely pursuits. But as weeks turned into months, her plans were stifled by unexpected health issues. Initially, she found herself frustrated and impatient, wrestling with the sudden halt on her ambitions. However, in quiet moments of reflection, she began to see this season of waiting as an opportunity to deepen her relationship with God. She started journaling her prayers and gratitude, feeling peace wash over her spirit as she encountered God in her stillness. It wasn't the life she had imagined, but it became one filled with unexpected blessings and growth.

Sometimes waiting can feel like a heavy burden, but it is often in those still moments that God reveals His greatest plans for us.

DAILY REFLECTION

What does waiting on God look like in your life right now, and how can you embrace this time as an opportunity for growth and deeper connection with Him?

PRAYER

Dear Lord, thank You for the gift of this season of life. Help me to trust in Your timing and to find joy and purpose in the times of waiting.

"Waiting is not a passive state; it is an active engagement with trust and hope."

TRUSTING GOD'S TIMING

"Commit your way to the Lord; trust in Him and He will do this."
Psalm 37:5

DEVOTIONAL

Once, there was a lovely grandmother named Doris who always planned every family gathering to perfection. From the decorations to the menu, everything was mapped out. One Thanksgiving, however, a surprise snowstorm left her daughter snowed in, and her son had to work late. Despite her initial panic, Doris decided to let go of her carefully curated plans. She invited a few neighbors over for an impromptu dinner and ended up having a wonderful time sharing laughter and stories. In that unexpected moment, she realized that love and connection thrived far better when she let go of the reins.

Sometimes, the magic happens when we loosen our grip and embrace the unexpected moments life offers.

DAILY REFLECTION

What areas of your life have you found difficult to release control over, and how might surrendering those burdens bring you peace and freedom?

PRAYER

Dear God, help me to release my grip on what I cannot control. Grant me the courage to embrace Your plans with an open heart, trusting in Your divine wisdom. Amen.

"Freedom blossoms when we let go of the need to control every detail of our lives."

GOD'S MERCY IS NEW EACH MORNING

"Because of the Lord's great love we are not consumed, for his compassions never fail. They are new every morning; great is your faithfulness." **Lamentations 3:22-23**

DEVOTIONAL

A dear friend of mine, whom I'll call Grace, found herself feeling a little lackluster in her retirement days. One morning, as the sun streamed through her kitchen window, she decided to try something new. She poured herself a steaming cup of tea and stepped outside to sit on her porch. In that quiet moment, she listened to the birds chirping and felt the warmth of the sun. With a smile, she realized that each new day offers a chance to explore, connect, and enjoy the simple beauty of life. That very moment felt like God's whisper: "Today is a gift—embrace it!"

Each morning is God's invitation to start anew; let's unwrap that gift with joy and gratitude.

DAILY REFLECTION

What is one way you can recognize and embrace God's mercy in your life today? How can this awareness reshape your perspective moving forward?

PRAYER

Dear Lord, thank You for the gift of each new morning. Help me to see Your mercy in the small moments and to share that love with those around me.

"Each dawn carries a fresh whisper of grace, a reminder that we are continuously cradled in God's love."

WALKING IN CONFIDENCE, NOT COMPARISON

"So do not throw away your confidence; it will be richly rewarded. You need to persevere so that when you have done the will of God, you will receive what he has promised." **Hebrews 10:35-36**

DEVOTIONAL

Once, a retired schoolteacher named Grace began to feel discontented as she compared her life to those of her friends. They seemed to craft perfect lives filled with travel and visits to exotic places, while Grace found joy in her quiet garden and cozy afternoons with a book. One day, while tending to her roses, she realized that her peace and happiness came from things that mattered most to her, not from what others deemed significant. In her moments of reflection, she found a renewed sense of confidence in her unique journey, celebrating her simple joys and the love she shared with family and friends.

Embrace your own path with gratitude, knowing that the beauty of your life is not defined by comparison but by the authenticity of your experiences.

DAILY REFLECTION

What does it look like for you to embrace your unique journey rather than measuring it against others? How can you celebrate your achievements, big or small, without feeling the pressure to compare?

PRAYER

Dear Lord, thank you for the beautiful path you have set before me. Help me to walk confidently in who I am, celebrating my own milestones and embracing the gifts I have been given.

"Your story is uniquely yours, and it deserves to be celebrated."

WHEN PRAYERS GO UNANSWERED

"The righteous cry out, and the Lord hears them; he delivers them from all their troubles.
The Lord is close to the brokenhearted and saves those who are crushed in spirit."
Psalm 34:17-18

DEVOTIONAL

Edith had spent years praying for her daughter's safety, asking God to guide her through life's challenges. One day, she received a phone call that her daughter had faced a minor car accident. Relieved that it wasn't serious, Edith was nonetheless disheartened—hadn't she prayed fervently for protection? A wise friend gently reminded her that life is unpredictable and, while prayers may not always yield the results we desire, God's presence is a steadfast comfort. With a warm cup of tea, Edith reflected on how sometimes, instead of immediate answers, her prayers turned into deeper conversations with God.

When prayers feel unanswered, remember that God is listening, cherishing every word, and drawing nearer during the tough times.

DAILY REFLECTION

What prayers have you offered that seem to have gone unanswered? How does it make you feel to reflect on those moments, and what might God be inviting you to learn or discover in the waiting?

PRAYER

Dear Lord, thank You for hearing my prayers, even when I struggle to see the answers. Help me to trust in Your perfect timing and to find peace in my journey of faith. Amen.

"Unanswered prayers can lead us to deeper understanding and greater faith."

FINDING JOY IN GOD ALONE

"You make known to me the path of life; you will fill me with joy
in your presence, with eternal pleasures at your right hand." **Psalm 16:11**

DEVOTIONAL

As retirement settles in, it becomes easy to fill our days with activities or relationships that bring temporary happiness, like gardening or coffee dates. But one afternoon, while tending to her roses, Clara felt the gentle breeze on her face and realized how often she rushed through moments of beauty to get to the next thing. In that stillness, she turned her heart to God, embraced the silence, and discovered a wellspring of joy bubbling up from within her. It was in the quiet presence of the Lord where her heart truly sang—surrounded by nature and His love, she found that joy is less about what we do and more about who we are with.

True joy is found in the presence of God, who invites us to delight in each moment.

DAILY REFLECTION

What are the specific moments in your day when you feel most connected to God's joy, and how can you nurture those moments?

PRAYER

Dear Lord, thank you for being a constant source of joy in our lives. Help us to seek you earnestly and to find delight in your presence every day.

"True joy is not found in our circumstances, but in the steadfast love and grace of God."

YOUR LIFE STILL HAS PURPOSE

"Likewise, teach the older women to be reverent in the way they live, not to be slanderers or addicted to much wine, but to teach what is good. Then they can urge the younger women to love their husbands and children, to be self-controlled and pure, to be busy at home, to be kind, and to be subject to their husbands, so that no one will malign the word of God."
Titus 2:3-5

DEVOTIONAL

Once upon a time in a cozy little town, there lived a retired schoolteacher named Mary. After years of shaping young minds, she found herself wondering what her purpose was now that she had hung up her teaching hat. One day, she noticed a group of neighborhood children playing in her backyard. Instead of retreating indoors, Mary decided to host a weekly story hour. With each tale she spun, she not only delighted the children but also re-discovered the joy and spark that teaching had always brought her. Before she knew it, she was back to inspiring the next generation, proving that her wisdom and love for storytelling had not faded—only transformed.
Never underestimate the value of your experiences, as they can light the way for others.

DAILY REFLECTION

What activities or relationships in your life bring you joy and allow you to share your unique gifts with others?

PRAYER

Dear Lord, thank You for the wisdom of years and the journey of life. Help me recognize the purpose You still have for me today and give me courage to embrace it fully.

"Every season of life holds the potential for new beginnings and meaningful contributions."

SPEAKING LIFE OVER YOURSELF

"The tongue has the power of life and death, and those who love it will eat its fruit."
Proverbs 18:21

DEVOTIONAL

Once, in a quaint little town, there lived a retired woman named Clara who loved to knit. She often made hats and scarves for the local children. One chilly afternoon, while she was knitting, she overheard someone say, "I can't do this," and it struck her. Clara realized that words have power! So, she took it upon herself to not only knit warmth but also to share words of encouragement with those around her. Every compliment she gave became a thread woven into the fabric of her community, and she found herself feeling more alive and vibrant with each positive word shared.

Life is too precious to waste on negativity; choose to speak love and life over yourself and watch how it transforms your days!s.

DAILY REFLECTION

What words do you speak over yourself each day, and how do they shape your view of who you are in this season of life?

PRAYER

Dear God, help me to recognize the power of my words. May I speak kindness, joy, and hope over myself, knowing that I am beloved and worthy of Your love.

"Your words are seeds; plant them wisely and watch your life bloom."

WHEN YOU FEEL SPIRITUALLY DRY

"A generous person will prosper; whoever refreshes others will be refreshed."
Proverbs 11:25

DEVOTIONAL

Once, a sweet grandmother named Mary found herself feeling spiritually parched. After years of volunteering, baking cookies for the church children's group, and sharing stories during Sunday school, she suddenly hit a wall. One day, while tending to her beloved rose garden, she noticed how the blooms seemed less vibrant and began to wilt. Inspired, she decided to bring a little water to those delicate petals and to her surprise, with just a bit of nurturing, those flowers began to flourish and bring her joy again. This experience reminded her to refresh her spirit by spending time in prayer and seeking God's presence once more.

Sometimes, to feel spiritually alive again, we need to pour a little love back into our own lives just as we do for others.

DAILY REFLECTION

What activities or practices help you reconnect with God when you feel distant from Him? Consider taking a moment to reflect on the things that spark joy in your spiritual journey.

PRAYER

Dear Lord, in times of spiritual dryness, remind us of Your unfailing presence. Fill our hearts with Your love and lead us gently back to the wellspring of joy in You.

"Even the driest seasons can lead us to deeper roots of faith."

HEALED BY HIS WORD

"But he was pierced for our transgressions, he was crushed for our iniquities; the punishment that brought us peace was on him, and by his wounds, we are healed."
Isaiah 53:5

DEVOTIONAL

There was once a grandmother named Elizabeth who had spent years pouring love into her family, but recently she found herself feeling lonely and a bit forgotten. One quiet afternoon, she decided to take a stroll in her garden, where vibrant flowers seemed to dance in the gentle breeze. As she wandered, she began to recite Scripture she had memorized: "I can do all things through Christ who strengthens me." With each step, her heart became lighter, and by the time she returned home, Elizabeth felt a renewed spirit, reminded that God's love and healing are always present, especially in the stillness of nature.

Never underestimate the power of spending time with God's Word; it has the ability to heal and refresh your spirit at any age.

DAILY REFLECTION

What words from Scripture have brought you comfort or healing in times of need? How can you embrace those healing promises today?

PRAYER

Dear Lord, thank You for the power of Your Word. Help me to lean on it for strength and healing, trusting that Your promises are true. May I find rest in Your presence today.

"His Word is a balm for weary hearts, bringing restoration and peace."

GOD'S LOVE THAT NEVER FAILS

"Give thanks to the Lord, for He is good; His love endures forever."
Psalm 136:1

DEVOTIONAL

Once, there was a retired woman named Clara who spent her days tending her garden. Each morning, she would revel in the beauty of blooming flowers, recalling the countless seasons she had watched pass. One day, an unexpected storm threatened to uproot her beloved plants. Clara ran out, covering them with old sheets and her own warmth. As she cared for her garden, she felt God's presence, reminding her that just as she rescued her flowers, His love continually nurtures and protects her through every storm of life.

Even in the later seasons of life, remember that God's love is a constant, ever-present force that will never fail you.

DAILY REFLECTION

What memories do you have of God's love in your life, and how has it sustained you through the seasons of change?

PRAYER

Dear Lord, thank you for your unwavering love that has been a constant in my life. May I feel your presence today, reassuring me of your faithfulness and grace.

"God's love is the unchanging anchor in the ever-shifting tides of life."

February 16

OVERFLOWING WITH GRATITUDE

"Give thanks to the Lord, for he is good; his love endures forever."
Psalm 107:1

DEVOTIONAL

Once, in a cozy little town, a retired woman named Grace decided to start a gratitude journal. Each morning, with her cup of tea warming her hands, she'd jot down three things she was thankful for. Some days, it was the sunrise painting the sky, and other days it was simply enjoying a quiet moment with a good book. As the months spun by, she noticed her heart felt lighter; each entry reminded her of life's little joys. Her friends began to notice too, and soon they gathered monthly to share their blessings, transforming their outlook on life, one thank-you at a time.

Life is a beautiful tapestry, and the threads of gratitude can brighten even the simplest moments.

DAILY REFLECTION

What moment in your life recently filled your heart with gratitude, and how can you share that joy with others today?

PRAYER

Dear God, thank you for the abundant blessings in our lives. Help us to recognize your gifts each day and share our gratitude with those around us.

Gratitude turns what we have into enough and more.

FORGIVING YOURSELF AND OTHERS

"Be kind and compassionate to one another, forgiving each other, just as in Christ God forgave you." **Ephesians 4:32**

DEVOTIONAL

Once, there was a grandmother named Doris who found herself still holding onto a misunderstanding with her childhood friend, Patty. They had both let a small disagreement fester over the years, causing laughter and warmth to fade into silence. One sunny afternoon, Doris baked a batch of her famous cookies and decided that life was too short for grudges. She knocked on Patty's door and offered not just cookies, but a heartfelt apology. To her delight, Patty embraced her with open arms, laughter spilling out as they reminisced about the good old days. Their rekindled friendship reminded Doris that forgiveness was the sweetest treat of all.

Forgiving yourself and others often leads to unexpected joys; hold onto those that matter and let go of the rest.

DAILY REFLECTION

What are the burdens you carry from your past that prevent you from fully embracing the present and future?

PRAYER

Dear Lord, help me to forgive myself and others, releasing the weight of past mistakes. Fill my heart with your love and grace, reminding me that I am worthy of peace and joy.

"Forgiveness is a gift we give ourselves as much as it is a gift we give to others."

GOD'S STRENGTH IN YOUR WEAKNESS

"But he said to me, 'My grace is sufficient for you, for my power is made perfect in weakness.' Therefore, I will boast all the more gladly about my weaknesses, so that Christ's power may rest on me." **2 Corinthians 12:9**

DEVOTIONAL

There was once a lovely woman named Martha who, in her retirement, took up knitting to make gifts for her grandchildren. At first, she struggled to even hold the needles, feeling clumsy and unsure. One afternoon, as she fumbled with yarn and stitches, she let out a laugh, realizing how much she loved the process—even the mess-ups! Each imperfect square gradually turned into beautiful blankets, reminding her that her efforts, no matter how fragile, reflected love and warmth for her family.

Embracing our weaknesses can lead to discovering new strengths we never knew we had.

DAILY REFLECTION

How have you seen God's strength lift you during times when you felt weak or overwhelmed?

PRAYER

Dear God, thank you for being my refuge in times of struggle. Help me to embrace my weaknesses, knowing that your strength shines brightest when I am most in need.

"God's strength is like a gentle breeze, giving lift to fragile wings."

ANXIOUS FOR NOTHING

"Cast all your anxiety on Him because He cares for you."
1 Peter 5:7

DEVOTIONAL

Ethel had always been a planner. With a color-coded calendar and a meticulous grocery list, she felt n control. But retirement brought unexpected free time, and sometimes anxiety crept in about how to fill those hours meaningfully. One day, she decided to join a quilting group at her local community center, thinking it would just be a fun way to pass the time. To her surprise, the delightful laughter and shared stories of the other women transformed her worries into joy. She learned that spontaneity can be even more beautiful than a perfectly planned day.

In moments of uncertainty, remember that every twist and turn of life can lead to unforeseen joys; it's okay to embrace the unexpected!

DAILY REFLECTION

What anxieties are you carrying today, and how might surrendering them to God lighten your heart?

PRAYER

Dear Lord, help me to release my worries and trust in Your perfect plan. Fill me with Your peace as I lean on You today.

"Peace is not the absence of trouble, but the presence of God."

LIVING A LEGACY OF FAITH

"A good person leaves an inheritance for their children's children, but a sinner's wealth is stored up for the righteous." **Proverbs 13:22**

DEVOTIONAL

Once, a grandmother named Evelyn decided to host a family gathering every month to share stories of faith, from her childhood to the lessons learned through struggles. As her grandchildren gathered around the table, they not only enjoyed her famous chicken pot pie but also listened intently to tales of bravery and prayer. Over the years, these dinners became a cherished tradition, instilling a sense of faith and belonging within the family—a living legacy that would continue for generations.

Your life 's a beautiful tapestry of experiences and faith—share your stories generously cnd watch as they inspire those you love to carry forward your legacy.

DAILY REFLECTION

What stories and memories of faith do you want to share with the younger generations in your family or community? How can you make those lessons come alive for them today?

PRAYER

Dear God, thank You for the gift of a life filled with faith. Help me to know how to share my journey and impart wisdom to others, nurturing their paths as they grow.

"Your faith is a tapestry woven with threads of love, hope, and memories that can inspire others."

PEACE IN THE MIDST OF CHANGE

"Peace I leave with you; my peace I give to you. I do not give to you as the world gives. Do not let your hearts be troubled and do not be afraid." **John 14:27**

DEVOTIONAL

As a young girl, Lila always dreamed of the day she could retire and spend her time gardening, painting, and traveling. Now that she's reached this stage of her life, she finds herself in a whirlwind of unexpected changes—family dynamics shifting, health challenges emerging, and even her beloved garden facing pests she never encountered before! One sunny afternoon, overwhelmed by it all, she decided to take her coffee into the garden for a moment of quiet reflection. As she sat there, surrounded by bees buzzing and flowers blooming, she realized that even though things were changing around her, the beauty of creation remained steadfast. She took a deep breath and felt a wave of peace washing over her, reminding her that she could adapt, grow, and find joy even amidst uncertainty.

Life is a series of changes, but by embracing the present moment, we can discover tranquility in our hearts despite life's unpredictable shifts.

DAILY REFLECTION

What changes are happening in your life right now, and how might you invite peace into those moments of transition?

PRAYER

Dear Lord, thank you for being a steady presence in our lives. Help us to embrace the changes around us, finding your peace in each new chapter we face.

"Peace is not the absence of change, but the assurance that God is with us through every transition."

WHEN YOU FEEL INADEQUATE

"I praise you because I am fearfully and wonderfully made; your works are wonderful, I know that full well." **Psalm 139:14**

DEVOTIONAL

Once upon a time in a cozy little town, there lived a retired woman named Betty who loved knitting. One day, she decided to create a beautiful blanket for her granddaughter. As she sat in her sunlit living room, she began to doubt her skills, comparing her work to the far more intricate patterns she saw online. Just then, her granddaughter came in, excitedly asking for a "Betty blanket" because they were always warm and filled with love, no matter how simple the stitches. It dawned on Betty that the true value of her creation wasn't in perfection but in the love and memories woven into every loop.

You are enough just as you are; your unique gifts are what make life colorful and special.

DAILY REFLECTION

What moments make you feel inadequate, and how can you bring those feelings to God for comfort and strength?

PRAYER

Dear Lord, help me to know that I am enough in Your eyes. Fill me with Your peace as I face the uncertainties of this season in my life.

"Your worth is not defined by your accomplishments, but by the love you share and the lives you touch."

GOD IS YOUR REFUGE

"The Lord is my rock, my fortress and my deliverer; my God is my rock, in whom I take refuge, my shield and the horn of my salvation, my stronghold." Psalm 18:2

DEVOTIONAL

Once upon a time, in a cozy little town, there lived a retired woman named Edith who swore by her garden. Every morning, she would tend to her flowers as if they were her own children. One afternoon, a sudden storm threatened to blow everything away, leaving her worried and anxious. As she scrambled to protect her beloved blooms, she remembered her favorite quilt—passed down from her grandmother—that always made her feel safe. Snuggling under that quilt with a cup of tea afterwards, she realized that like her quilt, God wraps her in comfort during life's storms.

In the storms of life, remember that God is your safe place, always there to shelter you and soothe your soul.

DAILY REFLECTION

What does seeking refuge in God look like for you in this season of your life? How can you create moments where you can feel His presence and comfort?

PRAYER

Dear Lord, thank You for being my safe haven and for the peace You provide. Help me to lean into Your love and guidance during this time of reflection and rest.

"In the shelter of His wings, we find our truest peace."

CHOOSING OBEDIENCE OVER COMFORT

"For I have come down from heaven not to do my own will but the will of him who sent me." John 6:38

DEVOTIONAL

Once upon a time in a cozy little town, there lived a retired teacher named Mildred. After years of guiding young minds, Mildred found solace in gardening. Every Saturday, she would tend to her lovely roses, believing it to be her little slice of comfort. One day, a neighbor asked her to lead a weekly Bible study for the women in her church. At first, she hesitated, wondering how much easier it would be to stay in her garden. But she decided to step out of her comfort zone, realizing that her words could inspire and uplift others. By choosing obedience over comfort, Mildred learned that teaching a new generation of heart was as fulfilling as any blooming flower.

Sometimes, stepping out of our comfy routines allows us to blossom in ways we never imagined.

DAILY REFLECTION

What does choosing obedience over comfort look like in your daily life, and how can you embrace that choice today?

PRAYER

Dear Lord, help me to seek Your guidance and strength as I navigate the often-difficult choices in life. May I find joy in obedience and trust Your plans for me, even when they lead me out of my comfort zone.

"True comfort is often found in the courageous act of following God's call."

BE STILL AND KNOW

"I make known the end from the beginning, from ancient times, what is still to come. I say, 'My purpose will stand, and I will do all that I please.'" **Isaiah 46:10**

DEVOTIONAL

Once, there lived a delightful lady named Martha who loved to fill her days with busy activities—gardening, volunteering, and even quilting. But in the hustle and bustle, she often forgot to carve out moments for herself. One sunny afternoon, while sipping tea on her porch, Martha noticed the blossoms dancing in the breeze and the clouds softly drifting by. It was in that moment of peace that she realized how refreshing it was to simply be still, savoring each breath and each fleeting moment of beauty.

Life can slow down beautifully, and amidst the calm, there are treasures waiting to be discovered; take time each day to embrace the stillness and let your heart reconnect with the wonders around you.

DAILY REFLECTION

What does it mean for you to "be still" in your daily life, and how can you create space for God's presence in the quiet moments?

PRAYER

Dear Heavenly Father, thank you for the gift of stillness. Help me to embrace these moments of peace and draw closer to You as I rest in Your love.

In the quiet, God whispers truths that often go unheard in the clamor of life.

PRESSING ON WHEN YOU'RE WEARY

"Therefore, since we are surrounded by such a great cloud of witnesses, let us throw off everything that hinders and the sin that so easily entangles. And let us run with perseverance the race marked out for us, 2 fixing our eyes on Jesus, the pioneer and perfecter of faith. For the joy set before him he endured the cross, scorning its shame, and sat down at the right hand of the throne of God." **Hebrews 12:1-2**

DEVOTIONAL

One sunny afternoon, Margaret decided to tackle her sprawling garden, which had become overgrown during her busy years. As she weeded, she felt a wave of fatigue wash over her. Instead of waving the white flag, she paused, took a deep breath, and remembered her joy in nurturing those blooms. With renewed spirit, she played her favorite tunes, danced a little shuffle between the rows, and found that not only was her body reinvigorated, but her heart felt joyful too.

Sometimes, the journey seems heavy, but a little music, laughter, and perspective can turn weariness into joy.

DAILY REFLECTION

What does pressing on look like for you in this season of your life, especially when you feel weary or discouraged? How can you embrace the strength that comes from within and the support of those around you?

PRAYER

Dear God, please grant me the energy and courage to keep moving forward, even when I feel spent. Surround me with your warmth and strength, reminding me that I am never alone in my journey.

"Even in weariness, the heart can find strength to rise again."

GOD'S GENTLE CORRECTION

"My son, do not despise the Lord's discipline, and do not resent his rebuke, because the Lord disciplines those he loves, as a father the son he delights in." **Proverbs 3:11-12**

DEVOTIONAL

Once, a sweet grandmother named Clara decided to take up gardening after retirement. She was so eager to see her flowers bloom that she often overwatered them, thinking they needed more love. One day, a friend stopped by and gently pointed out that less is sometimes more. Clara chuckled, realizing that her good intentions needed a little nudge of wisdom. With her friend's guidance, she found the perfect balance, and soon her garden flourished like never before, turning into a colorful display of life.

Sometimes, God's gentle correction helps us grow in ways we might not see ourselves, reminding us that even our best intentions can benefit from a loving touch.

DAILY REFLECTION

What areas in your life is God gently nudging you to reassess or change? How can you respond to His loving guidance today?

PRAYER

Dear Lord, thank You for Your gentle guidance in our lives. Help me to be open to Your corrections and to trust in Your perfect timing and love.

"Correction is not condemnation, but an invitation to grow closer to God."

HOPE THAT WILL NOT DISAPPOINT

"And hope does not put us to shame, because God's love has been poured out into our hearts through the Holy Spirit, who has been given to us." **Romans 5:5**

DEVOTIONAL

Once, a retired schoolteacher named Margaret discovered a box of old letters from her former students tucked away in her attic. As she read through the notes filled with gratitude and fond memories, her heart swelled with joy. Just when she thought her teaching days were behind her, Margaret realized those connections had shaped lives, including her own. With each letter, she felt a renewed sense of purpose and decided to start a monthly book club for the seniors in her community, cultivating new friendships and sharing stories. The hope she thought was dimmed rekindled brightly as she embraced the joy of giving back once more.

Hope is a gentle reminder that while our chapters may change, the story of our lives is still being written with love and purpose.

DAILY REFLECTION

What does hope mean to you in this season of your life, and how have you seen it lead you through challenges? Reflect on moments when your hope felt strengthened or renewed.

PRAYER

Dear God, thank you for the gift of hope that sustains us through all seasons. May we always find joy in your promises and assurance in your presence.

"Hope is the quiet whisper in our hearts that reminds us the best is yet to come."

BECOMING MORE LIKE CHRIST

"Follow God's example, therefore, as dearly loved children"
Ephesians 5:1

DEVOTIONAL

Once there was a lovely grandmother named Helen who always seemed to radiate joy, even on her toughest days. She spent her retirement volunteering at the local community center, sharing her love of baking with children who might not have enough at home. One day, a little girl asked her why she baked so much even when it wasn't her birthday. With a twinkle in her eye, Helen replied, "Just like Jesus fed the hungry, I want to share what I have with others. Plus, who can resist the smell of fresh cookies?" In that moment, Helen realized that each batch of cookies was not just a treat; it was her way of becoming more like Christ, sharing love and warmth with everyone around her.

Your everyday acts of kindness and love, big or small, are beautiful ways to reflect Christ to the world around you.

DAILY REFLECTION

What qualities of Christ do you desire to embody more in your daily life, and how can you take small steps toward that today?

PRAYER

Dear Lord, help me to seek Your heart and reflect Your love in all that I do. Guide me in my journey to become more like Christ, embracing grace and compassion each day.

"True transformation occurs when we allow His love to flow through us, shaping our thoughts, words, and actions."

FAITH OVER FEAR

"Therefore do not worry about tomorrow, for tomorrow will worry about itself. Each day has enough trouble of its own." **Matthew 6:34**

DEVOTIONAL

Once upon a time, in a cozy little town, lived a wise and spirited retiree named Margaret. She had always dreamt of traveling the world, but as she grew older, fears crept in—what if I get lost? Or what if I can't keep up? One sunny afternoon, she decided to host a tea party for some friends and shared her travel dreams, only to discover they had their worries too! Together, they laughed, shared stories of their "what-ifs," and made a pact to face their fears one adventure at a time. That summer, the group hopped on a bus to a nearby city, a small step that led to even bigger journeys and wonderful memories.

Sometimes, our dreams seem daunting because we let our fears take the driver's seat; however, when we lean on faith and invite friends along, we can conquer those worries together.

DAILY REFLECTION

What fears or uncertainties are holding you back from embracing God's promises in this season of your life? Take a moment to reflect on how your faith can guide you through these challenges.

PRAYER

Dear Lord, thank You for being our refuge and strength. Help us to trust in Your unwavering love and find courage in the face of our fears.

"When we choose faith over fear, we open the door to new possibilities and a deeper relationship with God."

WHEN GOD FEELS SILENT

"Ask, and it will be given to you; seek, and you will find; knock, and the door will be opened to you. For everyone who asks receives; the one who seeks finds; and to the one who knocks, the door will be opened." **Matthew 7:7-8**

DEVOTIONAL

There once was a lovely lady named Alice who had always found joy in her garden. After retiring, she spent countless hours nurturing her roses, yet one season, they failed to bloom. Day after day, she watered and pruned, but the silence from her garden grew heavy. One afternoon, while sitting by her fence, a butterfly landed on her shoulder, and it dawned on her: just as she had cultivated her garden with love, so too was she invited to cultivate a deeper relationship with God, even in the silence. Sometimes, the best things take time to blossom.

In the quiet moments when God seems distant, remember that growth is happening beneath the surface, often in ways we cannot yet see.

DAILY REFLECTION

What moments in your life have left you feeling like God was quiet? How did you navigate those times, and how might they influence your faith today?

PRAYER

Dear God, in those times when You seem distant, help me to trust You are still near. Remind me that Your presence is not always loud but can be found in the gentle whispers and quiet moments.

"In silence, God often speaks the loudest to our hearts."

BECOMING A VESSEL OF GRACE

"The wild animals honor me, the jackals and the owls, because I provide water in the wilderness and streams in the wasteland, to give drink to my people, my chosen, the people I formed for myself that they may proclaim my praise." **Isaiah 43:20-21**

DEVOTIONAL

As she stood in her garden, Martha marveled at the way the flowers bloomed brightly despite the dry summer. Each plant seemed to reach out, inviting the bees and butterflies to share in their beauty. She had lovingly tended to them, but this year, there was something different; she could feel the joy in her heart swelling every time she watered them. One sunny afternoon, she decided to share her flowers with a neighbor who had recently lost her husband. As she handed over a bouquet, she saw her friend's face light up, and in that moment, Martha realized that her simple act of kindness was like that water in the wilderness —bringing life and grace to those around her.

We become vessels of grace when we share our joy and kindness, blossoming in the lives of others.

DAILY REFLECTION

What does it mean for you, in this stage of life, to be a vessel of grace to others around you? How can you intentionally share kindness and love with those you encounter each day?

PRAYER

Dear Lord, thank you for the grace you've poured into my life. Help me to be a reflection of your love, sharing kindness and compassion with everyone I meet.

"Grace flows freely when we allow our hearts to be open and generous."

LEARNING TO DEPEND ON HIM

"Cast your cares on the Lord and He will sustain you;
He will never let the righteous be shaken." **Psalm 55:22**

DEVOTIONAL

Once, a lovely woman named Clara found herself feeling overwhelmed by daily decisions she hadn't anticipated in her golden years. From what to bake for her bridge club to figuring out the perfect flower arrangement for Sunday service, it all felt like too much. One day, she decided to take a walk in the park, pausing at a bench to observe the beauty around her. As birds chirped and blossoms swayed, Clara took a deep breath and whispered her worries to the Lord. Instantly, she felt lighter, as if someone had lifted a weight from her shoulders. From that day on, she invited God into her life's little details, discovering that He always had the perfect fit for all her concerns.

Trusting Him in both big and small matters allows us to wander through this season of life with joy and ease, knowing He's always got our back.

DAILY REFLECTION

What does it look like for you to fully depend on God in this season of your life? Are there areas where you find it easier to rely on your own strength rather than His?

PRAYER

Dear Lord, thank you for your constant presence in our lives. Help us to trust in you more fully and to lean on your strength, especially during times of uncertainty. Teach us how to surrender our fears and anxieties into your loving hands.

"Dependency on God is not a sign of weakness; it is the truest form of strength."

GOD'S TIMING IS PERFECT

"There is a time for everything, and a season
for every activity under the heavens" **Ecclesiastes 3:1**

DEVOTIONAL

Once, there was a lovely grandmother named Ruth who had waited years to travel across the country to see her grandchildren. Every time she thought it was the right moment, something else would come up—a health issue, bad weather, or conflicting schedules. Just when she was beginning to feel discouraged, a spontaneous opportunity arose when a family reunion was planned in her honor. As Ruth packed her bags, she realized that the delays had not only built her anticipation but also allowed her loved ones to come together in a way they never expected. When she finally arrived, she was overwhelmed with joy, feeling it was the perfect time to embrace her family.

Sometimes, our hearts can grow restless waiting, but God's perfect timing unveils the sweetest moments of life.

DAILY REFLECTION

What moment in your life have you noticed God's perfect timing, even when it didn't align with your own plans? Reflect on how that experience has shaped your faith.

PRAYER

Dear Lord, thank You for the gift of Your perfect timing in our lives. Help us to trust in Your plans, even when we can't see the full picture. Amen.

"Embrace each season of life, for in each moment God's hand is guiding you."

YOU ARE NOT ALONE

*"One who has unreliable friends soon comes to ruin,
but there is a friend who sticks closer than a brother."* **Proverbs 18:24**

DEVOTIONAL

Once there was a delightful grandmother named Edna who felt a little lost after retiring from her beloved teaching career. One afternoon, she decided to take a walk around her neighborhood, hoping fresh air would lift her spirits. As she strolled, she noticed some familiar faces—her former students now grown up, who waved warmly and invited her to join a community book club. Edna hesitated at first, thinking it would be odd to join, but she gathered her courage and went. To her surprise, she found laughter, friendship, and a wonderful chance to share her wisdom. In that instant, Edna realized she had always been part of a wider tapestry of companionship, even when she felt alone.

Even in the quiet moments of retirement, remember that new friendships and connections are waiting to blossom.

DAILY REFLECTION

What thoughts or feelings come to mind when you consider the ways God has been present in your life, even during times of solitude?

PRAYER

Dear God, thank you for being a comforting presence in our lives. Help us to always remember that we are never truly alone, as You walk with us every step of our journey.

"Even in the quiet moments, God whispers, 'You are never alone.'"

ABIDING IN THE VINE

"I am the vine; you are the branches. Whoever abides in me and I in them bears much fruit, for apart from me you can do nothing." **John 15:5**

DEVOTIONAL

Margaret had spent decades caring for her family, keeping her home, and volunteering. Now, in retirement, she found herself with plenty of time and yet felt a little lost. One afternoon, while sipping tea in her garden, she noticed how the flowers flourished when tended with love and attention. It struck her that her soul needed that same care and nurturing. She began dedicating her mornings to prayer, allowing God's presence to fill her heart. Suddenly, her days were not just filled hours, but blossomed with purpose and joy, just like her garden.

Remember, dear friend, that as you abide in the Lord, you will find your own unique purpose and joy blooming in this season of life.

DAILY REFLECTION

What does it mean for you to truly abide in the vine during this season of your life? How does staying connected to Christ shape your daily experiences and relationships?

PRAYER

Dear Lord, thank You for the gift of life and the time to rest in Your presence. Help me to remain rooted in You, drawing strength and joy from our relationship in every moment.

"Abiding in the vine is not just about staying connected; it's about flourishing where God has planted you."

TRUSTING THROUGH TRANSITIONS

"Jesus Christ is the same yesterday, today, and forever."
Hebrews 13:8

DEVOTIONAL

Mabel had spent decades caring for her family and volunteering in her community, finding joy in her routine. As her children moved away and her friends began to pass on, she felt the shadows of loneliness and uncertainty creeping in. On one particular evening, while sorting through old photographs, she came across a picture of herself as a young woman, smiling brightly, with the words "This too shall pass" written on the back. In that moment, she realized that just as seasons change, so do the chapters of her life. With a deep breath, Mabel chose to embrace the new opportunities that awaited her—traveling, learning, and forming new friendships—trusting that God was guiding her through each transition.
Trusting in God during life's many changes can open the door to unexpected blessings and new beginnings.

DAILY REFLECTION

What transitions are you currently navigating in your life, and how can trusting in God help you find peace amidst the changes? Consider the small ways He has shown His faithfulness in your past.

PRAYER

Dear Lord, thank you for walking with me through every season of life. Help me to trust You more deeply during this time of change, knowing that You have a perfect plan for me.

"Trusting God through transitions opens the door to new beginnings and renewed hope."

CHOOSING PEACE IN UNCERTAINTY

"Let the peace of Christ rule in your hearts, since as members of one body you were called to peace. And be thankful." **Colossians 3:15**

DEVOTIONAL

As we age, we often find ourselves navigating a sea of uncertainties—whether it's about health, family dynamics, or future plans. There was once a retired schoolteacher, Mary, who felt overwhelmed after her husband's passing. Each day brought new questions about how she would fill her time and find joy again. One morning, sitting quietly with a cup of tea, she noticed the vibrant colors of the flowers blooming just outside her window. In that moment, she decided to shift her focus from her worries to the simple pleasures around her. Gradually, she began volunteering at a local community center, discovering not only a renewed sense of purpose but also the comforting presence of kindred spirits.

In the midst of life's uncertainties, choosing to focus on the beauty and connections around us can bring peace to our hearts.

DAILY REFLECTION

What uncertain situation in your life is calling for an embrace of peace rather than fear?

PRAYER

Dear God, help me to find peace amid the uncertainties of life. May I trust in Your guidance and be filled with a calm spirit as I navigate each day.

"Peace is not the absence of chaos but the presence of God's comfort."

HOLDING ON TO GOD'S PROMISES

"My comfort in my suffering is this: Your promise preserves my life."
Psalm 119:50

DEVOTIONAL

Once upon a time, in a cozy little village, there lived a retired woman named Grace. After years of working hard and raising her children, Grace found herself with more time on her hands but sometimes felt overwhelmed by the uncertainties of life. One sunny afternoon, as she tended to her beloved garden, she noticed a tiny seedling pushing its way through the soil. It reminded her of the many promises God made, and she realized that just like her garden needed care and patience to flourish, so too did her faith. Each day, she remembered to tend to her spiritual garden as well, watering it with prayer and nurturing it with God's word, allowing His promises to bloom beautifully in her heart.
Trust that God's promises are like seeds planted in your soul—nurture them, and watch them grow!

DAILY REFLECTION

What promises have you found most comforting in your journey of faith, and how can you hold onto them today?

PRAYER

Dear Lord, thank you for your unwavering love and the promises you have made to us. Help me to trust in your guidance and find peace in knowing that you are always by my side.

"God's timing is not just about waiting; it's about growing and discovering

LETTING GOD DEFINE YOUR WORTH

"See what great love the Father has lavished on us, that we should be called children of God! And that is what we are!" **1 John 3:1-2**

DEVOTIONAL

After decades of hard work, raising children, and nurturing relationships, Mary found herself questioning her worth in retirement. She often compared herself to others, wondering if her days still held significance. One quiet afternoon, while tending her garden, she noticed a bird tirelessly gathering twigs to create a nest. Despite its size, the bird worked diligently, confident in its purpose. Mary recognized that just as the bird found value in its smallness, she too had immeasurable worth simply because she was loved by God.

Your worth is not defined by accomplishments or comparisons; it is rooted in the unfathomable love God has for you.

DAILY REFLECTION

What does it mean for you to find your worth in God's love rather than in the opinions or accomplishments of the world around you?

PRAYER

Dear God, thank You for loving me just as I am. Help me to embrace the worth You have placed within me and to see myself through Your eyes each day.

"True worth is not measured by what we do, but by who we are in the heart of God."

ENCOURAGEMENT FOR THE WEARY SOUL

"God is our refuge and strength, a very present help in trouble."
Psalm 46:1

DEVOTIONAL

Just the other day, I stumbled upon a worn-out garden gnome in my yard. The poor thing seemed to have lost its charm, leaning a bit to one side with paint chipping away. I took a moment to clean it up, and as I restored its colors, I realized that sometimes we all need a little TLC. Just like that gnome, we can feel a bit ragged in our later years, but even when we feel like we're past our prime, God lovingly restores us, reminding us that our worth doesn't fade with time.

Remember, dear friend, just as the gnome found new life once again, so too can you find renewed joy and strength in the Lord every day.

DAILY REFLECTION

What has been weighing heavy on your heart lately, and how can you invite God's comfort into those areas of your life?

PRAYER

Dear Lord, I ask for your gentle embrace to wrap around those feelings of weariness. Refresh her spirit and remind her of your everlasting love, bringing new hope and strength to each day.

"Even in your weariness, God is crafting a beautiful story of renewal."

WHEN YOU FEEL SPIRITUALLY STUCK

"I waited patiently for the Lord; he turned to me and heard my cry. He lifted me out of the slimy pit, out of the mud and mire; he set my feet on a rock and gave me a firm place to stand. He put a new song in my mouth, a hymn of praise to our God." **Psalm 40:1-3**

DEVOTIONAL

Once upon a time in a cozy little town, there lived a delightful retired woman named Ruth. With all the time in the world, you'd think she'd have her spiritual path all figured out. But lately, she felt as if she was trudging through thick mud, caught in the mundane routine of book clubs and gardening. One day, while sipping her coffee on the porch, she noticed the birds dancing in the trees and realized they weren't just going through the motions; they were celebrating life! Inspired, Ruth decided to shake up her routine. She joined a local art class, rediscovered her love for painting, and before she knew it, her heart began to sing again, filling her days with vibrancy and joy.

Even in retirement, it's important to embrace new adventures, for they can lead us out of spiritual ruts and open our hearts to fresh experiences.

DAILY REFLECTION

What is one area in your spiritual life where you feel a sense of stagnation, and how might God be inviting you to grow or rediscover your faith?

PRAYER

Dear Lord, I thank You for Your unwavering presence in my life. Help me to navigate this season of feeling stuck and guide me to new insights and joy in my walk with You.

"Even in the stillness, God whispers promises of renewal."

FAITH THAT MOVES MOUNTAINS

"He replied. "Because you have so little faith. Truly I tell you, if you have faith as small as a mustard seed, you can say to this mountain, 'Move from here to there,' and it will move. Nothing will be impossible for you."" **Matthew 17:20**

DEVOTIONAL

Once, a lovely retired woman named Betty faced a seemingly insurmountable challenge: her once beautiful garden had fallen into disarray. Weeds overran her petunias, and rusted garden tools littered the yard. Instead of feeling defeated, she recalled her childhood mantra, "One step at a time!" After rallying her friends for a weekend gardening party, they shared laughs, snacks, and stories as they turned the garden back into a vibrant oasis. What started as a daunting task transformed into a joyful gathering, and with faith and friendship, Betty learned she could indeed move mountains—just as long as she asked for a bit of help. *Sometimes, the mountains in our lives are best tackled with a little faith and the support of friends.*

DAILY REFLECTION

What mountains of doubt or challenge are standing before you today, and how can your faith help you move them aside? Consider the ways God has worked in your life before, and how He may be calling you to trust Him anew.

PRAYER

Dear God, thank You for the gift of faith and the strength it gives us. As I face the mountains in my life, help me to lean on You and to remember that with You, all things are possible.

"Faith is the tool that can reshape our realities and open pathways where none seem to exist."

THE GENTLE VOICE OF GOD

"My sheep hear my voice, and I know them, and they follow me."
John 10:27

DEVOTIONAL

Once, after years of working tirelessly, a retired woman sat alone on her porch, sipping tea while watching the garden she had nurtured for decades. Amidst the chirping birds and rustling leaves, she began to hear a soft whisper in her heart, reminding her of the dreams she had set aside in the busyness of life. As she listened more intently, memories of her love for painting surfaced—a gentle nudging from God encouraging her to pick up a brush again. With each stroke on her canvas, she felt a renewed sense of purpose and connection, discovering that God's gentle voice leads us back to our true passions, even in the later years of life. *In the serene moments of your day, remember to listen for the gentle voice of God that calls you back to your dreams and passions.*

DAILY REFLECTION

What moments in your daily life can you pause to listen for the gentle whispers of God?

PRAYER

Dear God, thank you for your gentle presence in my life. Help me to quiet my heart and listen for your voice in the busyness of each day. Amen.

"In the stillness, God's voice becomes a melody to our hearts."

LIVING WITH KINGDOM VISION

*"But seek first his kingdom and his righteousness, and all these things will be given to you as well." **Matthew 6:33***

DEVOTIONAL

Mary had always been an avid volunteer, even in her retirement. Despite the physical limitations of age, she found joy in mentoring young women in her community. One day, while sharing her life stories, she realized that her wisdom was a treasure that could illuminate the path for others. As she inspired the next generation, Mary felt a renewed purpose, showing that living with Kingdom vision means passing on the light of Christ, even as we enter our later chapters.

When we seek to serve and uplift others, we not only fulfill God's purpose for our lives, but we also enrich our own journey.

DAILY REFLECTION

What does it mean for you to view your daily life through the lens of God's Kingdom, even in this season of retirement? How can you embrace new opportunities to serve and share your wisdom with those around you?

PRAYER

Dear Lord, thank you for this season of rest and reflection in my life. Guide me to see the beauty and purpose in each day, that I may live with a heart aligned to your Kingdom.

"Embrace each day as a divine opportunity to reflect Christ's love in your community."

STANDING FIRM IN FAITH

*"Let us hold unswervingly to the hope we profess, for he who promised is faithful." **Hebrews 10:23***

DEVOTIONAL

Martha had spent her life nurturing her family and supporting her husband through his career, often putting her dreams on hold. Now in retirement, she found herself wrestling with feelings of purposelessness and doubt about her next chapter. One afternoon, she attended a women's gathering at her church where several women shared their journeys post-retirement. Inspired by their testimonies of finding new passions in faith and community service, Martha felt a spark igniting within her. As she reflected on the stories of resilience and hope, she realized that her faith in God's plan was a constant thread that could guide her into this new phase. That evening, she decided to volunteer at the local food pantry, convinced that God still had significant work for her to accomplish.

Trusting in God's faithfulness allows us to embrace new opportunities with courage and hope, even in the seasons of change.

DAILY REFLECTION

What are the moments in your life where you felt your faith waver, and how can those experiences strengthen your resolve to stand firm now?

PRAYER

Dear God, thank you for the gift of faith that guides us every day. Help us to lean on You in our uncertainties and give us the strength to remain steadfast in our trust.

"Faith is the anchor that holds us steady in the storms of life."

LETTING GO OF SHAME

*"Therefore, if anyone is in Christ, the new creation has come:
The old has gone, the new is here!"* **2 Corinthians 5:17**

DEVOTIONAL

Mabel had always been the caretaker in her family, juggling responsibilities for her husband, children, and later her grandchildren. Yet, as she entered her retirement years, the weight of past mistakes often loomed over her—those moments when she felt she had fallen short of being the 'perfect' mom or grandmother. One day, while cleaning out her attic, she stumbled upon an old photo album filled with memories of joy and love, reminding her of the laughter shared and the lessons learned. In that moment, Mabel realized that shame had held her back from fully embracing the beautiful woman she had grown into. She began to understand that her past did not define her and that God loved her, just as she was, allowing her to release the chains of shame that had bound her heart for too long.

Letting go of shame opens the door to fully embrace who you are and all the wonderful gifts you still have to offer.

DAILY REFLECTION

What burdens of shame have you carried into this season of your life, and how can you begin to release them today? Consider how they have shaped your journey and reflect on the freedom that awaits you in surrender.

PRAYER

Dear God, help me to release the shame I've held onto for too long. May I embrace your love and forgiveness, and find peace in knowing I am enough just as I am.

"Shame diminishes our light, but grace helps us shine bright."

ANCHORED IN HIS WORD

*"The grass withers and the flowers fall, but the word
of our God endures forever."* **Isaiah 40:8**

DEVOTIONAL

Once there was a grandmother named Grace who loved gardening. Every spring, she'd plant beautiful flowers, only to see them fade away come autumn. One day, while sipping her tea on the porch, she reflected on how her blooms would wither but remembered her favorite scripture about God's Word. It struck her that just like those flowers, life changes. Yet, God's promises are everlasting, providing peace and stability in her ever-changing world. With a smile, she decided to plant seeds of scripture in her heart, nurturing them to bloom in her life each day.

Just as flowers in a garden may fade, God's Word will always remain a source of strength and joy for you.

DAILY REFLECTION

What verses in the Bible have anchored your heart during life's storms, and how can you revisit those passages to strengthen your faith today?

PRAYER

Dear Lord, thank You for the steadiness of Your Word. Help me to remember and embrace the promises in Scripture as my anchor in every season of life.

"In His promises, we find our steadfast anchor, guiding us through every wave of uncertainty."

BRAVE IN THE SMALL THINGS

"Command them to do good, to be rich in good deeds, and to be generous and willing to share. In this way they will lay up treasure for themselves as a firm foundation for the coming age, so that they may take hold of the life that is truly life." **1 Timothy 6:18-19**

DEVOTIONAL

Once, a retired grandmother noticed her neighbor struggling with groceries. Instead of shying away or thinking it wasn't her place, she gathered some of her own extra items and knocked on the neighbor's door. That small act, which seemed simple to her, turned into a weekly ritual where the two shared stories over coffee each Saturday. The neighbor found community and hope in their conversations, while the grandmother discovered new purpose and joy in the companionship they built. What began as a small, brave step of kindness blossomed into a beautiful friendship, enhancing both their lives.

Bravery often starts with small gestures, and in those moments, we can find profound connections and purpose.

DAILY REFLECTION

What small act of courage can you embrace today that may seem insignificant but could have a big impact on your life or someone else's?

PRAYER

Dear Lord, thank You for the gift of each day. Help me to see and embrace the small opportunities to be brave, trusting that these moments matter in Your eyes.

"Bravery is not just in grand actions but in the quiet moments of choosing love and honesty."

YOUR PAIN HAS A PURPOSE

"For our light and momentary troubles are achieving for us an eternal glory that far outweighs them all." **2 Corinthians 4:17**

DEVOTIONAL

As a retired woman, you may find your days filled with quiet reflection and memories—both sweet and bittersweet. Consider the story of Martha, a lively grandmother who faced a daunting health issue that kept her from her beloved gardening. Initially disheartened, she found solace in creating a gardening club for local children, teaching them the joy of planting. Through her pain, she discovered a new purpose, nurturing young minds and hearts while finding joy in her newfound role. Her struggles became a bridge to connect with life's beauty once again.

Embrace the belief that your struggles, as painful as they may feel, are shaping you for a purpose that can brighten the lives of others.

DAILY REFLECTION

What experiences in your life have caused you pain, and how might God be using those moments to shape your purpose today?

PRAYER

Dear Lord, thank You for the ways You can turn our pain into purpose. Help me to see the beauty in my struggles and the lessons You want me to learn from them.

"Every tear we shed today can water the seeds of purpose that bloom tomorrow."

A GOD WHO REDEEMS

"I will repay you for the years the locusts have eaten — the great locust and the young locust, the other locusts and the locust swarm — my great army that I sent among you."
Joel 2:25

DEVOTIONAL

There was once a lovely woman named Margaret, who spent her busy years raising children and pursuing her career. Now retired, she often found herself reminiscing about the dreams she put aside, feeling like time had taken much from her. One sunny afternoon, she decided to join a local art class, rediscovering the joy of painting she had abandoned. Not only did she find her creativity blossoming, but she also formed deep friendships with other kindred spirits. As they painted and laughed together, Margaret realized that while life had its seasons, God was still, and always would be, in the business of redeeming and restoring.

No matter how many years have passed, God has beautiful plans for your heart and can restore your joy in unexpected ways.

DAILY REFLECTION

What areas of your life have you seen God's redemptive hand at work, and how can you embrace that truth today?

PRAYER

Dear God, thank you for being the Redeemer in our lives. Help me to see and embrace the beauty of your redemption in every moment. Amen.

"God's redemption is not just a story; it is a promise that unfolds in our lives every day."

BECOMING SPIRITUALLY RESILIENT

"The Lord your God is with you, the Mighty Warrior who saves. He will take great delight in you; in his love he will no longer rebuke you, but will rejoice over you with singing."
Zephaniah 3:17

DEVOTIONAL

As a retired woman, you have witnessed countless seasons of change in your life, from career pursuits to family milestones. There may have been moments when you felt overwhelmed, perhaps when your children left home or when you faced the loss of a dear friend. Each time, you found the strength to adapt, learning to lean into your faith. The wisdom gathered over the years reminds you that it's okay to feel fragile, and yet you still carry the resilience born from trusting in God's unwavering love. It becomes a delightful surprise each day when you realize that even in your golden years, new beginnings await, inviting you to explore uncharted paths.

Trust in your inner strength and the everlasting love that surrounds you; these are the foundations upon which resilience is built.

DAILY REFLECTION

What challenges have you faced lately that have tested your spiritual strength, and how can you lean on your faith for resilience during this time?

PRAYER

Dear Lord, thank You for the gift of Your presence in our lives. Help us to find strength in You, especially during moments of uncertainty, and to trust in the journey You have laid before us.

"Resilience is not just about bouncing back; it's about growing stronger in the midst of life's storms."

OVERFLOWING WITH LIVING WATER

*"But whoever drinks of the water that I shall give him will never thirst. But the water that I shall give him will become in him a spring of water welling up to eternal life." **John 4:14***

DEVOTIONAL

Imagine a sunny afternoon with a gentle breeze, where you sit in your garden, surrounded by blooming flowers. This garden, much like your life, requires care and nurturing. Just as you have taken the time to cultivate your plants and watch them flourish, so too does the Living Water offered by Jesus bring life to your soul in retirement. As you sip your afternoon tea, think of the way your heart can bloom and overflow with kindness, wisdom, and joy, reaching those around you—just like birds flocking to a sweet-smelling garden.

In this new season of life, may you be the flower that continues to bloom, bringing joy and comfort to those who cross your path. Remember that your well of experiences has so much to offer and can nurture others in ways that you may not even realize.

DAILY REFLECTION

Let your life be a refreshing spring of living water to family and friends, overflowing with love, laughter, and encouragement.

PRAYER

What small act of kindness can you sprinkle into someone's day this week?

Dear Lord, thank You for filling me with Your endless love and joy. Help me to be a source of encouragement and comfort to those around me. May I always let Your Living Water flow through me as I embrace this wonderful season of life. Amen.

CHOOSING REST OVER RUSH

*"Consider how the wild flowers grow. They do not labor or spin. Yet I tell you, not even Solomon in all his splendor was dressed like one of these." **Luke 12:27***

DEVOTIONAL

Margaret had spent her whole life rushing from one obligation to another. After retirement, she found herself with an abundance of time yet still felt the pressure to fill each day with activity. One sunny afternoon, she decided to take a walk in the nearby park. As she strolled slowly, she noticed the beauty of the flowers, the laughter of children, and the joy of the world around her. It dawned on her that the essence of life wasn't in the busyness, but in the moments she allowed herself to simply be present. From then on, she consciously carved out time each week to simply enjoy the stillness, embracing the beauty of each moment.

Choosing rest over rush allows you to savor the beauty of life that has always been waiting for you.

DAILY REFLECTION

What does it feel like to truly rest in the peace of God, rather than rushing through each moment? How might your life look different if you embraced calm and stillness instead of the urgency to always be busy?

PRAYER

Dear Lord, help me to embrace the gift of rest that You offer. Teach me to find peace in my days and to savor each moment as a precious part of my journey with You.

"Rest is not a luxury; it is a necessary rhythm of life."

A HEART THAT SEEKS GOD

"Look to the Lord and his strength; seek his face always."
Psalm 105:4

DEVOTIONAL

Once upon a time, there was a lovely grandmother named Doris who had embraced the joys of retirement. With her days now free from the rush of a career, she discovered a new passion for gardening. As she planted her flowers, she often found herself talking to God, sharing her thoughts and dreams. One sunny afternoon, while tending to her roses, Doris found herself reflecting on how God's love surrounds her like the sunshine. It was in those quiet moments in her garden that she felt the gentle nudge of the Holy Spirit guiding her to serve her community, reminding her that seeking God can lead to beautiful blooms in both her garden and her life.

When we seek God in the everyday moments, we uncover the treasures of His presence that fill our hearts with joy and purpose.

DAILY REFLECTION

What does it mean for your heart to genuinely seek God in this season of your life, and how can you draw nearer to Him each day?

PRAYER

Dear Lord, thank you for being a constant presence in our lives. Help me to cultivate a heart that seeks You in every moment and to find joy in Your guidance as I navigate this new phase.

"Seeking God is the journey that leads us to the peace and joy we desire."

OBEDIENCE IN THE LITTLE THINGS

"Teach me, Lord, the way of your decrees, that I may follow it to the end. Give me understanding, so that I may keep your law and obey it with all my heart." **Psalm 119:33-34**

DEVOTIONAL

Margaret had a small garden filled with colorful flowers, but they weren't thriving. One afternoon, as she tended to them, she noticed a few weeds creeping in. Instead of ignoring them, she took a moment to pull them out, realizing that this little act of care would help her garden flourish. That evening, she sat by her window, sipping tea, and felt a warmth in her heart—sometimes, it's the little things that lead to beautiful results.

Each act of obedience in daily life, no matter how small, can lead to unexpected blessings and growth.

DAILY REFLECTION

Embrace the little moments; they often hold the keys to greater joy and fulfillment in your journey.

PRAYER

Dear Lord, thank You for the gift of each day and the simple moments that fill our lives. Help me to be attentive to Your whispers and to walk obediently in the little things that bring me closer to You.

"Obedience in the little things can open doors to the extraordinary."

THE GIFT OF QUIET MOMENTS

*"The one who has knowledge uses words with restraint, and whoever has understanding is even-tempered. Even fools are thought wise if they keep silent, and discerning if they hold their tongues." **Proverbs 17:27-28***

DEVOTIONAL

Margaret had always been a busy woman, bustling through life with a packed schedule and never enough hours in the day. Now, in her retirement, she found herself with quiet mornings that stretched luxuriously before her. One day, she sat on her porch with a cup of tea, listening to the whisper of the wind through the trees and the distant sound of birds. It was in that unhurried moment, wrapped in the softness of stillness, that she felt God's presence enveloping her like a warm blanket. She sensed the beauty of being still, realizing that in the quiet, He was speaking to her heart.

In the calm of quiet moments, we discover the space to listen for God's whispers and the peace that comes from being present in the stillness.

DAILY REFLECTION

What are some quiet moments in your day that bring you peace and joy? How can you intentionally create more of these moments for yourself?

PRAYER

Dear Lord, help me to embrace the quiet moments in my life. May they become sacred spaces where I find your presence and rejuvenate my spirit. Thank you for the gift of stillness.

"In the stillness, we often hear the whispers of our heart and the love of our Creator."

HE CARRIES YOUR BURDENS

"He replied, 'Blessed rather are those who hear the word of God and obey it'"
Luke 11:28

DEVOTIONAL

In her quiet evenings, Mary often sat by her window, gazing at the garden she had lovingly cultivated over the years. With her husband gone and children settled elsewhere, she sometimes felt the weight of solitude pressing heavily upon her heart. One evening, as she pruned her beloved roses, she felt a gentle breeze that seemed to whisper to her spirit, reminding her that she wasn't alone in her struggles. As if the flowers themselves offered comfort, she realized that her burdens were shared and that she could give her worries to a loving God who cared deeply for her. Now, each time she feels overwhelmed, she takes a moment to breathe deeply and remember the reminder of that evening: she is supported, cherished, and never truly alone.

You are not meant to carry your burdens alone; lean into faith and trust that God's care surrounds you.

DAILY REFLECTION

How have you seen God carry your burdens in your life, and how can you invite Him to lighten your load today?

PRAYER

Dear Lord, thank you for always being there to carry my burdens. Help me to trust in Your love and presence as I navigate the challenges I face.

"His strength carries you, even when you feel weak."

YOUR JOURNEY IS SACRED

*"Rejoice always, pray continually, give thanks in all circumstances;
for this is God's will for you in Christ Jesus."*
1 Thessalonians 5:16-18

DEVOTIONAL

Once upon a time, there lived a wise woman named Grace who embraced her retirement with open arms. She filled her days with gardening, volunteering, and visiting loved ones. With each passing season, she found joy in the little things—watching the flowers bloom, sharing laughter with friends, and lending a helping hand. As she looked back on her journey, Grace realized that every moment, every twist and turn, had led her to a deeper understanding of love, gratitude, and the sacredness of life.

Your journey, filled with experiences and lessons, is a sacred tapestry woven by the hands of God.

DAILY REFLECTION

What moments in your life have felt especially sacred, and how can you celebrate those as part of your ongoing journey?

PRAYER

Dear God, thank you for every precious moment that has shaped my life. Help me to embrace my journey with gratitude and grace, recognizing the sacredness in each step along the way.

"Your journey is a beautiful tapestry, woven with threads of faith, love, and resilience."

VICTORY IN CHRIST

*"For everyone born of God overcomes the world.
This is the victory that has overcome the world, even our faith." **1 John 5:4***

DEVOTIONAL

Once upon a time, there was a delightful woman named Margaret, who spent her retirement days tending her fabulous garden. Each flower she planted was like a new prayer she whispered to God. One sunny afternoon, while watering her daisies, she noticed some pesky weeds trying to invade. Instead of getting upset, she joyfully rooted them out, remembering how life sometimes brings challenges that seem overwhelming. With God's strength in her heart, she found victory not just in her garden but in her spirit, realizing it was faith that truly allowed her to flourish.

Embrace each challenge as an opportunity to experience the sweet victory that comes from your faith in Christ.

DAILY REFLECTION

What does it mean for you to experience victory in your daily life, and how can Christ's love lead you to that triumph? Consider the moments where you've seen His hand at work.

PRAYER

Dear Lord, thank you for the gift of each new day and the victories you bring into our lives. Help me to lean on you, trusting in your strength and love as I navigate this season of life.

"Victory in Christ is not about winning the fight, but about finding peace in His presence."

RENEWAL IN CHRIST

*"to be made new in the attitude of your minds; and to put on the new self, created to be like God in true righteousness and holiness." **Ephesians 4:23-24***

DEVOTIONAL

Once upon a time, there was a woman named Claire who had spent her life caring for others. In her retirement, she found herself grappling with a sense of emptiness. One day, while tending to her garden, she noticed a small flower pushing through the soil, determined to bloom despite the harsh winter. Inspired by its resilience, Claire realized that just like that flower, she too was invited to embrace renewal. She began exploring new hobbies, volunteering at a local shelter, and connecting with old friends. Using the time and freedom of her retirement, she rediscovered her passions and found joy in new beginnings.

Even in the later seasons of life, God offers fresh starts and opportunities for renewal as we embrace new paths and passions.

DAILY REFLECTION

What areas of your life do you feel God is inviting you to renew in Him today? How can you embrace this season of change and growth with an open heart?

PRAYER

Dear Lord, thank You for the gift of renewal in our lives. Help us to seek You in all things and to trust Your ways as we embrace this new chapter. Amen.

"Renewal in Christ brings fresh beginnings, no matter our age."

WHEN YOU NEED REASSURANCE

*"May the God of hope fill you with all joy and peace as you trust in him, so that you may overflow with hope by the power of the Holy Spirit." **Romans 15:13***

DEVOTIONAL

Once there was a woman named Eleanor who, after retiring, often found herself worried about her future. On a particularly cloudy day, she decided to visit her favorite garden, a place where she had spent many joyful hours planting flowers and nurturing their growth. As she strolled through the vibrant blooms, she noticed how each flower was different yet harmonious in its own way. Just as the garden thrived with diversity, Eleanor realized her life too was filled with beautiful moments, friendships, and experiences—each contributing to her unique journey.

Even in times of uncertainty, remember that the beauty of your life, like a garden, flourishes in the most unexpected ways.

DAILY REFLECTION

What moments in your life have left you feeling uncertain, and how have you sought reassurance during those times? Reflect on how God's presence has played a role in your journey.

PRAYER

Dear Lord, thank you for being our constant source of love and support. In moments of doubt, help us to feel your comforting presence and the strength that comes from your promises.

"Even in seasons of change, God's embrace remains steadfast."

ROOTED IN GOD'S WORD

*"But blessed is the one who trusts in the Lord, whose confidence is in him. They will be like a tree planted by the water that sends out its roots by the stream. It does not fear when heat comes; its leaves are always green. It has no worries in a year of drought and never fails to bear fruit." **Jeremiah 17:7-8***

DEVOTIONAL

Once upon a time in a cozy neighborhood, there lived a lovely retired woman named Marge. Every morning, she would sip her tea on the porch, surrounded by her flower garden. One sunny day, while trimming her beloved roses, she noticed how deep their roots reached into the ground, drawing strength from the rich soil. That moment sparked a realization: just as her flowers relied on good soil, she needed to stay rooted in God's Word to flourish in life's challenges and joys. Marge began reading her Bible daily, finding comfort and guidance that bloomed in her heart just like her garden.

Stay rooted in God's Word, and watch as your life blossoms beautifully, bringing joy and peace into every season.

DAILY REFLECTION

What does being rooted in God's Word look like for you in this season of your life? How can you cultivate deeper connections with scripture amidst the changes you experience?

PRAYER

Dear Lord, thank You for Your everlasting Word that provides strength and comfort. Help me to dwell in it daily, allowing it to guide my thoughts and actions. May I find peace and purpose in every verse I embrace.

"Just as a tree flourishes when its roots dig deep into nourishing soil, so too does our spirit thrive when anchored in God's Word."

FAITH FOR THE FUTURE

"The Lord himself goes before you and will be with you; he will never leave you nor forsake you. Do not be afraid; do not be discouraged." **Deuteronomy 31:8**

DEVOTIONAL

I once met a lovely woman in her 70s who had spent her life being a caregiver for her family. Now in retirement, she felt a little lost, unsure of what the future held. One day, she decided to take a leap of faith and joined a local volunteer group. Much to her surprise, the warmth and joy brought into her own life through helping others sparked a renewed passion within her. She realized that while her roles had changed, God still had a purpose for her, and she looked toward the future with hope and excitement.

Embracing your future with faith opens up new possibilities and purpose, proving that every season of life holds its own unique offerings.

DAILY REFLECTION

What dreams and hopes do you secretly hold for the years ahead, and how can you lean on your faith to bring them to life?

PRAYER

Dear Lord, thank you for the gift of each day. Help me to trust in Your plans for my future and to embrace whatever comes with an open heart.

"Faith allows us to embrace tomorrow with joy, knowing that each new day is filled with His grace."

CHOOSING JOY DAILY

"I delight greatly in the Lord; my soul rejoices in my God. For he has clothed me with garments of salvation and arrayed me in a robe of his righteousness, as a bridegroom adorns his head like a priest, and as a bride adorns herself with her jewels." **Isaiah 61:10**

DEVOTIONAL

After a long career of service and dedication to her family and community, Ruth found herself wondering what it meant to embrace her golden years fully. One sunny morning, as she sat with a cup of tea in her garden, she noticed the vibrant colors of her flowers dancing in the gentle breeze. A small child passed by, laughing and playing, reminding her of the simple joys that life offers if we pause to notice. Inspired by this moment, Ruth decided to start each day by reflecting on the blessings around her, choosing to find joy in the small things—like the warmth of the sun or the sound of laughter. It became her daily ritual, transforming her perspective and enriching her life in delightful ways.

Every day is an opportunity to choose joy, even in the smallest moments that surround us.

DAILY REFLECTION

What small choice can you make today to embrace joy, even in the ordinary moments of your life? Consider what brings a smile to your face and how you can invite that joy into your daily routine.

PRAYER

Dear Lord, thank You for the gift of today and the joys that await us. Help us to see the beautiful moments, big and small, and to choose joy in all circumstances. Amen.

"Joy blooms in the heart that chooses to celebrate life's little wonders."

GOD'S PRESENCE IN THE WAITING

"and teaching them to obey everything I have commanded you. And surely I am with you always, to the very end of the age.'" **Matthew 28:20**

DEVOTIONAL

Once, a widow named Margaret found herself in a season of waiting. Each day seemed like a repetitive loop of quiet moments, with only the gentle tick of the clock as company. One afternoon, while tending to her garden, she noticed new buds emerging from the soil, hidden beneath the surface for so long. It struck her then that just as the plants had been growing while she waited, so too was God nurturing her heart, whispering love and promise amid uncertainty. She began to find joy in the small things, realizing that her time in waiting was also a time of preparation—a gentle reminder that God was ever-present, knitting together the beautiful tapestry of her life.

In these quiet moments of waiting, remember that God is gently crafting new beginnings, even when we cannot see the full picture.

DAILY REFLECTION

What are some ways you recognize God's presence during times of waiting in your life?

PRAYER

Dear Lord, thank You for being with me in every season of my life, especially when I find myself waiting. Help me to embrace this moment and feel Your presence surrounding me with love and peace.

'In the stillness of waiting, God whispers His promises to our hearts."

A HEART OF HUMILITY

"Humble yourselves before the Lord, and he will lift you up." **James 4:10**

DEVOTIONAL

In her later years, Margaret often found herself reflecting on her life. She realized that the moments she cherished most were not the accolades or the big events, but the quiet afternoons spent serving at the local shelter or listening to a friend's troubles over a cup of tea. One day, as she helped serve lunch, a young mother, overwhelmed and weary, expressed her deep gratitude. In that moment, Margaret felt a profound joy, knowing that her small acts of service were truly meaningful. She came to see that in lifting others up, she found her own heart lifted in return.

As we embrace our retirements, let us remember that a humble heart opens the door to deeper connections and a richer, more fulfilling life.

DAILY REFLECTION

What does it mean for you to live each day with a heart of humility? How can you embrace the beauty in serving others and recognizing their worth in your interactions?

PRAYER

Dear Lord, open my heart to the gift of humility. Help me to see the value in others and to find joy in serving, reflecting Your love through my actions. Thank You for the grace to grow in this beautiful trait.

"True humility is not thinking less of yourself, but thinking of yourself less."

WALKING IN GOD'S STRENGTH

"The Lord is my strength and my shield; my heart trusts in him, and he helps me. My heart leaps for joy, and with my song I praise him." **Psalm 28:7**

DEVOTIONAL

As a grandmother, Jane found herself reflecting on her younger years while watching her grandchildren play. One afternoon, she volunteered to join them on a nature walk. At first, she felt every creak and strain of her aging joints, but then she remembered a promise she had made to herself: to embrace each moment with joy and gratitude. With each step, she felt a renewed strength bubbling up within her. Instead of focusing on her limitations, she savored the laughter and wonder surrounding her. That day, Jane discovered that in the joys of connection, God provided a renewed spirit that made her heart soar.

Sometimes, our true strength is revealed in the moments we choose to engage with life, rather than withdraw from it.

DAILY REFLECTION

What does walking in God's strength look like for you in this season of your life? How can you embrace His power in your daily activities and interactions with others?

PRAYER

Dear Lord, thank You for being our constant source of strength. Help us to lean on You in every moment of our days and to trust that You equip us for the journey ahead.

"Strength is not the absence of weariness, but the assurance that we are never alone."

COMPASSION LIKE CHRIST

"When he saw the crowds, he had compassion on them, because they were harassed and helpless, like sheep without a shepherd." **Matthew 9:36**

DEVOTIONAL

Once upon a time in a cozy little neighborhood, there lived a retired woman named Edith. With her garden in full bloom and her knitting needles always clicking, she found joy in the little things. One sunny afternoon, she noticed a new neighbor, a frail elderly man, struggling with his groceries. Without hesitation, Edith grabbed her basket, filled it with the goodies she had prepared, and marched over to offer her help. As they chatted and shared a laugh, Edith realized that sometimes, a simple act of kindness can brighten someone's day just as much as a sunny garden.

Compassion, like Christ, thrives in the small acts of kindness we offer each day.

DAILY REFLECTION

How can you show compassion to someone around you today, and what small act might reflect Christ's love in their life? Consider how your experiences can guide your support for others in meaningful ways.

PRAYER

Dear Lord, thank you for filling our hearts with your love. Help us to extend that love to others through our actions and words, just as Christ did. May our lives reflect your compassion every day.

"Compassion is the heart's response to the needs of others, echoing the love of Christ."

OVERCOMING SPIRITUAL BURNOUT

*"Therefore encourage one another and build each other up, just as in fact you are doing." **1 Thessalonians 5:11***

DEVOTIONAL

Once, there was a woman named Helen who had devoted her life to serving others in her church and community. In her retirement, she found that the very passion that once fueled her became a source of fatigue. She realized that while she loved giving, she had forgotten to care for her own spirit. One quiet afternoon, Helen took a long walk in nature, allowing herself to breathe and reflect. Amid the gentle rustle of leaves, she felt God whispering that it was okay to take a step back and nurture her own heart. This moment of tranquility rekindled her joy and renewed her spirit.

Remember, dear friend, even in the season of giving, tending to your own soul is not selfish but rather a beautiful act of love towards yourself and those you care for.

DAILY REFLECTION

What are the ways you've noticed spiritual burnout creeping into your life, and how can you invite God to renew your spirit today?

PRAYER

Dear Lord, thank you for the gift of rest and renewal. Help me to take the time I need to rejuvenate my spirit and draw closer to You. Amen.

"Rest is not idleness; it's the quiet place where faith is replenished."

THE HOPE OF THE RESURRECTION

*"Jesus said to her, 'I am the resurrection and the life. The one who believes in me will live, even though they die; and whoever lives by believing in me will never die. Do you believe this?'" **John 11:25-26***

DEVOTIONAL

Imagine a cozy afternoon in her favorite armchair, surrounded by the delightful scent of blooming roses from the garden. She reminisces about her dear friend who recently passed, their laughter echoing through many shared moments. With every flower that blooms, she feels a connection, remembering that friendship and love transcend even the harshest realities. Just as winter gives way to spring, so too does the hope of resurrection bring warmth to her heart, knowing one day they'll be together again in a beautiful garden far beyond this life.

Sometimes, it takes a little faith to remember that love, like flowers, never truly fades; it is a promise of blooming joy in the life to come.

DAILY REFLECTION

What does the hope of the resurrection mean to you in your current season of life, and how does it inspire you to embrace each day with joy?

PRAYER

Dear Lord, thank you for the promise of resurrection and the hope it brings us. Help us to live fully in light of your eternal love, finding joy and purpose in every moment we share with others.

"Resurrection hope fills our days with light, reminding us that every ending is a new beginning."

POURING OUT, BEING FILLED

*"Whoever believes in me, as Scripture has said,
rivers of living water will flow from within them." **John 7:38***

DEVOTIONAL

Once upon a sunny afternoon, Marie decided to host a tea party for her neighbors. As she brewed fragrant chamomile and set out her finest china, she wondered how she could fill everyone's cups—not just with tea but with joy. Each guest shared stories, laughter, and even a few tears, and by the time the sun set, Marie felt as if her heart was as full as her teapot. Little did she know, while she thought she was pouring into others, they were filling her soul in return, weaving a beautiful fabric of friendship that brightened her golden years.

Surrounding yourself with joy and sharing it will always refill your own cup, even as you pour into others.

DAILY REFLECTION

What does it mean for you to pour out your heart and soul into the lives of others, and how have you seen God fill you in moments of giving?

PRAYER

Dear Lord, help me to be a vessel of your love, pouring out kindness and encouragement to those around me. Fill me with your joy and peace as I share your blessings with others.

"Pouring out your love is the very act that fills your spirit with God's abundance."

GOD'S PROVISION IS ENOUGH

*"I was young and now I am old, yet I have never seen the righteous forsaken or their children begging bread." **Psalm 37:25***

DEVOTIONAL

Once, in her golden years, Margaret found herself feeling anxious about her finances. Though her retirement savings seemed adequate, unexpected expenses loomed large. One day, while sipping tea in her garden, she noticed a friendly neighbor placing fresh vegetables on her doorstep. This simple act of kindness reminded her that she was not alone. Each time she faced uncertainty, it became clear that God had been weaving a beautiful tapestry of support around her, often through the hands of those in her community.

Each day, let us remember that God's provision is not just about our material needs; it transcends into the warmth of friendship and the love of family, reminding us that we are always cared for.

DAILY REFLECTION

What is a recent moment in your life where you felt God's provision, and how can you embrace that feeling of abundance even in the little things?

PRAYER

Dear God, thank you for your constant presence in our lives. Help us to recognize and cherish your provisions, knowing that they are more than enough for our needs.

"God's grace fills our hearts with enough to share and enough to feel whole."

WOMEN OF PURPOSE

"She is clothed with strength and dignity; she can laugh at the days to come."
Proverbs 31:25

DEVOTIONAL

Meet Margaret, a spirited grandmother who discovered a new passion for gardening after retiring. As she tended to her vibrant flowers and vegetables, she realized that this simple hobby brought her not only joy but a sense of purpose. Each bloom reminded her of the beauty that can emerge at any age, and with every harvest, she found new ways to share the fruits of her labor with her family and neighbors. Her garden became a gathering place that nurtured relationships and fostered laughter, proving that her purpose was not confined to a career but blossomed in new, unexpected ways.

Every season of life holds the potential for new purpose; embrace it with joy and an open heart.

DAILY REFLECTION

What passions have remained in your heart that you've yet to explore? How can you take small steps toward fulfilling those dreams now?

PRAYER

Dear Lord, thank You for the journey of life and the purpose You have instilled in each of us. Guide our hearts to seek out the dreams You have planted within us, and give us the courage to follow them.

"Every season of life can lead to beautiful new beginnings."

COURAGE TO BEGIN AGAIN

"Be strong and courageous. Do not be afraid or terrified because of them, for the Lord your God goes with you; he will never leave you nor forsake you."
Deuteronomy 31:6

DEVOTIONAL

In her cozy sunroom, Margaret often reflected on her life. She had raised her children, nurtured her career, and now found herself in a quiet space, where the days sometimes felt too still. One afternoon, a flyer for a local painting class caught her eye. With hesitation, she thought about the years since she had picked up a brush, feeling a pang of self-doubt. Yet, as she moved toward the class for the first time, she felt a spark—something new and exciting was unfolding in her life. Embracing this new beginning allowed her to express herself in ways she never expected, and she discovered joy in creating again, surrounded by new friends who inspired her spirit.

Every new beginning is a chance to discover a vibrant part of yourself that still longs to grow and flourish.

DAILY REFLECTION

What new beginnings are you being called to embrace in this season of your life?

PRAYER

Dear God, grant me the courage to embrace new beginnings, even when the path seems uncertain. Help me to trust in Your guidance and find joy in each step forward. Amen.

"Every ending carries the seed of a new beginning."

FAITHFUL IN THE HIDDEN PLACES

"I will give you hidden treasures, riches stored in secret places, so that you may know that I am the Lord, the God of Israel, who summons you by name." **Isaiah 45:3**

DEVOTIONAL

Imagine a lovely grandmother named Ruth who spends her afternoons tending to her garden. Each morning she is up early, nurturing her flowers and plants, drawing strength from the silence of the dawn. She finds joy in the simple, unseen work that transforms her yard into a vibrant paradise. One day, a neighbor passing by stops to admire her blooms and tells her how her garden brightens the entire street. Ruth hadn't realized that her hidden efforts bore such beautiful witness to those around her.

In this season of life, remember that your small, faithful acts in hidden corners can bring beauty and joy to others, even when it feels unnoticed.

DAILY REFLECTION

What hidden places in your life have you overlooked where God may be calling you to be faithful and present? How can you nurture those areas with love and attention?

PRAYER

Dear Lord, thank you for your presence in the quiet moments of our lives. Help us to recognize the beauty of being faithful in hidden places, trusting that even the smallest acts of love and service hold great significance in Your eyes.

"Even in the quiet corners of our days, our faithfulness sparks a light that shines in unseen ways."

LIVING LIGHT IN A HEAVY WORLD

"Carry each other's burdens, and in this way you will fulfill the law of Christ."
Galatians 6:2

DEVOTIONAL

One sunny afternoon, a retired woman named Margie decided to organize a tea gathering for her friends from church. With laughter and stories shared over warm scones and fragrant tea, they honored their journeys—both the burdens and the blessings. In the midst of sharing her own struggles of loneliness and fear, Margie felt the weight lift as her friends encircled her with love and prayers. Each person left feeling lighter, carrying not only their burdens but also a sense of belonging that softened the hardness of life's realities.

Our relationships can become beacons of light, illuminating the darkness in a heavy world; we are strengthened and uplifted when we come together in love and support.

DAILY REFLECTION

What heaviness are you carrying today that might be lifted by leaning into the light of God's presence? How can you choose to let that weight be transformed into strength and purpose?

PRAYER

Dear Lord, thank you for the gift of your light that guides me through the heaviness of life. Help me to embrace your grace and reflect your love in all I do.

"When we let go of the burdens, we create space for the blessings."

TRUSTING GOD WITH THE UNKNOWN

"You hem me in behind and before, and you lay your hand upon me."
Psalm 139:5

DEVOTIONAL

Julia sat on her porch, sipping her morning tea and watching the world wake up. She had spent years planning every detail of her life, from her career to her children's futures. Now in retirement, she found herself facing new seasons of life that felt uncertain and daunting. One day, a friendly neighbor invited her to join a book club she had never considered. Tentatively, she accepted, unsure of what to expect. To her surprise, she made new friends and discovered a passion for reading romantic novels, which led to delightful discussions that filled her heart with joy. In those moments, Julia realized that trusting God with her future meant stepping into the unknown with faith.

When you embrace life's uncertainties, you open the door to unexpected blessings.

DAILY REFLECTION

What unknowns are weighing on your heart today, and how can trusting in God ease those worries? What steps can you take to surrender these concerns to Him?

PRAYER

Dear Lord, thank You for being our guiding light in times of uncertainty. Help us to lean on Your wisdom and grace as we navigate the unknowns in our lives.

"God holds the future in His hands, just as He has held your past."

EMBRACING GOD'S REFINING

"See, I have refined you, though not as silver;
I have tested you in the furnace of affliction." **Isaiah 48:10**

DEVOTIONAL

Once upon a time, there was a wise grandmother named Edna who loved baking. One day, while making her famous cookies, she accidentally spilled a whole bag of salt instead of sugar into the mixing bowl! Instead of tossing the batch, she decided to embrace the mishap. After adding sweetness to balance it out, the result was a delightful treat that became the talk of the family. Edna realized that sometimes life's little mistakes lead to the greatest blessings and teach us valuable lessons about being refined.

Embracing God's refining process helps us transform our experiences, even the salty ones, into something joyful and sweet.

DAILY REFLECTION

What does it mean for you to embrace the refining process that God has in store for your life during this season of retirement? How can you open your heart to His gentle guidance and transformation?

PRAYER

Dear God, thank You for the beautiful journey of life and the wisdom that comes with every season. Help me to trust in Your refining process and to embrace the changes You bring with an open heart.

"Like gold in the fire, we are purified and made radiant in His love."

GRATITUDE IN THE GRIND

*"I am not saying this because I am in need, for I have learned to be content whatever the circumstances. I know what it is to be in need, and I know what it is to have plenty. I have learned the secret of being content in any and every situation, whether well fed or hungry, whether living in plenty or in want." **Philippians 4:11-12***

DEVOTIONAL

Once upon a time, there was a vibrant retiree named Martha who devoted her days to tending to her garden. While she initially daydreamed about traveling and adventure, she soon found joy in the morning dew on her petunias and the cheerful chirps of her backyard birds. As she pruned and watered, she began to see her everyday tasks as sacred rituals, each one a delightful lesson in gratitude. With each bloom, she found purpose and peace right where she was, discovering that the grind of daily life is filled with moments to cherish.

Every day holds a sprinkle of grace, waiting for you to uncover it, even in the most routine tasks.

DAILY REFLECTION

What are the little moments in your day-to-day routine that spark gratitude in your heart, even amidst the hustle of life?

PRAYER

Dear Lord, thank You for the gift of today. Help me to see the beauty in the mundane and to cultivate a spirit of gratitude in every moment.

"Gratitude transforms the ordinary into the extraordinary."

HOLDING ON TO HOPE

*"There is surely a future hope for you, and your hope will not be cut off." **Proverbs 23:18***

DEVOTIONAL

In her cozy living room, Margaret often found herself flipping through old photographs, reminiscing about the vibrant life she had lived. One rainy afternoon, she stumbled upon a picture of her and her late husband on a hiking trip, both beaming with joy at the peak of a mountain, surrounded by breathtaking views. As tears welled up in her eyes, she realized that while his absence left a void, the memories they shared were treasures that would forever light her path. Inspired by these moments, Margaret decided to organize nature walks with her friends, fostering connections that honored her past while embracing her present. Each step they took together filled her heart with laughter and new hope for the future.

Even in the midst of change and loss, the love and joy we've experienced can inspire us to seek new connections and rediscover our purpose.

DAILY REFLECTION

What are some moments in your life when hope has carried you through, and how can you rekindle that hope in your current season?

PRAYER

Dear God, thank you for the gift of hope that fills our hearts. Help us to see your light shining brightly in our lives, guiding us through each day with trust and faith.

"Hope is the quiet companion that whispers courage into our fears."

GOD'S STILL SMALL VOICE

*"After the earthquake came a fire, but the Lord was not in the fire.
And after the fire came a gentle whisper." **1 Kings 19:12***

DEVOTIONAL

One sunny afternoon, Margaret decided to take a leisurely stroll in her favorite park. With a light breeze caressing her face, she found herself lost in the beauty of blooming flowers and chirping birds. Suddenly, she felt a nudge to sit on a nearby bench. As she sat there, a little girl approached her with a dandelion bouquet, exclaiming, "These are for you!" Margaret laughed, realizing that in that simple moment, God was reminding her of the joy and kindness present in the everyday, often overlooked details of life.

In the quiet moments, allow yourself to listen for God's gentle whisper guiding your heart and encouraging little joys each day.

DAILY REFLECTION

When was the last time you took a moment to pause and listen for God's still small voice in the midst of your day-to-day life? How might slowing down invite you to hear Him more clearly?

PRAYER

Dear God, I invite You into my quiet moments today. Help me to listen attentively for Your gentle whispers among the noise of life. May Your presence fill my heart with peace and guidance.

"In the stillness, I find the comfort of His whisper."

THE BEAUTY OF FORGIVENESS

*"Bear with each other and forgive one another if any of you has a grievance against someone. Forgive as the Lord forgave you." **Colossians 3:13***

DEVOTIONAL

In her golden years, Margaret often reflected on her life with gratitude, but also with a hint of sorrow over a quarrel with her sister that had lasted for decades. One sunny afternoon, while tending to her garden, she felt a stirring in her heart—an urge to reach out and mend the rift. With a little courage, she picked up the phone and dialed her sister's number. Much to her surprise, the conversation flowed easily, and before she knew it, they were both laughing and reminiscing about old times. That moment became a gentle reminder that forgiveness can bloom anew at any age.

Forgiveness is a beautiful gift we give ourselves, allowing us to blossom into the fullness of joy in this season of life.

DAILY REFLECTION

What burdens are you carrying today that might be lifted by the grace of forgiveness? Can you think of someone in your life who would benefit from your willingness to forgive, including yourself?

PRAYER

Dear Lord, help me to embrace the gift of forgiveness, both for myself and for others. May my heart be open and my spirit be free as I let go of past hurts and embrace Your loving grace.

"Forgiveness is the gentle release of the weight we carry, allowing our hearts to blossom anew."

WHEN YOU FEEL SPIRITUALLY EMPTY

"As the deer pants for streams of water, so my soul pants for you, my God. My soul thirsts for God, for the living God. When can I go and meet with God?" **Psalm 42:1-2**

DEVOTIONAL

As a retired woman, you may find that the hustle and bustle of daily life has quieted down, but this can sometimes lead to feelings of emptiness as you seek purpose and connection. Picture a beloved grandmother who spent countless hours nurturing her grandchildren. One day, she sat in her garden, pondering the beauty around her, yet still feeling a tug of emptiness in her heart. She realized that in the busyness of love and family, she had set aside those quiet moments with God that once filled her spirit. By intentionally setting aside time each day to connect through prayer and scripture, she found the joy in her soul once more, like a flower blooming anew in spring.

The essence of spiritual renewal lies in intentionally carving out time to nurture your relationship with God, as our souls often reflect our attention and devotion.

DAILY REFLECTION

When was the last time you felt truly connected to your faith, and what steps might you take to rekindle that connection today?

PRAYER

Dear Lord, as I journey through moments of emptiness, fill my heart with Your presence and peace. Help me to seek You in the quiet and remember the love that surrounds me.

"Even in seasons of emptiness, God's love is the rich soil from which new growth can emerge."

PEACE THAT TRANSCENDS

"You will keep in perfect peace those whose minds are steadfast because they trust in you." **Isaiah 26:3**

DEVOTIONAL

In the quiet of her garden, Eleanor found solace among the blooming flowers. After years of busy schedules and endless responsibilities, retirement offered her a chance to slow down and reflect. One afternoon, while tending to her roses, she realized that the peace she longed for was not just a momentary escape, but rather a deep-rooted assurance born from her faith. Each petal she cared for reminded her that beauty thrives in hope and trust, bringing her closer to the serenity she sought.

True peace is cultivated in the heart, nourished by trust in God and the simple joys surrounding us.

DAILY REFLECTION

What does peace mean to you in this season of life, and how can you invite more of it into your daily moments?

PRAYER

Dear God, thank you for the gift of peace that you freely offer. Help me to embrace it fully in my heart and share it with those around me.

"Peace is not the absence of trouble, but the presence of God in our hearts."

CARRYING GOD'S LIGHT

"Arise, shine, for your light has come, and the glory of the Lord rises upon you."
Isaiah 60:1

DEVOTIONAL

Maggie had always been the nurturing type, caring for her family and friends. Now in her retirement, she felt somewhat adrift, unsure of how to fill her days meaningfully. One afternoon, she decided to volunteer at her local soup kitchen, where she served meals and shared laughter with those in need. As she interacted with the guests, she realized that her smile and kindness illuminated the room. By offering her time and warmth, Maggie discovered that she was not only serving others but also igniting the divine light within herself.

In this season of life, your light can shine brightly, bringing hope and warmth to those around you.

DAILY REFLECTION

What does it mean for you to carry God's light into your daily life? How can you share that light with those around you, perhaps in small acts of kindness or words of encouragement?

PRAYER

Dear Lord, thank you for the gift of Your light that guides us through every season of life. Help me to reflect Your love and warmth in my words and actions today.

"Your light is a beacon that can brighten even the darkest days."

STANDING ON GOD'S PROMISES

"Your kingdom is an everlasting kingdom, and your dominion endures through all generations. The Lord is trustworthy in all he promises and faithful in all he does."
Psalm 145:13

DEVOTIONAL

After 65 wonderful years, Sarah found herself reflecting on her life's journey. As she sorted through old photographs, she came across a letter from her late husband, filled with promises of love and support. These words echoed in her heart, reminding her of the faithfulness she had experienced throughout her life. In seasons of joy and sorrow, the promises of God were like a solid foundation, steady and unwavering, just as her husband had promised her love would be. With a heart full of gratitude, she recognized that while life may change, God's faithfulness remains constant.

Trusting in God's promises allows us to find peace and constancy in every season of life.

DAILY REFLECTION

What promises of God can you lean on today to bring comfort and assurance into your life? Consider how these promises can shape your outlook and actions as you enter this new season.

PRAYER

Dear Lord, thank You for the promises You have sealed in my heart. Help me to stand firm in trust and to remember that Your faithfulness never wavers, even as seasons change.

"God's promises are a lighthouse that guides us through the fog of uncertainty."

FINDING REST IN HIS LOVE

*"Truly my soul finds rest in God; my salvation comes from him. Truly he
is my rock and my salvation; he is my fortress, I will never be shaken." **Psalm 62:1-2***

DEVOTIONAL

In her retirement, Mary found herself with more time than ever, yet often felt more restless than she did in her busy career. One afternoon, she sat on her porch with a cup of herbal tea, watching the gentle sway of the trees in the breeze. As she slowed down, she began to breathe deeper, recalling the many times in her life when God had been her anchor amid storms. In that moment of stillness, she felt an overwhelming sense of peace envelop her, a reminder that in resting, she was walking closer with Him. It became clear to Mary that this season of her life was not just a time for leisure, but a divine invitation to discover more of His love and grace.

The greatest rest comes not in doing less, but in trusting more deeply in God's unfailing love.

DAILY REFLECTION

What does it mean for you to find rest in His love during this beautiful season of your life? How can you embrace that love more fully each day?

PRAYER

Dear Lord, help me to feel the warmth of Your love enveloping me, bringing peace and rest to my heart. May I seek refuge in Your presence and find comfort in the promises of Your Word.

"In His love, we find the sweetest rest for our weary souls."

WALKING BY FAITH, NOT SIGHT

*"Consequently, faith comes from hearing the message, and
the message is heard through the word about Christ." **Romans 10:17***

DEVOTIONAL

Once, there was a retired woman named Grace who found herself uneasy in her new daily routine. After years of busyness, the quietness felt daunting, and she often wondered what purpose lay ahead. One day, while sipping tea and gazing out of her window, she noticed a tiny seedling pushing through the earth in her garden. It reminded her that growth takes time and is not always visible. Just like the seed, she realized that her faith was rooted deep within her, even if the fruits weren't immediately apparent. Trusting in God's plan for her life, she decided to nurture herself with prayer and Bible study, allowing her faith to flourish amidst the uncertainties.

Walking by faith often means trusting God's timing and plan, even when the path ahead isn't clear.

DAILY REFLECTION

What does it mean for you to trust in God's plan during uncertain times in your life? How can you lean into faith when the path ahead seems unclear?

PRAYER

Dear God, thank you for being my guiding light even when the shadows linger. Help me to embrace the journey of faith, trusting in your timing and your perfect plans for my life.

"Faith is not the absence of doubt; it's the willingness to trust despite it."

GOD'S GRACE THROUGH EVERY SEASON

"Praise be to the Lord, to God our Savior, who daily bears our burdens."
Psalm 68:19

DEVOTIONAL

As the seasons change outside her window, Margaret gazes at the vibrant hues of autumn leaves, reflecting on her journey through life. In her younger years, she often felt rushed and overwhelmed, juggling work and family responsibilities. Now, in retirement, she finds herself savoring the quiet moments, often recalling how God's grace was a steadfast companion through every challenge. Whether navigating career changes, raising children, or facing losses, Margaret recognizes that God's presence was like a gentle hand holding hers, guiding her through each season of life, reminding her that grace doesn't wane with age; it flourishes.

In every season of life, God's grace is the constant that upholds and nurtures us.

DAILY REFLECTION

What are some ways you've experienced God's grace in the different seasons of your life, and how can you share those lessons with others today?

PRAYER

Dear God, thank you for your unwavering grace through every chapter of our lives. Help us recognize your presence and beauty in each season, guiding us to embrace what lies ahead with faith and love.

"God's grace is like a gentle breeze, reminding us that we are never alone, regardless of the season we are in."

GRACE FOR TODAY

"Let us then approach God's throne of grace with confidence, so that we may receive mercy and find grace to help us in our time of need." **Hebrews 4:16**

DEVOTIONAL

After years of busy schedules, juggling work, family, and community commitments, Mary found herself with an abundance of free time in her retirement. At first, she was unsure how to fill her days. However, one afternoon she decided to volunteer at a local shelter. As she served meals and shared smiles with those in need, she realized that grace wasn't just about receiving but also about sharing. The warmth and gratitude she felt filled her heart more than any busy day ever had. Every moment became a gift, reminding her that grace s active and alive in the everyday acts of kindness we offer to others.

Embrace each day, knowing that God's grace is sufficient to fill your heart and guide your steps.

DAILY REFLECTION

What does it mean for you to receive God's grace in your daily life, and how can you reflect that grace to those around you?

PRAYER

Dear Lord, thank you for your abundant grace that sustains us each day. Help me to recognize your blessings in my life and share your love with others. Amen.

"Grace is not just a gift we receive; it's a light we are meant to share."

BECOMING A PRAYERFUL WOMAN

"Devote yourselves to prayer, being watchful and thankful." **Colossians 4:2**

DEVOTIONAL

Evelyn had always been the one to care for others—her children, her friends, her community. Now, in retirement, she found herself with more time than she knew what to do with. One afternoon, as she dusted off the shelves in her living room, she stumbled upon an old journal filled with her thoughts and prayers from years past. Inspired, she decided to revive that practice, dedicating a few quiet moments each day to connect with God. As she prayed, she felt a deep sense of peace wash over her and a rekindling of hope for not just her life but for the lives of those she held dear. Little did she know, her intentional prayers began to weave threads of support and connection among her family and friends, reminding her that her influence continues even in this season of life.

Every prayer you offer can bring comfort and connection, reminding you and those you love that you are never alone.

DAILY REFLECTION

What does prayer mean to you at this stage in your life, and how can you deepen your dialogue with God in your daily routine?

PRAYER

Dear Lord, thank you for the gift of prayer. Help me to draw closer to you, filling my heart with peace and purpose as I embrace this beautiful season of life.

"Prayer is the gentle art of opening one's heart to the Divine, where every word is met with unwavering love."

GOD'S STRENGTH IN YOUR STORY

"Have I not commanded you? Be strong and courageous. Do not be afraid; do not be discouraged, for the Lord your God will be with you wherever you go." **Joshua 1:9**

DEVOTIONAL

Once there was a retired teacher named Martha, who had devoted her life to shaping young minds. After retirement, she found herself in a new chapter, feeling unsure about her purpose. One afternoon, while visiting a local community center, she noticed a group of young girls struggling with their reading. Drawing on her years of experience, she volunteered to help them, sharing her love for stories and the joy of reading. Through this simple act, Martha not only reignited her passion but discovered God's strength in her ability to uplift others, reminding her that her story was far from over.

Your life's narrative may shift in retirement, but always remember that God's strength fuels your purpose; embrace every opportunity to uplift those around you.

DAILY REFLECTION

What experiences in your life have showcased God's strength, guiding you through challenges and shaping your story?

PRAYER

Dear God, thank you for being my constant source of strength. Help me to see your hand in my journey and to trust in your plans for my life. Amen.

"Your story is a testament to the strength God provides, even in the quiet moments."

RESTORING YOUR SOUL

" he refreshes my soul. He guides me along the right paths
for his name's sake." **Psalm 23:3**

DEVOTIONAL

As Margaret settled into her favorite armchair with a cup of chamomile tea, she reflected on the years gone by—filled with busy schedules, family commitments, and the hustle of daily life. Since retiring, she had found the golden opportunity to slow down and explore her passions, whether it was gardening or painting. Yet, there were days when the stillness left her feeling lost, as if she couldn't quite find her purpose in this new season. One afternoon, as she wandered through a local park bursting with colors of autumn, a gentle breeze whispered through the trees, reminding her of the beauty in simply existing and allowing her soul to breathe. In that moment, Margaret realized that restoring her soul meant embracing this time to reconnect with herself, her memories, and her Creator.

In retirement, creating space for your soul to rest and rejuvenate is not just a luxury; it is a sacred investment in your well-being.

DAILY REFLECTION

What activities or moments in your life bring you true peace and replenish your spirit?

PRAYER

Dear God, help me to find moments of quiet and reflection in my day. I open my heart to your love and guidance as I seek to restore my soul.

"True restoration comes from slowing down and embracing the stillness within."

TRUSTING GOD IN THE UNKNOWN

"Do not let your hearts be troubled. You believe in God; believe also in me."
John 14:1

DEVOTIONAL

Once upon a time in a quaint little town, a retired woman named Ruth found herself at a crossroads. After dedicating decades to her family and career, she faced the unexpected challenge of living alone. Confusion clouded her days, and worry whispered in her ears. One morning, while sipping her tea on the porch, she noticed a small, resilient flower blooming amidst the cracks of the sidewalk. Inspired by its strength, Ruth began to embrace the unknown ahead, trusting that God had a beautiful plan for her life, even if it looked different than before. Slowly, she explored new hobbies, connected with friends, and found joy in her newfound independence, realizing that life's uncertainties were an opportunity for God to show His goodness.

Trusting God in the unknown can reveal unexpected blessings and beauty in this new season of life.

DAILY REFLECTION

What unknowns in your life are you holding onto that might be more peaceful if surrendered to God's care? How might trusting Him transform your perspective today?

PRAYER

Dear God, thank you for being our constant guide in every season of life. Help me to lean on your promises and trust in your unfailing love as I navigate the unknowns ahead.

"Trusting God means stepping into the unknown with the assurance
that He is always by your side."

OVERFLOWING WITH COMPASSION

"Therefore if you have any encouragement from being united with Christ, if any comfort from his love, if any common sharing in the Spirit, if any tenderness and compassion, then make my joy complete by being like-minded, having the same love, being one in spirit and of one mind." **Philippians 2:1-2**

DEVOTIONAL

One sunny afternoon, Margaret noticed that her neighbor, Mrs. Jenkins, had been struggling to carry her groceries. Although they had exchanged pleasantries over the years, they weren't close friends. Yet, seeing Mrs. Jenkins struggle stirred something in Margaret. She immediately walked over, offered to help, and spent the afternoon chatting and sharing stories about their families. That simple act of compassion blossomed into a deep friendship, filled with laughter and support.

Compassion opens doors to new relationships and rekindles the joy of connection in our golden years.

DAILY REFLECTION

What does it mean for you to overflow with compassion in your daily life, and how might you express that to those around you today?

PRAYER

Dear Lord, thank you for the gift of compassion that flows from You. Help me to recognize and embrace opportunities to share this love and warmth with others every day.

"Compassion is love in action, reaching out to touch the hearts of those around us."

THE POWER OF A GRATEFUL HEART

"Enter his gates with thanksgiving and his courts with praise; give thanks to him and praise his name." **Psalm 100:4**

DEVOTIONAL

Mabel, a beloved grandmother, took to writing thank-you notes each week. One day, she decided to write a letter to her closest friends, expressing her deep appreciation for their support throughout the years. As she penned the heartfelt words, she was flooded with memories of laughter, shared struggles, and sunsets spent together. When her friends received the notes, they were so touched that they began to share their own stories of gratitude, reviving their bond and rekindling joy. Mabel realized that gratitude not only brightens her own heart but also empowers those around her to reflect on their own blessings.

In this season of life, cultivating a grateful heart can transform not just your perspective, but also the connections you cherish with others.

DAILY REFLECTION

What are the small moments in your life that bring you joy and gratitude, and how can you intentionally focus on them today?

PRAYER

Dear Lord, thank You for the gift of each day. Help me cultivate a heart filled with gratitude, recognizing the blessings that surround me in every moment.

A grateful heart turns ordinary moments into extraordinary blessings.

FAITH IN THE STORM

"When you pass through the waters, I will be with you; and when you pass through the rivers, they will not sweep over you. When you walk through the fire, you will not be burned; the flames will not set you ablaze." **Isaiah 43:2**

DEVOTIONAL

Martha spent many years dedicated to her career, often prioritizing work over herself. Now, in retirement, she found herself facing unexpected health challenges that left her feeling adrift, much like a boat in a stormy sea. One afternoon, as she sat in her garden, a gentle rain began to fall, reminding her of God's presence even in trying times. Just as the flowers bloom after rain, she realized her faith could help her navigate life's storms, reminding her that she was not alone on this journey.

Even in the storms of life, God is a constant presence, offering strength and comfort to guide us through.

DAILY REFLECTION

What storms are you facing in your life right now, and how can you consciously choose to lean on your faith during these challenging times? Reflect on the ways you have seen God's hand in your past struggles and how that can reassure you today.

PRAYER

Dear Lord, thank You for being our refuge in every storm. Help me to trust in Your presence and provision as I navigate life's uncertainties. Fill my heart with peace as I embrace the journey ahead.

"In every storm, faith is the anchor that holds us steady."

WHEN YOU FEEL INVISIBLE

"Do nothing out of selfish ambition or vain conceit. Rather, in humility value others above yourselves, not looking to your own interests but each of you to the interests of the others." **Philippians 2:3-4**

DEVOTIONAL

Once in a quaint little town, a retired woman named Edna found herself often overlooked during community activities. The younger members seemed to dominate the conversations, leaving her feeling invisible and unheard. One day, while volunteering at a local soup kitchen, she struck up a conversation with a shy teenager who had come to help. As Edna listened and encouraged her, she realized how valuable her words and presence were. In that moment, she discovered that her ability to uplift others brought her a sense of belonging and purpose far greater than the accolades she had sought.

Sometimes, when you feel invisible, remember that your voice is a gift waiting to be shared with someone who needs it.

DAILY REFLECTION

What are the ways you can remind yourself of your worth and the impact you have on those around you, even in this season of life?

PRAYER

Dear Lord, thank You for the unique purpose You give each of us. Help me to see my value and to share my light with others, even when I feel overlooked.

"In moments of feeling invisible, remember that even the quietest voices can leave a lasting echo in the hearts of others."

ROOTED IN GOD'S LOVE

"God is love. Whoever lives in love lives in God, and God in them."
1 John 4:16b

DEVOTIONAL

As I sat on my porch one sunny afternoon, I noticed how the vines in my garden had intertwined with the sturdy trellis I'd built years ago. What was once just an empty space now flourished with vibrant blooms, fully supported by the structure that surrounded it. Watching those flowers climb higher, I was reminded of how, just like them, we draw strength and beauty from being rooted in God's love. In seasons of change and uncertainty, it is this love that nurtures our spirit and encourages us to blossom, even as we embrace the golden years of our lives.

Let God's love be the trellis that supports you, allowing your heart to flourish in every season of life.

DAILY REFLECTION

What does it mean for you to feel deeply rooted in God's love as you embrace this season of your life? How has His love shaped your identity and purpose?

PRAYER

Dear God, thank you for your endless love that sustains me each day. Help me to remain anchored in your embrace, finding peace and joy in the knowledge that I am cherished by you.

"Being rooted in God's love gives us strength to grow and flourish, no matter the season of life."

A QUIET SPIRIT, A POWERFUL FAITH

"Rather, it should be that of your inner self, the unfading beauty of a gentle and quiet spirit, which is of great worth in God's sight." **1 Peter 3:4**

DEVOTIONAL

Mildred, a retired teacher, spent her days tending to her garden, a space that reflected her tender care. With each bloom, she would sit quietly, letting the gentle breeze carry her prayers to God. One day, a neighbor who often passed by stopped to express how her peaceful presence brightened the street. Mildred realized that in her sweet solitude, she was sharing her faith through her quiet spirit, teaching those around her more than words ever could.

In the quiet moments of your life, remember that your gentle spirit and faith are powerful testaments to God's love and grace.

DAILY REFLECTION

What does it mean for you to cultivate a quiet spirit in the midst of life's busyness and changes? How can you tap into that inner peace to strengthen your faith?

PRAYER

Dear Lord, help me to embrace the quiet moments of my day, filling my heart with your peace. Teach me to nurture a gentle spirit that reflects your love and strength. Amen.

"A quiet spirit is often the birthplace of a faith that moves mountains."

MOTHERING WITH GRACE

*As a mother comforts her child, so will I comfort you; and you will be comforted over Jerusalem. **Isaiah 66:13***

DEVOTIONAL

After years of nurturing her children, Ruth found herself with more time to reflect and embrace the beauty of grace-filled mothering. One afternoon, while visiting her daughter's home, she noticed her granddaughter struggling to complete a craft project. Instead of rushing in to fix it, Ruth quietly sat beside her, offering gentle encouragement. Together, they turned frustration into joy, reminding Ruth that her mothering spirit could still shine brightly in these moments of connection, even without the daily demands of raising a family.

Take the time to celebrate the little moments of connection with your loved ones, for they are the heartbeats of grace in mothering.

DAILY REFLECTION

What does it mean for you to embody grace in your relationships with your children and grandchildren as you navigate this cherished season of life? How can you offer support while also allowing them to grow?

PRAYER

Dear God, thank you for the gift of family. Help me to mother with grace, embracing each moment with love and understanding as I nurture those around me.

"Grace is not just a gift; it is the gentle strength we offer to those we love."

PERSEVERING IN PRAYER

*"Then Jesus told his disciples a parable to show them that they should always pray and not give up." **Luke 18:1***

DEVOTIONAL

In her quiet living room, Margaret often sipped tea while gazing out the window at the garden she had tended for years. One crisp autumn day, she noticed a stubborn weed growing right in the midst of her beloved flowers. While it seemed easier to let it be, Margaret decided to pull it out. Day after day, the weed persisted, but so did she, reminding herself that just as she needed sustenance for her plants, they too needed prayer for strength to flourish. The more she prayed, the more she felt peace grow within her, transforming her struggle into a beautiful testimony of perseverance in her life's garden.

Just as Margaret learned, every prayer nurtures our spirit, encouraging us to stay steadfast and hopeful in every season of life.

DAILY REFLECTION

What prayers have you set aside in your heart, waiting for God's timing? How might you reignite your passion for those conversations with Him?

PRAYER

Dear Lord, thank You for always being present and ready to listen. Help me to keep the faith and persevere in my prayers, trusting in Your perfect timing.

"Prayer is the quiet hand that calms the storm within us."

THE LORD IS YOUR SHEPHERD

*"He tends his flock like a shepherd: He gathers the lambs in his arms and carries them close to his heart; he gently leads those that have young." **Isaiah 40:11***

DEVOTIONAL

Once upon a time, there was a retired woman named Margaret who spent her days volunteering at a local community center. She often noticed the lonely faces of others her age and felt a stirring in her heart to do something meaningful. One afternoon, while preparing simple meals with her friends, she encountered a woman who shared her struggles and joys. That connection blossomed into a friendship, reminding Margaret that being a shepherd means ensuring others feel valued and loved. They laughed, shared stories, and discovered together the importance of companionship in this new chapter of life.

Each act of love and kindness not only enriches your life but also fulfills the calling to shepherd others with grace and compassion.

DAILY REFLECTION

What does it mean for you to allow the Lord to lead you like a shepherd, especially in this new season of your life? Are there areas where you feel the need for His guidance and care?

PRAYER

Dear Lord, thank you for being my Shepherd in every season of life. Help me to trust in Your guidance and find peace in Your presence as I navigate these days of retirement.

"Even in the quiet moments, you can hear His loving call leading you gently forward."

LETTING GO OF BITTERNESS

*"See to it that no one misses the grace of God and that no bitter root grows up to cause trouble and defile many." **Hebrews 12:15***

DEVOTIONAL

Maria had spent years harboring resentment towards her daughter for moving away. Every time she watched the empty chair at the dinner table, bitterness surged within her like an unwelcome guest. One afternoon, while sorting through old photos, she came across a picture of them laughing together at the beach, carefree and happy. It dawned on her that holding onto past grievances was stealing the joy of their present moments. With a deep breath, she picked up her phone and called her daughter, ready to let go and embrace the relationship anew.

Letting go of bitterness opens the door to healing and deeper connections in our lives.

DAILY REFLECTION

What is one memory or situation you find it challenging to release, and how might holding onto it be affecting your peace today?

PRAYER

Dear Lord, help me to release the burdens of bitterness I've been carrying. Fill my heart with your love and grace, guiding me to forgive and find peace in the freedom of letting go.

"Letting go of bitterness is a gift we give ourselves, opening the door to joy and healing."

WALKING IN SPIRITUAL FREEDOM

"So if the Son sets you free, you will be free indeed."
John 8:36

DEVOTIONAL

Once, a dear friend of mine took up painting in her retirement years. At first, she hesitated, fearful that her skills might not match the talent of others. However, after spending time in prayer and reflection, she felt a stir in her heart that encouraged her to embrace her creative expression. As she poured her joys and struggles onto the canvas, she realized the freedom she had found—not just in art, but in letting go of expectations and embracing who she was becoming in this new chapter of life.

Life is about discovering and claiming the freedom God offers us, encouraging us to step beyond our self-imposed limits and shine in our truest form.

DAILY REFLECTION

What does it mean to you to walk in spiritual freedom each day? How can you embrace joy in the moments you experience this freedom?

PRAYER

Dear Lord, thank You for the gift of freedom in our lives. Help us to embrace this gift fully and to walk in Your light each day, guided by Your love and grace.

"True freedom in Christ invites us to let go of our pasts and embrace the fullness of His presence today."

YOUR STORY ISN'T OVER

"In their hearts humans plan their course, but the Lord establishes their steps."
Proverbs 16:9

DEVOTIONAL

Margaret sat on her porch, a steaming cup of tea in hand, reflecting on the years gone by. She had envisioned a retirement filled with travel and adventures, yet due to health issues, her plans had shifted dramatically. As days turned into months, she found herself mulling over what life would look like now. One morning, she noticed a community garden that needed volunteers. Deciding to help, Margaret soon discovered a passion for gardening and a new circle of friends. In nurturing the plants, she also found new life growing within her spirit.

Your story isn't over; it's simply unfolding in a new way, and sometimes what seems like an ending is just the beginning of a beautiful chapter.

DAILY REFLECTION

What dreams or adventures have you set aside that may still be waiting for you to explore in this next chapter of your life?

PRAYER

Dear Lord, thank You for the gift of each new day and the stories yet to unfold. Help me to embrace the journey ahead with hope and joy.

Every moment is a blank page, waiting for your pen to write the next chapter of your story.

STRENGTH TO FORGIVE

"Do not take revenge, my dear friends, but leave room for God's wrath, for it is written: 'It is mine to avenge; I will repay,' says the Lord. On the contrary: 'If your enemy is hungry, feed him; if he is thirsty, give him something to drink. In doing this, you will heap burning coals on his head.' Do not be overcome by evil, but overcome evil with good. **Romans 12:19-21**

DEVOTIONAL

There lived a woman named Margaret who had spent her entire life caring for her family and friends. After a misunderstanding with her closest neighbor, she found herself harboring resentment that weighed heavily on her heart. One day, while tending her garden, she noticed how the flowers flourished with a little care and patience. Inspired, she decided to invite her neighbor over for tea, choosing reconciliation over bitterness. In that moment of openness, both women found healing and a deeper friendship, realizing that forgiveness bloomed just like the flowers with love and warmth.

True strength is not in holding onto grudges but in nurturing relationships through the gift of forgiveness.

DAILY REFLECTION

What grudges or past hurts have you been holding onto that weigh on your heart? How might letting go of these burdens free you to experience joy and peace in this season of life?

PRAYER

Dear Lord, grant me the courage to forgive those who have hurt me and to release these pains into Your loving care. May Your Spirit fill me with grace, enabling me to walk the path of peace and reconciliation.

"Forgiveness is not forgetting; it's letting go of the hurt."

FAITHFUL THROUGH THE SEASONS

"Every good and perfect gift is from above, coming down from the Father of the heavenly lights, who does not change like shifting shadows." **James 1:17**

DEVOTIONAL

Mabel sat on her porch, enjoying a cup of tea as the golden leaves danced in the breeze. Each season of her life has brought its challenges and joys, but she always found comfort in the constancy of her faith. Just as the trees shed their leaves in the fall only to bloom anew in spring, Mabel realized that the trials she faced were part of a divine rhythm that shaped her character and deepened her trust in God. Reflecting on her journey, she couldn't help but smile, knowing that she was surrounded by the many blessings she had collected through the years, gifts from a loving God who was faithful through every season.

In every stage of life, God remains unchanging, offering us hope and strength amidst transition.

DAILY REFLECTION

What seasons of life have shaped your faith journey? How can you embrace God's presence in the current season you are experiencing?

PRAYER

Dear Lord, we thank You for walking with us through every season of our lives. Help us to embrace change with grace and trust in Your unwavering faithfulness. Amen.

"Just as leaves change color with the season, so does our faith deepen through the experiences life brings."

CHOSEN AND CHERISHED

*"But you are a chosen people, a royal priesthood, a holy nation, God's special possession, that you may declare the praises of Him who called you out of darkness into His wonderful light." **1 Peter 2:9***

DEVOTIONAL

Once, in a cozy little home, there lived a retired woman named Mary. After decades of selfless work, raising a family, and volunteering in her community, she often found herself questioning her purpose now that her days were her own. One afternoon, while sifting through her old photos, she came across a cherished picture of herself, surrounded by friends she had uplifted and inspired throughout her life. In that moment, she realized that her worth wasn't tied to her job or her age but rather the love and wisdom she had shared, as well as the light she brought to others.

Never forget that your worth is not defined by what you do, but by who you are—chosen and cherished by God, and capable of spreading love and joy to those around you.

DAILY REFLECTION

What does it mean to you to feel chosen and cherished in this season of your life? How can you carry that sense of worth into your daily interactions with others?

PRAYER

Dear Lord, thank you for choosing me as your beloved daughter and for filling my heart with your love. Help me to embrace this truth each day, reminding me that I am cherished in every moment of my life.

"In every chapter of our lives, we remain God's chosen treasures."

GOD'S PEACE IN PRESSURE

"For I know the plans I have for you, declares the Lord, plans to prosper
*"The Lord gives strength to his people; the Lord blesses his people with peace." **Psalm 29:11***

DEVOTIONAL

As a retired woman, you may find that the days are quieter but can still hold unexpected pressures. Perhaps you've recently taken on the responsibility of caring for a family member or felt the weight of unfulfilled dreams. One lovely spring morning, a retired school teacher named Margaret walked in her garden, overwhelmed by feelings of inadequacy and anxiety about the future. She paused to watch a tiny bird build a nest, tirelessly weaving bits of grass and twigs together. That simple act reminded her that just as the bird trusted God to provide for its needs, she could, too, rely on His strength and peace, recognizing that pressure could lead her back to the Lord's quiet presence.

When life's pressures feel heavy, remember that God's peace is a gentle guide that reassures us in our times of uncertainty.

DAILY REFLECTION

What pressures are you feeling in this season of your life, and how might you invite God's peace into those moments?

PRAYER

Dear Lord, thank You for Your unchanging presence in our lives. Help us to surrender our worries and find refuge in Your perfect peace each day.

"God's peace is a gentle anchor in the storms of life."

A LIFE THAT BEARS FRUIT

"But the fruit of the Spirit is love, joy, peace, forbearance, kindness, goodness, faithfulness, 23 gentleness and self-control.Against such things there is no law." **Galatians 5:22-23**

DEVOTIONAL

Once, a retired teacher named Grace found herself feeling a bit disconnected after leaving her career. Looking for ways to stay engaged, she began volunteering at a local community center. Each day she spent with the children there reignited her passion for learning, and she discovered that her kindness and warm spirits were contagious. The laughter and excitement of the children filled her heart, reminding her that even in retirement, she had the power to nurture and inspire others.

In this chapter of your life, remember that you can cultivate fruits of the spirit that not only enrich your own heart but also bless those in your path.

DAILY REFLECTION

What are the unique gifts and experiences from your life that you can share with others to help them grow?

PRAYER

Dear Lord, thank You for the seasons of our lives and the fruit we can bear in Your service. Help me to recognize and nurture the gifts You've given me, so I can share them abundantly with those around me.

"Just as a tree bears fruit in its season, so too can we cultivate lives that bring nourishment and joy to others."

UNSHAKEABLE FAITH

"Those who trust in the Lord are like Mount Zion, which cannot be shaken but endures forever." **Psalm 125:1**

DEVOTIONAL

Once, a retired woman named Clara faced the upheaval of moving from her beloved home of over thirty years. The thought of leaving behind cherished memories and friendships seemed daunting, and she felt a whirlwind of uncertainty swirling around her. Yet, as she packed her belongings, she leaned into her faith, recalling the many seasons of life God had seen her through. Each box became a reminder of God's faithfulness, and instead of fear, Clara found surprising joy in the new journey ahead, trusting that her roots in faith would hold her steady.

Even in seasons of change, remember that your unshakeable faith can provide the strength to embrace new beginnings.

DAILY REFLECTION

What moments in your life have tested your faith, and how did you find strength to stand firm in those times? Have you considered how those experiences have shaped your unshakeable faith today?

PRAYER

Dear Lord, thank you for being our rock in every season of life. Help us to lean on your unfailing love and trust in your plans as we navigate the journey ahead.

"Faith is the anchor that steadies our soul amid life's storms."

CELEBRATING SMALL VICTORIES

"This is the day that the Lord has made; let us rejoice and be glad in it."
Psalm 118:24

DEVOTIONAL

Martha had a quiet morning routine that she cherished. Each day, she would brew her favorite tea, tend to her garden, and easily check off small tasks from her to-do list. One sunny afternoon, while pruning the roses, she realized how far she had come since her husband passed. She felt gratitude for the blooming flowers, the sweet song of the birds, and the small victories of mastering new recipes or reconnecting with old friends. With each small achievement, she celebrated not just what she had done, but how each effort fueled her spirit, reminding her of the gifts life still held.

Celebrating small victories brings light into our daily lives, welcoming joy in every moment we embrace.

DAILY REFLECTION

What small victory have you experienced recently that brought you joy, and how can you celebrate it in your own special way?

PRAYER

Dear God, thank You for the little victories that brighten our days. Help us to recognize and cherish these moments as we journey through life. May we always find reasons to celebrate, no matter how small.

"Each small victory is a step toward a heart full of gratitude and joy."

SERVING WITH A JOYFUL HEART

"Worship the Lord with gladness; come before him with joyful songs."
Psalm 100:2

DEVOTIONAL

Mabel, a retired schoolteacher, found herself feeling a bit lost after her last day in the classroom. Day after day, she enjoyed her newfound freedom but missed the connection with her students. One Sunday, she decided to volunteer in the church's children's ministry. As she engaged with the little ones, their laughter and curiosity reignited her spirit. Each week, she prepared lessons with excitement, singing along with the kids and discovering joy in their wide-eyed wonder. Mabel realized that serving others brought her heart much closer to God, embracing her role as a vessel of love and learning.

Embracing the call to serve nurtures joy in our hearts and fulfills our purpose in the golden years of life.

DAILY REFLECTION

What brings you the most joy when you think about serving others? How can you embrace those moments today?

PRAYER

Dear God, help me to serve others with a joyful heart, embracing the opportunities you place in my path. Let my actions reflect your love and bring light into the lives of those around me.

"Joyful service is a gift we give not only to others, but also to ourselves."

WHEN GOD REDIRECTS YOUR PATH

"The Lord makes firm the steps of the one who delights in him; though he may stumble, he will not fall, for the Lord upholds him with his hand." **Psalm 37:23-24**

DEVOTIONAL

After years of living a busy life filled with work and family commitments, Helen found herself wondering how to spend her retirement. Initially, she filled her days with activities that felt familiar, but her heart yearned for something deeper. One day, while volunteering at a local community center, she met a group of women who shared stories of faith and encouraged one another. Inspired by their camaraderie, Helen felt God gently redirect her path towards helping others. That new direction filled her days with purpose, joy, and new friendships, reminding her that sometimes, what God has in store is even more fulfilling than what we had planned.

Trust that God has a beautiful plan for this season of your life, and embrace the unexpected paths He sets before you.

DAILY REFLECTION

What do you feel God might be whispering to you about a new direction in your life right now? How can you open your heart to embrace His guidance?

PRAYER

Dear Lord, as I journey through this season of life, help me to remain open to the redirection You have planned for me. Guide my steps and grant me peace as I trust in Your wisdom.

"Every detour can be a divine detour, leading to unexpected blessings and new adventures."

HEALED AND WHOLE IN CHRIST

"Do not conform to the pattern of this world, but be transformed by the renewing of your mind." **Romans 12:2**

DEVOTIONAL

Mabel had spent years nurturing her family and friends, always putting their needs above her own. Now, with children grown and retirement in full swing, she found herself grappling with the identity shift that came with this new season. One afternoon, as she sat in her favorite garden chair, she felt whispers of doubt creeping in—was she still valuable? Then she decided to volunteer at a local community center, where she discovered a new purpose: mentoring young women who shared her struggles. This act of service not only brought joy to others but also reminded Mabel of her worth through Christ, who had lovingly crafted her for such a time as this.

Embrace each new chapter of life as an opportunity for renewal and purpose, trusting that in Christ, you are healed and whole.

DAILY REFLECTION

What areas of your life—whether physical, emotional, or spiritual—would you like to invite Christ into for healing and restoration?

PRAYER

Dear Lord, thank You for the promise of wholeness in You. We ask that You fill our hearts with Your peace and guide us towards the healing we seek. May we embrace the fullness of joy that comes from being whole in Christ.

"Through Christ, we are not just healed; we are made whole, embracing each moment with grace."

THE JOY OF OBEDIENCE

"If you are willing and obedient, you will eat the good things of the land;"
Isaiah 1:19

DEVOTIONAL

After retiring, Martha discovered that her days could easily slip into routine and monotony. One morning, she felt the gentle nudge to join a local book club, even though she was hesitant and unsure of her place among strangers. Much to her delight, as she embraced this opportunity, she found not only fulfilling friendships but also a renewed passion for learning and sharing insights. The joy that came from stepping out in obedience to that gentle prompting was a blessing she never imagined.

Living in the spirit of obedience can lead us to unexpected joys and deeper connections in our later years.

DAILY REFLECTION

What does obedience to God look like in your daily life, and how does it bring you joy in this season of your journey?

PRAYER

Dear Lord, thank You for being a guiding light in our lives. Help us embrace obedience with joy, trusting that Your ways are always best.

"Obedience isn't about following rules; it's about deepening our relationship with the One who loves us most."

COURAGE TO TRUST AGAIN

"And we know that in all things God works for the good of those who love him, who have been called according to his purpose." **Romans 8:28**

DEVOTIONAL

At 65, Clara found herself reflecting on her years spent navigating life's winding paths. After a difficult divorce that shook her trust, she hesitated to embrace new relationships. One sunny afternoon, a friendly neighbor invited her for coffee, gently easing her fears. Understanding that vulnerability is part of love, Clara chose to step out of her comfort zone, discovering that the warmth of friendship could blossom anew with time. Each shared laugh over coffee became a thread stitching her heart back together.

Trust can feel daunting, especially after heartache, yet the joy of new connections often lies just on the other side of fear. Embracing courage allows for the possibility of deeper, fulfilling relationships in this beautiful season of life.

DAILY REFLECTION

What experiences have shaped your ability to trust others, and how might God be inviting you to open your heart again? Reflect on moments of disappointment or hurt and consider how they might be transformed into opportunities for renewed faith and connection.

PRAYER

Dear Lord, help me to embrace the courage to trust again. Fill my heart with your love and guide me toward those who need my kindness and companionship. May I find strength in Your presence as I navigate this journey of opening myself once more.

"Trust is the bridge we build to connect our hearts with others, even after we've faced storms together."

RESTORING WHAT WAS LOST

*"Restore to me the joy of your salvation and
grant me a willing spirit, to sustain me."*
Psalm 51:12

DEVOTIONAL

After years of dedicated service as a teacher, Margaret found herself in a quiet house, a world that once felt vibrant now hushed. One afternoon, while sorting through old photographs, she stumbled upon a picture of her younger self, drenched in laughter during a summer camping trip with friends. That moment sparked an idea. Inspired by the memories, she decided to start a small book club, inviting neighbors and fellow church members to join her. As they gathered, sharing stories and laughter over cups of tea, Margaret felt the joy flood back into her life, just as it had years ago.

Sometimes, by reaching out and connecting with others, we can reclaim the joy and purpose that we thought was lost.

DAILY REFLECTION

What are the precious moments or passions in your life that you feel have been set aside or lost, and how might you begin to restore them now?

PRAYER

Dear Lord, help me to embrace the beautiful chapters still to come in my life. Open my heart to the opportunities to restore joy and purpose where I've felt a sense of loss.

"Every day is a new opportunity to reclaim the dreams that once stirred our souls."

FINISHING THE MONTH FAITHFULLY

"His master replied, 'Well done, good and faithful servant! You have been faithful with a few things; I will put you in charge of many things. Come and share your master's happiness!'" **Matthew 25:21**

DEVOTIONAL

Martha had always taken pride in the little things—the garden she tended, the friendships she nurtured, and the smiles she shared with her neighbors. As she approached the end of the month, she contemplated her accomplishments, both big and small, reflecting on how her simple acts of kindness created ripples of joy in her community. One afternoon, as she pruned her roses, she received a call from a friend who needed someone to talk to, and without hesitation, Martha adjusted her plans. That conversation turned into a lifesaving connection, reminding her that her dedication to others bore fruit in ways she hadn't even realized.

In the twilight years of life, it's the quiet faithfulness in our daily acts that opens the door to greater joy and purpose.

DAILY REFLECTION

What are the ways you can intentionally embrace the last days of this month with gratitude and purpose? How might you finish strong and faithful in your relationships and responsibilities?

PRAYER

Dear Lord, thank You for this month filled with grace and lessons. Help me to finish it well, with a heart full of gratitude and a spirit ready to embrace the blessings You have for me.

"Finishing strong is not about perfection; it's about faithfulness in every moment."

FAITH THAT PERSEVERES

"Blessed is the one who perseveres under trial because, having stood the test, that person will receive the crown of life that the Lord has promised to those who love him." **James 1:12**

DEVOTIONAL

Marie never imagined her retirement would come with challenges. After years of planning for restful days filled with hobbies and travel, she faced sudden health issues that kept her homebound. At first, she felt overwhelmed and lost, but she found strength in her faith and began to lean on her community. Each morning, she would sit by her window, sip her tea, and reflect on the blessings in her life, even amidst adversity. Slowly, her perspective shifted from fear to gratitude as she discovered new ways to connect with others and inspire those around her.

Even when faced with unexpected trials, your faith can be a source of strength and hope, enabling you to persevere and grow.

DAILY REFLECTION

What does perseverance look like in your daily life, and how has your faith guided you through challenging seasons? Reflect on a specific moment when you felt your faith carried you forward.

PRAYER

Dear Lord, thank You for the gift of faith and for the strength it provides. Help me to remain steadfast in my journey, trusting in Your love and guidance each step of the way.

"Faith is not just about believing; it's about holding on when the path gets difficult."

GOD'S TIMING IS ALWAYS RIGHT

"Let perseverance finish its work so that you may be mature and complete, not lacking anything." James 1:4

DEVOTIONAL

Mabel had always dreamed of traveling to Europe, but life's responsibilities kept her tied to the home front for years—caring for her family, her job, and her community. Now, retired and with her children grown, she finally booked a trip to see the charming streets of Paris. As she wandered through the Louvre, a neighbor from her hometown unexpectedly appeared, and they were able to reminisce and catch up on a friendship that had faded with time. Mabel realized that everything in her life, including those seemingly endless years of waiting, had perfectly prepared her for this very moment of joy and connection.

God's timing is a beautiful reminder that every season has purpose, and our dreams can flourish when we least expect them.

DAILY REFLECTION

What moments in your life have taught you the most about trusting in God's timing, and how can you embrace those lessons as you move forward?

PRAYER

Dear Lord, thank you for your perfect timing in our lives. Help me trust you more deeply and find peace in the seasons you've planned for me.

"Sometimes, waiting is the most powerful act of faith."

LIVING WITH OPEN HANDS

"We have different gifts, according to the grace given to each of us. If your gift is prophesying, then prophesy in accordance with your faith; if it is serving, then serve; if it is teaching, then teach; if it is to encourage, then give encouragement; if it is giving, then give generously; if it is to lead, do it diligently; if it is to show mercy, do it cheerfully." Romans 12:6-8

DEVOTIONAL

At the local community center, a retired woman named Margaret found herself surrounded by a group of eager knitters. She watched as they created blankets for newborns and warm scarves for the homeless. Although she had never knitted before, Margaret felt a tug in her heart to help. So, she decided to learn. In the process, she not only crafted beautiful pieces but also discovered deep connections with her fellow crafters. They shared stories, laughter, and even tears, creating a tapestry of friendship that was more precious than the yarn they worked with. In opening her hands to learn and share, Margaret found new purpose in her retirement.

When we live with open hands, we not only give of our gifts but also receive the blessings of connection and community in unexpected ways.

DAILY REFLECTION

What does it mean for you to live with open hands, embracing both the gifts of each day and the opportunities to serve others?

PRAYER

Dear Lord, thank You for the blessings You have poured into my life. Help me to remain open-hearted and open-handed, ready to share my time, love, and resources with those around me. Fill my spirit with joy as I give and receive.

"Living with open hands invites abundance into our lives, not just for ourselves, but for the world around us."

THE POWER OF GOD'S WORD

"In the beginning was the Word, and the Word was with God, and the Word was God."
John 1:1

DEVOTIONAL

One autumn day, Sara, a retired teacher, felt a wave of loneliness wash over her. With her children grown and her husband passed on, she often found herself reminiscing about the good old days. One afternoon, while dusting off her old Bible, she stumbled upon a passage that spoke directly to her weary heart. As she read, she felt a warm comfort wrap around her, reminding her that God was ever-present, guiding her, and that there was hope yet to be found in the new chapters of her life.

Seek solace and strength in the promises of God's Word, for it has the power to transform your loneliness into purpose and your fears into faith.

DAILY REFLECTION

What verses or stories from the Bible have profoundly impacted your life, and how can you share that wisdom with others today?

PRAYER

Dear Lord, thank you for the gift of Your Word, which brings comfort and guidance. Help me to embrace its truths with an open heart and share its light with those around me. Amen.

"God's Word is a lamp to our feet, illuminating our path and guiding us into deeper understanding."

ANCHORED IN HOPE

"We have this hope as an anchor for the soul, firm and secure."
Hebrews 6:19

DEVOTIONAL

In her younger years, Margaret often felt adrift. Life's currents swept her from one responsibility to another, leaving little time for reflection. But as she entered retirement, she discovered the beauty of stillness; moments spent in nature or with her grandchildren felt like warm embraces from God. One evening, sitting on her porch and watching the sun dip below the horizon, she realized that her faith had become her anchor, giving her a profound sense of peace and purpose even in this new season of life.

In the quiet seasons of life, remember that hope is your anchor, providing strength and stability through all storms.

DAILY REFLECTION

What anchors your hope today, and how can you remind yourself of that anchor in the days to come?

PRAYER

Dear Lord, help us to feel Your gentle presence surrounding us as we rest in Your promises. May our hearts be filled with hope, trusting in Your unwavering love.

"Hope is the gentle hand that steadies our heart when life's storms threaten to sway us."

TRUSTING GOD'S PROCESS

"Look at the birds of the air; they do not sow or reap or store away in barns, and yet your heavenly Father feeds them. Are you not much more valuable than they?" **Matthew 6:26**

DEVOTIONAL

Margaret sat on her front porch, watching the birds flit about. She had spent her life managing a busy household and a career, always planning every detail down to the last moment. Now, in retirement, her days felt uncertain, leaving her uneasy about the future. One sunny afternoon, as she observed the carefree birds, she was reminded that they didn't worry about tomorrow. Instead, they trusted the available resources, and Margaret realized that God had a plan for her too—she just needed to embrace the unfolding rather than control it.

Trusting God's process means allowing Him to care for us, just as He does for the birds.

DAILY REFLECTION

What areas of your life do you find challenging to trust God's timing and process? Take a moment to reflect on your journey and how God has guided you through changes in the past.

PRAYER

Dear Lord, thank You for being with us through every season of life. Help us to trust Your process, embracing the journey You have laid out for us. Grant us peace as we wait patiently for Your perfect timing.

"God's process is often a winding road, leading us to destinations we never imagined."

PURPOSE IN THE PAIN

"I have told you these things, so that in me you may have peace. In this world you will have trouble. But take heart! I have overcome the world." **John 16:33**

DEVOTIONAL

Mabel had always been the one who cared for others. After years of dedicating her life to family and community, she found herself alone and facing unexpected health challenges. Some days were filled with frustration and loneliness, yet in those moments, she stumbled across a group of women at her church sharing their own struggles. As Mabel listened, she realized that her experiences of pain had created a space for connection and understanding. Those shared moments turned into a support group, bringing each woman closer as they comforted one another and lifted each other's spirits.

Every challenge faced can become an opportunity to connect and encourage others who are walking similar paths.

DAILY REFLECTION

What pain or challenge in your life has led you to discover deeper meaning or purpose? How might that experience shape your understanding of your journey ahead?

PRAYER

Dear Lord, as I navigate the complexities of my life, help me to see the purpose woven through my pain. May I find comfort in your presence and strength to embrace my journey.

"Sometimes, it is through our most difficult experiences that our true purpose emerges, shining brightly in the shadows."

FINDING REST IN SURRENDER

"There remains, then, a Sabbath-rest for the people of God; for anyone who enters God's rest also rests from their works, just as God did from his. Let us, therefore, make every effort to enter that rest, so that no one will perish by following their example of disobedience." **Hebrews 4:9-11**

DEVOTIONAL

In the quiet of her home, Helen often found herself overwhelmed with the tasks of maintaining her garden, balancing family visits, and volunteering in the community. One afternoon, as she sat on her porch watching the leaves dance in the wind, she felt the weight of her responsibilities pressing down. With a deep breath, she closed her eyes and whispered a simple prayer, asking God to take her worries. In that moment, she realized that she didn't need to control everything; surrendering her concerns allowed her to feel an unexpected lightness in her spirit.

Sometimes, finding rest in surrender means recognizing that it's okay to let go and allow life to unfold in its own beautiful way.

DAILY REFLECTION

What are the areas in your life where you find it hardest to let go and trust God? Take a moment to reflect on how surrendering those worries may bring you peace.

PRAYER

Dear Lord, thank You for inviting us to lay down our burdens at Your feet. Help us find rest in surrender and embrace the peace that only You can provide. Amen.

"Surrender is not the end of your strength; it's the beginning of God's grace."

SPIRITUAL REFRESHMENT

"God is faithful, who has called you into fellowship with his Son, Jesus Christ our Lord."
1 Corinthians 1:9

DEVOTIONAL

Mabel, a 65-year-old retiree, found herself feeling a bit disoriented after leaving her job. Each day melded into the next, and she longed for purpose and vibrancy. One afternoon, as she sat on her porch sipping tea, she observed a butterfly fluttering around the blooming flowers. It was as if the butterfly had been resting too, waiting for the right moment to emerge and revel in the beauty of the garden. Inspired, Mabel decided to volunteer at her local library, sharing her love of books with children. She felt a renewed sense of connection and purpose, understanding that God had more plans for her than she'd ever imagined.

Embrace the freedom of your retirement to explore the new avenues of service and joy that God has laid before you.

DAILY REFLECTION

What activities or practices bring you a sense of spiritual renewal and joy in your everyday life? How can you intentionally incorporate them into your routine this week?

PRAYER

Dear God, thank You for the gift of this day and the calming moments that come with it. Please help me to find refreshment in Your presence and to embrace the beauty of each moment.

"In the quiet corners of life, we discover the whispers of God's love."

A NEW SONG IN YOUR HEART

"Sing to the Lord a new song; sing to the Lord, all the earth."
Psalm 96:1

DEVOTIONAL

Marjorie always loved to sew. For years, her sewing machine was a constant companion, creating clothes and gifts for family and friends. After retiring, she found herself surrounded by a sea of fabric scraps. One day, inspired by a colorful array of remnants, she decided to create a patchwork quilt. With each stitch, she not only crafted warmth for her home but also wove memories of those she loved. This quilt became her new song—a tapestry of gratitude, love, and creative fulfillment that resonated deeply in her heart.

Embrace the fresh chapters of life with a spirit of creativity and gratitude, for every new experience can enrich your soul's melody.

DAILY REFLECTION

What new melodies is God inviting you to sing in this season of your life? How can you open your heart to embrace these songs of joy and gratitude?

PRAYER

Dear Lord, thank you for the gift of each new day. Help me to recognize the songs of hope and love that you whisper to my heart, guiding me toward deeper joy and fulfilment.

"Every day holds the potential for a fresh anthem of praise."

CONFIDENT IN HIS CALLING

"Therefore, my dear brothers and sisters, stand firm. Let nothing move you. Always give yourselves fully to the work of the Lord, because you know that your labor in the Lord is not in vain." **1 Corinthians 15:58**

DEVOTIONAL

Mabel spent countless years as a devoted teacher, investing in her students' lives and their future. After retiring, she felt uncertain about her new role, questioning how she could still serve and share her gifts. One day, while volunteering at a local community center, she met a young single mother who needed guidance and encouragement. As Mabel shared her experiences and offered support, she realized that her calling to teach and uplift never truly ended; it simply transformed into a new chapter. Her heart swelled with joy, knowing that her wisdom was still making a difference.

You are never too old to embrace the calling that God has given you; your life experiences have unique value that can bless others in unexpected ways.

DAILY REFLECTION

What are the unique gifts and experiences you have gained throughout your life that can be used to fulfill God's calling for you in this season? Reflect on how He may be inviting you to serve and share your wisdom.

PRAYER

Dear Lord, thank You for the journey that has brought me to this moment. Help me to embrace Your calling with confidence, knowing that every experience shapes my purpose.

"Embracing His calling means celebrating the wisdom gained through a life well-lived."

HEALING TAKES TIME

"Yet the Lord longs to be gracious to you; therefore he will rise up to show you compassion. For the Lord is a God of justice. Blessed are all who wait for him!" **Isaiah 30:18**

DEVOTIONAL

Mabel, a retired schoolteacher, spent a season in quiet reflection after her husband's passing. Each day, she would take a stroll around her neighborhood, breathing in the scents of blooming flowers and listening to birds chirping. While some days felt heavier than others, she learned to cherish the small moments of joy—like the smile of a neighbor or the warmth of the sun on her face. Over time, she began to find comfort in her memories and the love that still surrounded her, discovering that healing isn't just an end goal but a gradual embracing of life.

Healing takes time, and it's in the gentle acceptance of each moment that we find our strength.

DAILY REFLECTION

What healing journey are you currently on, and how can you be gentle with yourself as you navigate it?

PRAYER

Dear Lord, thank You for the promise of healing and the reminder that it unfolds in Your perfect timing. Help me to embrace each step of my journey with patience and trust.

"Just as the seasons change gradually, so too does the soul find its renewal."

PEACE WHEN YOU DON'T UNDERSTAND

"Finally, be strong in the Lord and in his mighty power."
Ephesians 6:10

DEVOTIONAL

Once, in a cozy little town, there lived a woman named Martha who loved to tend her garden. One spring, she decided to plant a variety of flowers, excited for the beauty they would bring. As summer approached, a sudden storm swept through, uprooting her tender blooms and leaving her feeling lost and confused. She spent restless nights wondering why such devastation had struck her peaceful corner of the world. Yet, as the months rolled by, she noticed a beautiful patch of wildflowers growing in the very spot where destruction had occurred. These flowers became a symbol of resilience and unexpected beauty in her life, showing her that even in chaos, peace could follow.

When the storms of life uproot your plans, trust that something beautiful may emerge when you least expect it.

DAILY REFLECTION

What areas of your life feel uncertain or confusing right now, and how might trusting in God's plan provide you with peace?

PRAYER

Dear God, thank you for the comfort you offer even when we face uncertainty. Help me to lean into your promises and trust that you are guiding my steps each day.

"Peace is not found in understanding everything; it is found in trusting Someone who knows all."

YOUR PRAYERS MATTER

"The Lord is far from the wicked, but he hears the prayer of the righteous."
Proverbs 15:29

DEVOTIONAL

In the quiet of her sunlit kitchen, Martha often reflected on her many years spent nurturing her family and friends. One day, feeling particularly grateful, she decided to send a heartfelt note to each of her children, letting them know how much they meant to her. As she prayed for them, she felt an overwhelming sense of peace, believing her words and prayers could make a difference in their lives. To her surprise, a few days later, her daughter called, sharing how she had faced a tough week but felt strengthened when she sensed her mother's prayers surrounding her. Martha realized that even in retirement, her prayers held weight and power, touching her loved ones in more ways than she could see.

Your prayers are a beautiful gift, weaving a tapestry of love and support that reaches far beyond what you can see.

DAILY REFLECTION

What are the ways you can see your prayers impacting the lives of those around you, even if it's in small, quiet moments?

PRAYER

Dear Lord, thank You for hearing my prayers and for the gentle whispers of hope You share with me. Help me to remember that every prayer, no matter how small, carries weight in Your eyes.

"Your prayers are seeds planted in faith, growing into blessings you may never fully see."

WHEN GOD FEELS DISTANT

"'Keep your lives free from the love of money and be content with what you have, because God has said, "Never will I leave you; never will I forsake you."' **Hebrews 13:5**

DEVOTIONAL

In her garden, Margaret often found solace, pulling weeds and tending to her flowers. One afternoon, as she sat on her favorite bench, she reflected on a season of her life when she felt God's presence so vividly; yet now, in her retirement years, a sense of quietness had replaced those moments of warmth. Just as the seasons of a garden change, Margaret realized her relationship with God was also undergoing a transformation, inviting her to seek Him differently—through prayer walks, devotions, and quiet moments of gratitude.

When God feels distant, remember that He is still with you, guiding and nurturing your spirit through every season of your life.

DAILY REFLECTION

What moment in your life do you feel God has felt the most distant, and how did that experience shape your faith journey?

PRAYER

Dear God, in moments when we feel far from You, remind us of Your everlasting presence. Help us to draw near with open hearts and find comfort in Your love. Amen.

"Even in the silence, God is crafting a beautiful story with our lives."

HIS MERCY IS ENOUGH

"But because of his great love for us, God, who is rich in mercy, made us alive with Christ even when we were dead in transgressions—it is by grace you have been saved."
Ephesians 2:4-5

DEVOTIONAL

Consider the sweet journey of Ruth, who after years of raising children and caring for her family, found herself pondering her purpose in retirement. One day, feeling particularly aimless, she stumbled upon a neighbor in distress—an elderly woman struggling with her groceries. As Ruth lent a hand, she felt a warmth in her heart that reminded her of the mercies she had received throughout her life. In that moment, guiding her neighbor became a divine appointment, revealing how God's mercy flows through acts of kindness and love, reminding Ruth that her life still held great significance.

Even in retirement, remember that His mercy is enough for you and can flow through you, bringing light to others.

DAILY REFLECTION

What does it mean to you that God's mercy has been present in every chapter of your life, guiding you through both challenges and joys? How can you embrace the sufficiency of His mercy today?

PRAYER

Dear Lord, thank you for your endless mercy that covers us every day. Help us to lean into your grace and find comfort in knowing that it is always enough for our needs.

"His mercy is a gentle embrace that holds us through every season of life."

WALKING BOLDLY WITH GOD

"But we do not belong to those who shrink back and are destroyed, but to those who have faith and are saved." **Hebrews 10:39**

DEVOTIONAL

As she stood in front of her window, watching the leaves turn golden with the changing season, Margaret reflected on the years gone by. After decades dedicated to family and career, she found herself at a crossroads of peace and uncertainty. Embracing each day, she decided to pick up painting, something she had long dreamed of but set aside for years. With each brushstroke, she let her creative spirit flourish, finding joy in the simple act of creation. It was in those moments that she realized walking boldly with God meant stepping into new beginnings, not dwelling on the past.

In this beautiful chapter of life, it's important to remember that walking boldly with God invites us to embrace new opportunities, no matter our age.

DAILY REFLECTION

What does it mean for you to walk boldly with God in this new season of life? How can you embrace His guidance and strength in your daily routine?

PRAYER

Dear God, thank you for the gift of each day. Please help me to walk boldly with You, trusting in Your promises and leaning on Your love in every moment.

"Boldness is not the absence of fear, but the courage to step forward with faith."

LESS OF ME, MORE OF HIM

He must become greater; I must become less."
John 3:30

DEVOTIONAL

Margaret had spent years putting everyone else first—her family, her community, and even her church. Now, in her retirement, she found herself reflecting on what it truly meant to let go. One afternoon, while tending to her vibrant garden, she noticed the flowers blooming beautifully, but only because she'd spent time nurturing their roots in the soil. It struck her that just as her flowers needed care to grow, her spirit needed to prioritize God above all else. Through prayer and quiet moments with Scripture, she began to see how letting go of her need for control allowed God's love and purpose to flourish within her life.

When we make space for God in our hearts, we find that He fills our lives with more joy, peace, and purpose than we could ever imagine.

DAILY REFLECTION

What does it mean for you to embrace less of yourself and more of God in this season of your life? How can you invite His presence into your daily routines and interactions with others?

PRAYER

Dear Lord, as I navigate this new chapter in my life, help me to open my heart wider to Your love and guidance. May I discover the joy of putting You first and allowing Your light to shine through me each day.

"In the quiet moments of surrender, He fills the spaces within us."

THE JOY OF TRUSTING

"But the Lord is faithful, and he will strengthen you and protect you from the evil one." **2 Thessalonians 3:3**

DEVOTIONAL

In her small garden, Martha found joy in nurturing her flowers. Each morning, she watered them and whispered words of encouragement, despite the challenges of the changing seasons. One day, after a particularly strong storm, she worried that her blooms would be lost. Yet as the sun broke through the clouds, she discovered her garden had not only survived but thrived, adorned with vibrant colors anew. It reminded her that, just like her flowers, her faith could flourish even in the storm, under the watchful care of her Lord.

Trusting in God, especially in life's later chapters, can bring forth unexpected beauty and strength just when you need it most.

DAILY REFLECTION

What are some areas in your life where you feel challenged to fully trust, and how might surrendering those worries bring you peace and joy?

PRAYER

Dear God, thank you for the gentle reminders of your presence in our lives. Help me to trust you more deeply with each passing day, finding joy in your steadfast love and guidance.

"Trusting in the Lord is like resting in a warm embrace, where worries fade and hope blossoms."

A LIGHT FOR THE WORLD

*"In the same way, let your light shine before others, that they may see your good deeds and glorify your Father in heaven." **Matthew 5:16***

DEVOTIONAL

One sunny afternoon, Margaret decided to volunteer at a local shelter, something she had always talked about but never had the time to do while working. As she served warm meals and shared smiles, she noticed how her presence brought joy to both the staff and the guests. One gentleman, looking particularly downcast, beamed when she stopped to chat, sharing his hopes and dreams. That brief conversation lit up not only his face but also filled Margaret with a warmth she hadn't expected. In that moment, she realized that her time and kindness, though seemingly small, were like a candle illuminating the darkest corners.

Your golden years are not just a time for rest—embrace opportunities to shine your light and make a difference in the lives of others.

DAILY REFLECTION

What are the unique ways you can share your wisdom and love with those around you, becoming a light in their lives?

PRAYER

Dear Lord, thank you for the light you've given us. May our hearts shine brightly as we share your love and joy with others.

"Your light is meant to shine brightly, illuminating the path for those who follow."

SPIRIT-LED LIVING

*"But the Advocate, the Holy Spirit, whom the Father will send in my name, will teach you all things and will remind you of everything I have said to you." **John 14:26***

DEVOTIONAL

As she embraced the quiet moments of retirement, Ruth found herself reflecting on the days when her life was filled with bustling activities and responsibilities. One afternoon, while sipping her tea, she felt a gentle nudge to call an old friend she hadn't spoken to in years. Hesitant at first, she followed that soft prompting, and the conversation naturally flowed, healing old wounds and rekindling a cherished friendship. It struck Ruth that this Spirit-led interaction gave her joy and purpose in a new season of life.

Embrace the gentle nudges of the Holy Spirit; they may lead you to unexpected blessings and purpose in your retirement years.

DAILY REFLECTION

What does it mean for you to be led by the Spirit in your daily life? Can you recall moments when you felt a gentle nudge towards a decision or an action that brought peace or joy?

PRAYER

Dear God, thank you for your presence in our lives. Help us to hear your voice and follow your leading, trusting in your wisdom each day.

"Spirit-led living opens our hearts to the beauty of divine direction."

HE SEES EVERY TEAR

"And even the very hairs of your head are all numbered."
Matthew 10:30

DEVOTIONAL

As a retired woman, there may be times when you feel overlooked or insignificant, lost in a world that seems to rush past. Yet, consider the story of Margaret, who after her husband's passing, found solace in her garden. Every morning, she would tend to her flowers, often shedding quiet tears over memories shared. One day, as she knelt in the soil, she noticed the way the sun warmed her face and the vibrant petals swayed gently in the breeze. It was then she felt a profound peace, realizing that while life can bring sorrow, beauty and love continue to flourish, and someone is watching over every tear she sheds.

In life's trials, remember that every tear has meaning and you are never alone in your struggles.

DAILY REFLECTION

What tears have you shed in the quiet moments of your life, and how have those experiences shaped who you are today?

PRAYER

Dear Lord, thank You for being our comfort in times of sorrow. Help us to remember that every tear we shed is seen by You, and that Your love surrounds us even in our weakest moments.

"Every tear is a testament to a heart that has loved deeply and has been seen completely."

THE BEAUTY OF DEPENDENCE

"The Lord replied, "My Presence will go with you, and I will give you rest.""
Exodus 33:14

DEVOTIONAL

Mabel often found herself reminiscing about her youthful days of independence, where she raced through life, juggling work, family, and community commitments. But now, in her retirement, she felt a twinge of uncertainty, wondering how to navigate this new phase without a clear purpose. One day, while sipping tea with her friend Lucy, Mabel shared her feelings of being unneeded. Lucy gently reminded her that dependence on God and their friendship was a beautiful gift, one that deepened their connection and allowed for shared joy and support. It dawned on Mabel that leaning on others and on God wasn't a sign of weakness, but one of strength and wisdom.

Embracing dependence on God and community can lead to richer relationships and a more fulfilling life in retirement.

DAILY REFLECTION

What does being dependent on God look like in your daily life, and how can it lead to newfound strength and beauty in this season of your life?

PRAYER

Dear God, thank you for the gift of this season and the assurance that we are never alone. Help us to lean into you, finding peace and joy in our dependence on your love and guidance.

"In the quiet moments of life, dependence blooms into strength."

A LIFE OF OVERFLOW

*"You prepare a table before me in the presence of my enemies.
You anoint my head with oil; my cup overflows."* **Psalm 23:5**

DEVOTIONAL

Once upon a time, there was a retired woman named Grace who took up volunteering at a local soup kitchen. Each week, she mixed ingredients with love, serving meals and sharing smiles. At first, it felt like just another way to fill her time, but soon she noticed the joy and gratitude of those she served. The more she gave, the more she received; she found her heart overflowing with a sense of purpose and connection. Grace realized that by sharing what she had, she created a ripple effect of kindness that uplifted not only others but herself as well.

True fulfillment comes when we pour out our blessings into the lives of others.

DAILY REFLECTION

What does a life of overflow mean for you in this season of your life, and how can you cultivate joy and generosity in your daily interactions?

PRAYER

Dear Lord, thank you for the richness of life you've bestowed upon us. Help me to share my blessings with others and to live each day with a heart full of gratitude.

"Though seasons change, the abundance of God's love remains ever-flowing."

THE LORD WILL PROVIDE

"'Bring the whole tithe into the storehouse, that there may be food in my house. Test me in this,' says the Lord Almighty, 'and see if I will not throw open the floodgates of heaven and pour out so much blessing that there will not be room enough to store it.'" **Malachi 3:10**

DEVOTIONAL

After years of working tirelessly, Margaret found herself in a new rhythm of life in retirement. One sunny afternoon, as she was sorting through old boxes, she came across a forgotten stash of envelopes filled with uncashed checks from her volunteer work. As she sifted through the papers, she realized that these little pieces of paper represented countless moments of joy and fulfillment. Feeling a gentle tug on her heart, she decided to donate a portion of them to her local community center. That small act brought unexpected blessings—not just for those who received, but for herself as well, renewing her purpose and reminding her that the Lord indeed provides when we are willing to give.

Trust that as you open your heart to share your blessings, the Lord will not only provide for others but enrich your own life in ways you never imagined.

DAILY REFLECTION

What are some ways you've experienced God's provision in your life, and how can you trust Him to provide for your needs in this new season?

PRAYER

Dear Lord, thank you for the abundant ways you have cared for us throughout our lives. Help us to trust in your provision as we embrace the opportunities and challenges that come with each new day.

"God's provisions are often found in the simplest moments of our lives."

STANDING IN SPIRITUAL AUTHORITY

*"Very truly I tell you, whoever believes in me will do the works I have been doing, and they will do even greater things than these, because I am going to the Father." **John 14:12***

DEVOTIONAL

Once, there was a woman named Martha, who after retiring, found herself feeling somewhat adrift. She had spent her life serving others in her career and raising her family, but now she struggled to find her place in a world that was shifting. One day, while stirring a pot of soup, she felt a gentle nudge to reach out to her neighbor, who had been ill. It turned out that her visit brought comfort not just to the neighbor, but to Martha herself. She realized that even in retirement, her influence and spiritual authority could shine in the lives of those around her.

You have the power to nurture and uplift others, reminding you that your spiritual authority can manifest in the simplest acts of kindness.

DAILY REFLECTION

What does it mean for you to stand firm in your faith and exercise the authority God has given you in your daily life? How can you embody His strength in your relationships and community?

PRAYER

Dear Lord, thank you for the gift of wisdom and strength in every season of life. Help me to walk confidently in the spiritual authority you have bestowed upon me, sharing your love and truth with those around me.

"Your words carry power; let them resonate with grace and strength."

FAITH OVER FRUSTRATION

"Rejoice in hope, be patient in tribulation, be constant in prayer."
Romans 12:12

DEVOTIONAL

Mabel had a beautiful garden filled with blooming flowers, but one summer, an unrelenting drought turned her vibrant oasis into a parched landscape. Feelings of frustration swelled within her as she watched the withering plants. One afternoon, while sitting on her porch with a cup of tea, she recalled the verse "Trust in the Lord" and decided to lay her worries before Him in prayer. The very next day, the skies opened up, and refreshing rain poured down. Mabel learned that even in the dry spells of life, faith can water our spirits.

In times of trial and frustration, remember to bring your burdens to God in prayer, knowing He is our source of strength and comfort.

DAILY REFLECTION

What frustrations have been weighing on your heart lately, and how can recalling God's faithfulness help you navigate through them?

PRAYER

Dear Lord, thank You for being our constant source of strength. Help us to lean on You during moments of frustration, trusting that You are working everything for our good.

"When frustration creeps in, let faith be your anchor."

RENEWED BY GRACE

*"For by grace you have been saved through faith, and that not of yourselves; it is the gift of God, not of works, lest anyone should boast." **Ephesians 2:8-9***

DEVOTIONAL

After decades of pouring your heart into family, career, and community, you may find yourself at a crossroads, feeling a bit lost in this new season of life. One evening, as she sat with a cup of tea, Emily reflected on her journey. She had spent years caring for her loved ones, but now, she felt the quiet tug within her heart to explore her own dreams. Inspired by this moment, she took a painting class. With each brushstroke, she discovered not just her artistic talent but also a deeper sense of self—a unique flair that she had set aside for too long. It reminded her that grace allows us to grow and renew, even in the twilight of life.

Embrace this season of renewal, for even in retirement, your journey of grace is just beginning.

DAILY REFLECTION

What does it mean to you to experience renewal in this season of your life, and how can you open your heart more fully to the grace that surrounds you each day?

PRAYER

Dear Lord, thank You for the gift of Your grace that renews our spirits. Help me embrace this season of my life with open arms, trusting in Your plan and the beauty of new beginnings.

"Grace is the gentle whisper that assures us we are never too old to start anew."

THE GIFT OF HIS PRESENCE

*"And I will ask the Father, and he will give you another helper, to be with you forever, even the Spirit of truth, whom the world cannot receive, because it neither sees him nor knows him. You know him, for he dwells with you and will be in you." **John 14:16-17***

DEVOTIONAL

In her quiet evenings, Martha found joy in the garden she had tended for years. As she pruned the rose bushes, she reflected on the many seasons of her life and all the moments spent outdoors. One evening, while watering her flowers, she noticed a little bird taking refuge in the branches above. Its song filled the air with a gentle melody, reminding her of an unseen presence always nearby. Just as the bird seemed at ease in her garden, she understood that God's presence was like that: a comforting reassurance that filled her heart with peace in moments of solitude.

Even as life changes and seasons pass, we can always find solace in the comforting presence of God, who is with us every moment.

DAILY REFLECTION

What does it mean to you to experience God's presence in your everyday life, especially during these golden years? How can you create space to invite Him in more fully?

PRAYER

Dear Lord, thank You for the gift of Your presence in our lives. Help us to recognize and celebrate Your companionship each day, drawing strength and joy from our relationship with You.

"In the quiet moments, His presence speaks the loudest."

Halfway Through Our Journey

You are now halfway through this devotional journey.

Many women discover this book through the thoughtful reviews shared by readers like you.

If these pages have supported your faith and daily reflection, would you consider sharing a short review on Amazon?

Your voice may help someone else find encouragement today.

devo.anchoredgraces.com/retired

FINISH STRONG IN FAITH

"I have fought the good fight, I have finished the race, I have kept the faith. Now there is in store for me the crown of righteousness, which the Lord, the righteous Judge, will award to me on that day—and not only to me, but also to all who have longed for his appearing."
2 Timothy 4:7-8

DEVOTIONAL

In her retirement years, Clara found joy in volunteering at her local community center. She embraced each moment with the same fervor she had in her career, fostering friendships and inspiring others with her zest for life. One chilly autumn morning, she organized an event to uplift the spirits of fellow seniors, sharing stories of faith that united them. As they laughed and encouraged one another, Clara realized that her journey didn't end; it evolved into something more impactful. By living out her faith actively and engagingly, she discovered that finishing strong in this chapter of life meant pouring love and hope into the lives around her.

Every day is a new opportunity to share your faith and strengthen your community, leaving a lasting legacy of love and encouragement.

DAILY REFLECTION

What does finishing strong in your faith look like for you in this season of life? Are there new ways you feel called to deepen that faith and share it with others?

PRAYER

Dear Lord, thank you for the journey of faith we've walked together. As I approach each new day, help me finish strong, filled with hope and love, sharing your light with those around me.

"Filling our later years with faith's purpose is the crowning glory of a life well-lived."

FREEDOM IN CHRIST

"It is for freedom that Christ has set us free. Stand firm, then, and do not let yourselves be burdened again by a yoke of slavery." **Galatians 5:1**

DEVOTIONAL

There's a wise woman in our community, now in her sixties, who spent many years caring for her elderly parents. While she adored them, she often felt confined by the responsibilities that consumed her days. When they passed, she found herself at a crossroads, unsure of what to do with her newfound freedom. Rather than retreating into solitude, she embraced the time to explore her passions—painting, gardening, and volunteering. Through discovering what brought her joy, she realized that her worth wasn't tied to her caregiving role but found fully in Christ's love, which freed her to embrace new chapters of life.

Embrace the freedom found in Christ, for it opens the door to new possibilities and passions waiting to be explored.

DAILY REFLECTION

What does freedom in Christ mean for you in this season of your life, and how can you embrace that freedom day by day?

PRAYER

Gracious Father, thank you for the gift of freedom found in Your Son, Jesus. Help me to lean into this freedom as I navigate each new day, trusting in Your plan for my journey.

"In Christ, every moment holds the potential for new beginnings and endless possibilities."

GOD'S LOVE NEVER FAILS

"Love never fails."
1 Corinthians 13:8

DEVOTIONAL

Once, a retired woman named Helen found herself feeling lost after her children moved away. She spent her days reminiscing about busy family life and felt pained by the silence in her home. One afternoon, as she was tidying up, she stumbled upon a dusty box of letters from her late husband. Each note was filled with expressions of love and encouragement. In reading those words, she felt enveloped by God's eternal love, reassuring her that even in solitude, she was never truly alone.

Remember, dear friend, in every change and challenge, God's love is the anchor that holds us steady.

DAILY REFLECTION

What experiences in your life have shown you that God's love remains steadfast, even in the challenging moments?

PRAYER

Dear God, thank you for the unwavering love You pour into our lives. Help me to embrace Your presence each day, trusting that Your love will guide and sustain me through all seasons of life.

"Even in the twilight of our years, God's love shines brightest, inviting us to rest in His promises."

COURAGE TO FOLLOW GOD'S CALL

"But Jesus immediately said to them: 'Take courage! It is I. Don't be afraid.'"
Matthew 14:27

DEVOTIONAL

In her retirement years, Mary found herself sitting quietly, enveloped in an unfamiliar stillness that often invited doubt and uncertainty about her next steps in life. One afternoon, during a walk in her neighborhood, she noticed a small group of young mothers struggling to organize a community event. The hesitant voice inside her urged her to help, but she pondered if her age and experience made her relevant in their world. With a deep breath, Mary approached them and offered her assistance, and soon, her wisdom and calm presence became the heart of the gathering, proving that following God's gentle nudges could create vibrant connections during any season of life.

Every act of courage, no matter how small, can lead to new adventures and meaningful connections, reminding us that following God's call can be a beautiful journey at any age.

DAILY REFLECTION

What dreams or passions has God placed in your heart that you've yet to explore? How might you take a small step toward those today?

PRAYER

Dear Lord, grant me the courage to recognize and embrace Your call on my life. Help me to trust in Your guidance as I seek to follow where You lead.

"Courage is not the absence of fear, but the willingness to act in faith regardless of it."

TRUE FREEDOM THROUGH FAITH

"I will walk about in freedom, for I have sought out your precepts."
Psalm 119:45

DEVOTIONAL

Embrace each day with the confidence that your faith provides; it is in seeking God's wisdom that we discover true freedom.

True freedom comes when we let go of worldly concerns and trust fully in the plans God has for our lives.

DAILY REFLECTION

What does true freedom mean to you in this season of your life, and how can your faith guide you toward embracing it fully?

PRAYER

Dear Lord, thank you for the gift of faith that brings us true freedom. Help us to embrace this gift each day and to find joy in your presence.

"True freedom comes not from the absence of burdens but from the presence of faith."

FAITH IN THE EVERYDAY

"Be on your guard; stand firm in the faith; be courageous; be strong. Do everything in love."
1 Corinthians 16:13-14

DEVOTIONAL

As you navigate this beautiful season of your life, embrace the strength and courage that your faith provides in every moment.

Every day presents an opportunity to express love and strengthen your faith, reminding you that each small act of kindness weaves God's grace into the fabric of your daily life.

DAILY REFLECTION

What everyday moments can you cherish as opportunities to deepen your faith and connection with God?

PRAYER

Dear Lord. thank You for the gift of this day. Help me to see Your presence in the simple, ordinary moments of my life. Amen.

"Faith is not just a feeling; it's a daily practice of trust and gratitude."

ABIDING IN PEACE

*"Now may the Lord of peace Himself give you peace at all times and in every way. The Lord be with all of you." **2 Thessalonians 3:16***

DEVOTIONAL

In this season of life, embrace the quiet moments, for they often carry the most profound gifts of peace and connection to your spirit.

May you find serenity not only in the stillness of your days but also in the warmth of cherished memories and the love that surrounds you.

DAILY REFLECTION

What does it mean for you to truly abide in peace during this season of your life? How can you create a sanctuary of serenity in your daily routines?

PRAYER

Dear Lord, help me to find your peace in every moment of my day. May I rest in your loving presence and share that tranquility with those around me.

"Peace is not found in the absence of trials, but in the presence of God."

LIVING FOR AN AUDIENCE OF ONE

*"Whatever you do, work at it with all your heart, as working for the Lord, not for human masters, since you know that you will receive an inheritance from the Lord as a reward. It is the Lord Christ you are serving." **Colossians 3:23-24***

DEVOTIONAL

As you embrace this season of life, remember that your worth is not defined by others or their expectations; you are living for a higher purpose and a loving God who sees your heart.

DAILY REFLECTION

What does it mean for you to live your life with the understanding that you are ultimately accountable to God alone, rather than to the expectations of others?

PRAYER

Dear Heavenly Father, thank You for Your unwavering love and guidance in our lives. Help us to focus on pleasing You and to find joy in each moment, knowing that our worth comes from being Your beloved daughters.

"Life becomes truly beautiful when it's lived for an audience of One."

FINDING STILLNESS WITH GOD

"The Lord is good to those who wait for him, to the soul who seeks him. It is good that one should wait quietly for the salvation of the Lord." **Lamentations 3:25-26**

DEVOTIONAL

In her cozy living room, Mary sipped her herbal tea, the quiet of the afternoon wrapping around her like a warm blanket. After years of bustling through work and family obligations, the stillness felt both foreign and beautifully inviting. As she gazed out the window, watching the leaves sway gently in the breeze, a sense of peace washed over her, guiding her to a realization: in this season of life, moments of calm were a gift, a time to simply be with God. In those serene pauses, she found not only comfort but also clarity in her purpose, cherishing the whispers of love that the Lord offered in silence.

True stillness can lead to the sweetest moments of communion with God, reminding us that in our quietest hour, His presence can fill the space with profound meaning.

DAILY REFLECTION

What does finding stillness with God mean for you in this season of your life? How can you create a space for quiet communion with Him amidst the everyday busyness?

PRAYER

Dear Lord, thank You for the gift of this moment. Help me to embrace the stillness and find Your presence in the quiet spaces of my life.

"Amidst the noise of the world, God whispers to those who pause and listen."

THE STRENGTH OF SURRENDER

"No temptation has overtaken you except what is common to mankind. And God is faithful; he will not let you be tempted beyond what you can bear. But when you are tempted, he will also provide a way out so that you can endure it." 1 **Corinthians 10:13**

DEVOTIONAL

Once upon a time, there was a spirited woman named Edith who spent her days tending to her garden, filled with vibrant flowers and freshly blooming vegetables. As she aged and faced health challenges, she found herself overwhelmed by the changes in her once manageable routine. One morning, as she sat on her garden bench, she saw a beautiful butterfly struggle against a strong wind. Instead of fighting, it simply surrendered to the breeze, allowing itself to be carried to new flowers. Inspired, Edith realized that in surrendering her worries and accepting help from loved ones, she could find peace and joyously embrace this new season of life.

Surrendering doesn't mean giving up; it means trusting God to lead you to a new purpose and peace in every season of your life.

DAILY REFLECTION

What does it mean for you to let go of control and trust in God's plan for this season of your life? How might surrendering bring you peace and strength?

PRAYER

Dear Lord, as I navigate this new chapter, help me to lay my burdens at Your feet. Teach me the art of surrender, that I may find strength in letting go and peace in trusting You.

"Surrendering is not giving up; it is opening our hearts to a new kind of strength."

BECOMING A WOMAN OF INFLUENCE

"Let us not become weary in doing good, for at the proper time we will reap a harvest if we do not give up." **Galatians 6:9**

DEVOTIONAL

Judith always believed that her influence in her community had dwindled since retiring. Yet, one afternoon at the local senior center, she noticed a younger woman struggling to connect with others. Remembering her own challenges when she first moved to town, Judith decided to share her story. She invited the woman to have coffee, and they ended up weaving a beautiful friendship that encouraged both of them. The ripples of that simple act of kindness spread as they began organizing activities together, bringing joy and connection to many others.

Every small act of kindness can blossom into impactful relationships, reminding us that we are never too old to influence the lives around us.

DAILY REFLECTION

What influences have shaped your life, and how might you harness those experiences to inspire others in your community today?

PRAYER

Dear Heavenly Father, may my heart be open to the ways I can impact those around me. Guide me to share my wisdom and love with others, reflecting Your grace in all I do.

"True influence is not about power, but the ability to uplift and inspire those around us."

TRUST WHEN YOU CAN'T SEE

"For we walk by faith, not by sight"
2 Corinthians 5:7

DEVOTIONAL

In her early retirement, Marjorie found herself grappling with her purpose. After decades of raising children and building a career, she faced days when the future felt unclear and daunting. One afternoon, while tending to her garden, she noticed the tiny buds appearing on her once-bare rosebush. Though the flowers were not yet visible, she understood that underneath the surface, life was flourishing, preparing for the bloom that would soon grace her garden. This simple moment taught her the beauty of trust; she realized that just as nature operates in cycles, so too does life unfold in God's perfect timing, often beyond what we can currently see.

Sometimes, we must trust that God is working behind the scenes, nurturing our lives, even when the path ahead feels hidden in shadows.

DAILY REFLECTION

What are the areas in your life where you feel challenged to trust, especially when you can't see the next step ahead? Take a moment to reflect on how faith can guide you through uncertain times.

PRAYER

Dear God, as I journey through my days, help me to trust in Your plans, even when they remain unseen. May Your peace fill my heart and guide my steps as I rest in Your loving promises.

"True faith is believing not just in the promise, but in the One who promises."

GRACE THAT COVERS ALL

"But where sin increased, grace increased all the more."
Romans 5:20

DEVOTIONAL

In her early years, Mildred often felt overwhelmed by the pressures of life—raising children, working long hours, and tending to her home. One evening, as she sat in her favorite chair with a cup of tea, she reflected on her journey. Though she had made mistakes and faced regrets, she began to understand the depth of God's grace covering each stumble. As the sun set and painted the sky with soft hues of gold and pink, she realized that this grace was like a comforting quilt wrapped around her heart, reminding her that she was loved, cherished, and never alone, no matter what had come before.

Remember that grace is not only abundant; it is specifically crafted by God to embrace every moment of your life, reminding you that you are valued beyond measure.

DAILY REFLECTION

What are the ways you have experienced God's grace in your life, and how can you carry that grace forward in your interactions with others today?

PRAYER

Dear Lord, thank You for the grace that envelops us no matter where we've been or what we've faced. Help us to recognize and share this precious gift in our everyday lives, bringing comfort to ourselves and those around us.

"Grace is not just a one-time gift; it flows endlessly, inviting us into a deeper relationship with our Creator."

LETTING GOD LEAD

"But when he, the Spirit of truth, comes, he will guide you into all the truth. He will not speak on his own; he will speak only what he hears, and he will tell you what is yet to come."
John 16:13

DEVOTIONAL

After spending years nurturing her family and managing the hustle of a career, Margaret found herself at a crossroads in retirement. Initially, she busied herself with activities and errands, feeling the need to fill her time. One quiet afternoon, while sipping tea on her porch, she felt a gentle nudge to explore her community in a different way. She started volunteering at the local shelter, and it was within those humble walls that she rediscovered her purpose and passion. As she embraced this new path, she realized that letting God lead her into unfamiliar territory brought unexpected joy and fulfillment to her days.

God invites us to let go of our own plans and to trust in His guidance, often opening doors to new opportunities we never imagined.

DAILY REFLECTION

What does it mean for you to truly let God lead in your life during this season of retirement? How can you invite Him into your daily decisions and moments of reflection?

PRAYER

Dear Lord, I thank You for the journey I have walked with You. Please help me to trust Your guidance and embrace the paths You set before me, knowing that You know what is best for my heart and soul.

"Letting God lead is not a surrender of our dreams, but an invitation for His greater vision to unfold in our lives."

REJOICING IN TRIALS

"Consider it pure joy, my sisters and brothers, whenever you face trials of many kinds, because you know that the testing of your faith produces perseverance." **James 1:2-3**

DEVOTIONAL

In her golden years, Mary found herself facing unexpected challenges that seemed to cloud her sunny disposition. Sprains, an unanticipated house repair, and difficulties with neighbors felt like a wave crashing over her peaceful shore. Yet, one evening while sitting on her porch, she spotted a group of children playing joyfully amidst the rain. Their laughter and cheerfulness sparked a thought: much like the rain nourishes the flowers, perhaps her trials could yield new growth in her spirit. With this revelation, she chose to embrace the struggles, seeking joy in the little moments rather than letting difficulties dim her light.

Embracing trials with a joyful heart can transform challenges into stepping stones for deeper faith and appreciation in this cherished season of life.

DAILY REFLECTION

What trials are you currently facing, and how might you see God's hand in them as you rejoice in His presence?

PRAYER

Dear God, help me to embrace the challenges of each day with a heart full of trust and joy. May I find Your grace in every trial and peace in every moment.

"Joy blooms in the garden of our trials when we tend to it with faith."

THE POWER OF SPIRITUAL DISCIPLINE

"No discipline seems pleasant at the time, but painful. Later on, however, it produces a harvest of righteousness and peace for those who have been trained by it." **Hebrews 12:11**

DEVOTIONAL

In the quiet moments of her day, Margaret often reflects on the string of small routines she has woven into her life. It began with a simple commitment to rise early for her morning coffee with God, and over time, this had blossomed into a cherished ritual that grounded her amid the chaos of life. She also found joy in nurturing her garden, viewing it not just as a hobby but as a manifestation of her spiritual discipline. Each plant was a reminder of her faith: needing care, patience, and consistency to flourish. Through these moments, Margaret understood that while discipline might sometimes feel burdensome, the rewards of peace and growth in her spiritual life were more than worth the effort.

Just as the blooms in her garden transformed with time and care, so too can our spiritual lives flourish through consistent discipline and dedication.

DAILY REFLECTION

What spiritual disciplines have you embraced in your life, and how have they shaped your relationship with God?

PRAYER

Dear Heavenly Father, thank You for the gift of time in this season of life. Help me to cultivate spiritual disciplines that draw me closer to You and nurture my soul.

"Spiritual discipline is the gentle practice of making space for God in our daily lives."

YOUR PAST DOES NOT DEFINE YOU

*"For I will forgive their wickedness
and will remember their sins no more."* **Hebrews 8:12**

DEVOTIONAL

In her earlier years, Martha often found herself regretting choices she made, from career mistakes to strained relationships. As she reminisced about these moments, she felt weighted down by the past. But one day while sorting through an old box of letters, she found one from a friend who had once encouraged her to embrace the beauty of second chances. Inspired by those words, Martha decided to volunteer at a local shelter. Helping others reminded her that while her past shaped her, it didn't have to hold her back; instead, it could lead her to a fulfilling purpose in the present.

Your past experiences enrich your wisdom, but they do not define your worth or future.

DAILY REFLECTION

What experiences from your past have you clung to that no longer serve you? How might letting go of these narratives allow you to embrace the abundant life waiting ahead?

PRAYER

Dear Lord, thank you for the gift of new beginnings. Help me to release my past and walk in the freedom you've promised, embracing the joy of each new day.

"Your past is a chapter, not the whole story."

CHOOSING JOY OVER ANXIETY

"Finally brothers and sisters, whatever is true, whatever is noble, whatever is right, whatever is pure, whatever is lovely, whatever is admirable—if anything is excellent or praiseworthy—think about such things." **Philippians 4:8**

DEVOTIONAL

In her cozy living room, Clara often reminisced about her earlier days—raising her children, tending a garden, and sharing laughter with friends. One rainy afternoon, a flurry of anxious thoughts crept in, spiraling her into worry about the future and the changes that retirement had brought. Yet, as she absentmindedly flipped through an old photo album, smiles and cherished memories caught her heart. It dawned on her that each photo was a reminder of joyful times that outshone her current worries. Embracing these thoughts, she decided to pick up the phone and call her closest friend to share a laugh, realizing that choosing joy was a powerful antidote to anxiety.

In this season of life, remember that joy is a choice you can make each day, even amidst uncertainty.

DAILY REFLECTION

What are some gifts of joy you can choose to embrace today, even as worries try to creep in?

PRAYER

Dear Lord, help me to see the beauty in each moment and to choose joy over anxiety. Fill my heart with peace and guide my thoughts toward gratitude and love.

"Joy is not the absence of anxiety, but the choice to dance with hope amid it."

DELIGHT IN THE LORD

"Take delight in the Lord, and he will give you the desires of your heart."
Psalm 37:4

DEVOTIONAL

Once, a woman named Edith found joy in her morning routine of sipping tea on her sunlit porch. Each day, she would pause to read her Bible, and it became a moment she cherished deeply. One day, as she lingered over a verse about God's goodness, she was struck by how her life had changed since retiring. What once felt daunting—filling her time—had transformed into an opportunity to explore her passions, volunteer, and deepen friendships. It was through these daily moments of delight that she felt a renewed connection to the Lord, appreciating how His faithfulness permeated her quiet mornings.

Find joy in the simple moments with God, for it is in these times that your heart truly opens to His blessings.

DAILY REFLECTION

What brings you joy in your daily life, and how can you invite more of the Lord's presence into those moments? Consider the simple things that make your heart smile.

PRAYER

Dear Lord, thank You for the gift of each day. Help me to see Your hand in the beauty around me and to find deep delight in Your presence.

"Delighting in the Lord opens our hearts to the abundance of His grace."

FINDING BALANCE IN GOD'S DESIGN

"Set your minds on things above, not on earthly things."
Colossians 3:2

DEVOTIONAL

As a retired woman in her 60s, life has shifted in so many ways, bringing both freedom and uncertainty. One day, while tending to her beloved garden, Mary found herself overwhelmed by clutter in her home and the pace of life. With a short burst of wind, a single leaf from a nearby tree danced in front of her, reminding her to focus on the beauty around her instead of the chaos. That moment led Mary to reorganize her priorities, creating space for her passion for volunteering and nurturing relationships that mattered. With a heart full of gratitude, she discovered that balance comes from intentionally choosing what to give her time and energy to, reflecting God's design for her life.

In the beauty of simplicity, we find the balance that God desires for us, reminding us to focus on what truly matters.

DAILY REFLECTION

What areas of your life feel out of balance right now, and how can you invite God into those spaces for His guidance and peace?

PRAYER

Dear Lord, thank You for this season of life where I can draw closer to You. Help me to find harmony in the responsibilities and joys that fill my days as I seek to honor Your design.

"Embracing balance in our lives allows us to fully experience the richness of God's gifts."

HOPE IN THE WILDERNESS

"Why, my soul, are you downcast? Why so disturbed within me? Put your hope in God, for I will yet praise him, my Savior and my God." **Psalm 42:11**

DEVOTIONAL

In the quiet of her morning routine, Clara often found herself reminiscing about the brighter days of raising her children and the bustling energy of her career. Now, in her cozy home filled with memories, she sometimes felt as though she was wandering through a wilderness of loneliness. One day, while tending to her little garden, she noticed a small patch of wildflowers struggling to bloom amidst the weeds. Just as she tended to those flowers with love and patience, she realized that God was tending to her heart, planting seeds of hope and reminding her that beauty could still flourish, even in the wilderness.

In life's quieter seasons, we are invited to nurture our inner gardens, trusting that hope can sprout anew when we tend to our souls.

DAILY REFLECTION

What wilderness experiences have shaped your life, and how do you see hope emerging from them?

PRAYER

Dear Lord, as I navigate through the wilderness of life, help me to recognize the glimmers of hope you place in my path. Fill my heart with gratitude and remind me of your steadfast love.

"Even in the deepest valleys, hope can blossom like wildflowers after the rain."

YOU ARE GOD'S MASTERPIECE

"For we are God's handiwork, created in Christ Jesus to do good works, which God prepared in advance for us to do." **Ephesians 2:10**

DEVOTIONAL

Once upon a time, there lived a woman named Evelyn who had dedicated her life to her family and community. In her golden years, she often felt as if she had lost her purpose, wondering if there was still a way for her to contribute. One day, while tending to her garden, she discovered a wilted flower amongst the vibrant blossoms. With a little care and attention, that flower flourished, inspiring Evelyn to realize that even in this later stage of life, she could offer love and beauty to those around her. She began volunteering at a local shelter, sharing her warmth and wisdom, discovering that her experiences were valuable gifts that could uplift others.

You are a beautiful creation, and even in retirement, the good works you were meant to do are waiting to be revealed through your unique talents and stories.

DAILY REFLECTION

What unique gifts and experiences has God woven into the tapestry of your life that make you feel like His masterpiece? Reflect on how each chapter has shaped you into the beautiful woman you are today.

PRAYER

Dear God, thank you for creating me in Your image and for the unique story You've written for my life. Help me to see the beauty in every season and to embrace my role as Your masterpiece.

"You are not just a creation; you are God's cherished masterpiece, crafted with love and purpose."

LIVING LOVED AND KNOWN

*"The Lord appeared to us in the past, saying: "I have loved you with an everlasting love; I have drawn you with unfailing kindness." **Jeremiah 31:3***

DEVOTIONAL

In her quiet mornings, Margaret would sit by the window, sipping her tea as the sun began to rise. Each day seemed to blend into the next, but one morning, as she watched the birds flutter about, it struck her: these little creatures never worried about their worth or their place in the world. They instinctively knew they were loved and cared for. In that moment, Margaret understood that just as the birds were known to the Creator, so too was she, cherished and seen in every stage of her life, particularly in her retirement.

You are not defined by what you accomplish but by the love that surrounds you and the joy that fills your heart, reminding you that you are always known and beloved.

DAILY REFLECTION

What does it feel like to be truly loved and known by God in this season of your life? How has His love shaped your identity and relationships with others?

PRAYER

Dear God, thank you for your unwavering love that surrounds us each day. Help me to fully embrace the depth of Your affection and to share that love with those around me.

"Embracing God's love allows us to walk confidently in the beauty of who we are."

THE VOICE THAT CALMS

*"But whoever listens to me will live in safety and be at ease, without fear of harm." **Proverbs 1:33***

DEVOTIONAL

In the quiet moments of life, like sipping tea on the porch or tending to a garden, remember that tuning in to the gentle voice of wisdom can bring peace even in tumultuous times.

Embrace the calming presence of God's voice, for it brings comfort and reassurance amid life's changes.

DAILY REFLECTION

What calming voice do you hear in the moments of life's chaos? How can you invite that voice into your day-to-day experiences?

PRAYER

Dear Lord, thank You for being the gentle voice that calms our hearts. Help us to listen for Your guidance and to find peace in Your presence each day. Amen.

"In the stillness, His voice brings peace to the soul."

RETURNING TO YOUR FIRST LOVE

"Yet I hold this against you: You have forsaken the love you had at first. Consider how far you have fallen! Repent and do the things you did at first." **Revelation 2:4-5**

DEVOTIONAL

In this season of life, it's a beautiful opportunity to reflect on the deeper loves in our lives, including the joys and passions that once brought us comfort and excitement.

Returning to your first love means rekindling the passion for God and the simple joys of life that made you feel most alive.

DAILY REFLECTION

What have you learned about love in your journey with God, and how can you rekindle that passion today?

PRAYER

Dear Lord, help me to remember the joy of my early days with You. Ignite my heart anew and guide me as I seek to deepen my relationship with You each day.

"Love is the bridge that connects our hearts to God's purpose."

PERSEVERANCE THROUGH PRAYER

"If you believe, you will receive whatever you ask for in prayer."
Matthew 21:22

DEVOTIONAL

When Clara retired, she suddenly found herself drowning in a sea of quiet days. Initially, she felt lost, but soon she discovered a new rhythm in her life through prayer. Every morning, she would sit by her kitchen window with a cup of tea, asking God for clarity about her purpose in this new season. One day, as she spoke her heart's desires aloud, she felt a gentle nudge inside, encouraging her to volunteer at a local community center. Through her newfound commitment, Clara not only rekindled her own joy but became a beacon of hope for others, realizing that prayer had opened doors she never expected.

True perseverance in our later years often springs from the quiet strength of prayer, and there lies new purpose waiting for us if we keep asking and seeking.

DAILY REFLECTION

What challenges have you faced lately that could benefit from your unwavering prayer? How can you invite God into those moments to strengthen your perseverance?

PRAYER

Dear Lord, thank You for the gift of prayer and the strength it brings. Help me to rely on You in every moment, trusting in Your plan and timing as I navigate life's seasons.

"Prayer is the bridge that connects our struggles to God's boundless hope."

FLOURISHING IN EVERY SEASON

"Look to the Lord and his strength; seek his face always."
1 Chronicles 16:11

DEVOTIONAL

Margaret always loved her garden. In spring, she would plant tulips, eagerly anticipating their vibrant blooms. As summer rolled in, she nurtured her veggies, savoring fresh tomatoes and peppers. When autumn came, she harvested what she had sown, and though winter brought frost and dormancy, she found joy in planning her next year's garden. Each season brought its own beauty and lessons, reminding her that life, much like her garden, flourishes in cycles.

Embrace each season of life, knowing that growth and beauty are found in every stage of your journey.

DAILY REFLECTION

What does it mean for you to flourish in this season of your life, and how can you embrace the changes that come with it?

PRAYER

Dear Lord, thank You for the gift of each season in our lives. Help us to find joy in every moment and to be open to the beauty that surrounds us, even in times of change.

"Embrace the seasons of life, for each one brings its own unique beauty and purpose."

GOD'S PRESENCE IN YOUR ROUTINE

"Be strong and take heart, all you who hope in the Lord."
Psalm 31:24

DEVOTIONAL

Every morning for the past five years, Margaret sat by her kitchen window with a steaming cup of tea, watching the world awaken. As flowers bloomed and birds chirped, she began to notice that these moments were more than just a routine; they were invitations from God. One day, she caught herself humming a hymn, realizing that her quiet mornings had become a sacred space where she felt His presence. Through the simplicity of daily rituals, Margaret found beauty in God's company, reminding her that even in the mundane, the divine is present, guiding her heart and thoughts.

Embrace the ordinary moments of your day as sacred encounters with God, for His presence is woven into your routine.

DAILY REFLECTION

What small moments in your daily routine can you acknowledge as God's gentle nudges or reminders of His presence?

PRAYER

Dear Lord, thank You for the quiet moments of each day where You meet us. Help us to recognize and embrace Your presence in our routines, bringing peace and joy to our lives.

"Every moment is an opportunity to encounter the divine in the ordinary."

LIVING WITH HOLY CONFIDENCE

*"Now to him who is able to do immeasurably more than all we ask or imagine, according to his power that is at work within us, to him be glory in the church and in Christ Jesus throughout all generations, for ever and ever! Amen." **Ephesians 3:20-21***

DEVOTIONAL

In her golden years, Mary found herself volunteering at the local community center. At first, she felt unsure, wondering if her contributions would truly make a difference. However, as she spent time with younger women and offered her wisdom, she witnessed a transformation—not only in them but in herself. Through cooking classes and shared stories, she developed friendships that enriched her days, realizing that her past experiences were invaluable treasures, just waiting to be shared. With each passing week, Mary discovered that stepping out in faith opened her heart to the joy and strength she never realized she possessed.

Living with holy confidence means embracing your worth and recognizing the unique gifts you bring to the world, allowing God's light to shine through you in ways you may not even see yet.

DAILY REFLECTION

What does it mean for you to walk each day with a holy confidence, trusting in God's promises and purpose for this season of your life?

PRAYER

Dear Lord, thank You for the gift of this new chapter in life. Help me to embrace each day with confidence, knowing that You are my guide and strength. May I reflect Your love in all that I do.

"Confidence in God transforms ordinary moments into extraordinary journeys."

RELEASING THE WEIGHTS YOU CARRY

*"Therefore we do not lose heart. Though outwardly we are wasting away, yet inwardly we are being renewed day by day." **2 Corinthians 4:16***

DEVOTIONAL

Mabel had spent years caring for her family, volunteering in her community, and holding on to past grievances that weighed heavily on her heart. One afternoon, as she sat quietly by the window, she noticed the vibrant colors of the garden outside, blooming without reservation. It struck her that just as the flowers released their faded petals to embrace the new growth, she too could let go of her burdens. It was time for her to welcome the possibility of a lighter spirit, freeing herself from the expectations and regrets that had outweighed her joy.

Sometimes, we carry weights that cloud our ability to appreciate the beauty around us; releasing these burdens is essential for newfound joy in this season of life.

DAILY REFLECTION

What burdens or concerns are you holding onto that may be weighing you down more than you realize?

PRAYER

Dear God, help me to recognize the weights I carry. Grant me the courage to release them into Your loving hands and to embrace the freedom of Your grace.

"Letting go is not forgetting; it's choosing to be free from the hold those memories have on our hearts."

FAITH THAT TRANSFORMS

*"He saved us, not because of righteous things we had done,
but because of his mercy. He saved us through the washing of
rebirth and renewal by the Holy Spirit."*
Titus 3:5

DEVOTIONAL

Once there was a retired teacher named Elsie who spent her days painting and gardening. She had a quaint little home with a blooming garden, but sometimes, she felt a sense of emptiness—missing the purpose she once had in her classroom. One afternoon, as she tended to her flowers, she noticed one that appeared to be lifeless. With patience and care, she nurtured it with water and sunlight, eagerly watching it blossom into a beautiful bloom. Just as that flower revived through time and attention, Elsie realized that faith could transform her life in ways she hadn't considered. She began volunteering at a local community center, where her teaching spirit flourished once again, igniting her heart with renewed joy and purpose.

Even in retirement, faith, like a garden, needs nurturing to bring forth beautiful transformations in our lives.

DAILY REFLECTION

*What areas of your life are you inviting God to
transform through your faith today?*

PRAYER

Dear God, thank you for the gift of faith that holds the power to change us. Help us to open our hearts to Your work in our lives and embrace the transformation You offer.

"Faith isn't just a belief; it's the spark that ignites change from the inside out."

PRAISE BEFORE THE BREAKTHROUGH

"Let everything that has breath praise the Lord. Praise the Lord."
Psalm 150:6

DEVOTIONAL

As a retired woman, you may find yourself reflecting on the various seasons of your life. There was a time when you faced a daunting challenge, perhaps caring for a sick loved one, navigating the complexities of work-life balance, or adjusting to an empty nest. Remember the moments when you chose to lift your voice in praise, even when the answer seemed far off. Those were the moments your spirit found strength, where joy broke through disappointment, and hope shone like a beacon, guiding your steps.

In times of uncertainty, let your heart praise God in advance for the breakthroughs yet to come; your grateful spirit will illuminate the path ahead.

DAILY REFLECTION

What are the moments in your life where you found it difficult to see the light, yet through praise, you felt a glimmer of hope? How did that shape your understanding of God's goodness?

PRAYER

Dear Lord, thank You for the blessings yet to come. Help me to praise You even when my circumstances seem dim, trusting that Your light will always shine through.

"Praise is the bridge that carries us from despair to hope."

ROOTED IN GOD'S TRUTH

"But whose delight is in the law of the Lord, and who meditates on his law day and night. That person is like a tree planted by streams of water, which yields its fruit in season and whose leaf does not wither— whatever they do prospers." **Psalm 1:2-3**

DEVOTIONAL

Once, a grandmother named Helen spent her mornings tending to a small garden in her backyard, nurturing each plant with care and patience. Over the years, the flowers flourished, and their vibrant colors brought joy not only to her but to the neighbors passing by. Helen often reflected on how her gardening parallels her relationship with God; just as she fed the plants with nourishment, she turned to Scripture for strength and wisdom, allowing His truth to guide her life. In her quiet moments, she found herself rooted in God's promises, drawing sustenance from His love and grace.

In this season of your life, nurture your spiritual roots with God's truth, and watch as your faith blossoms in ways you never imagined.

DAILY REFLECTION

What truths from God's word have you held onto throughout your life, and how can they continue to guide you in this new season?

PRAYER

Dear God, thank You for being a steadfast foundation in my life. Help me to remain deeply rooted in Your truth, trusting in Your promises each day.

"Deep roots lead to a fruitful life."His purpose in the waiting."

CONFIDENCE IN HIS PLAN

"'For my thoughts are not your thoughts, neither are your ways my ways,' declares the Lord. 'As the heavens are higher than the earth, so are my ways higher than your ways and my thoughts than your thoughts.'" **Isaiah 55:8-9**

DEVOTIONAL

After years of working tirelessly, Helen found herself at a crossroads in retirement. She had once envisioned travel, new hobbies, and spending time with family, but life felt uncertain. One afternoon, while sorting through old photos, she stumbled upon a picture of herself climbing a mountain with her friends. Remembering the thrill of the challenge, Helen felt a spark of inspiration. As she began volunteering at a local community center, she realized that this new chapter held opportunities to uplift others, offering her a renewed sense of purpose.

In this season of life, it's important to trust that God's plan for your future is filled with promise, even when it looks different than you expected.

DAILY REFLECTION

What areas of your life do you find challenging to trust in God's plan, and how can you seek His guidance in those moments?

PRAYER

Dear Lord, thank You for Your steadfast presence in our lives. Help us to rest in the assurance that Your plans for us are good and full of hope.

"Embracing God's plan invites peace into our hearts, even when the path is unclear."

WHEN YOU FEEL SPIRITUALLY DRY

"Therefore, my beloved sisters, as you have always obeyed, not only in my presence but now much more in my absence, continue to work out your salvation with fear and trembling, for it is God who works in you to will and to act in order to fulfill his good purpose." **Philippians 2:12-13**

DEVOTIONAL

Once there was a retired woman named Helen who had spent her life teaching children in her community. Now, in her quiet days, she found herself feeling spiritually dry and distant from her faith. One afternoon, while pruning her rose bushes, she noticed how some of them had become overgrown and needed careful trimming. As she worked, she reflected on how the bushes, like her spirit, required attention and nurturing to bloom. Afterward, during her daily prayer, she felt a gentle reminder that even in seasons of dryness, God is always at work, ready to cultivate new growth within her heart.

In the times we feel spiritually dry, remember that God is patiently working in us, preparing us for a beautiful new season of growth.

DAILY REFLECTION

What are the different ways you can invite the Holy Spirit to refresh your spirit during this dry season in your life?

PRAYER

Dear Lord, in moments of spiritual dryness, help me to seek Your presence and find comfort in Your love. Grant me the patience to wait on You and the wisdom to recognize the gentle whispers of Your guidance.

"Even in the desert, the sun rises, reminding us that hope is never truly lost."

GOD IS IN THE DETAILS

"Are not five sparrows sold for two pennies? Yet not one of them is forgotten by God."
Luke 12:6

DEVOTIONAL

As she sat at her kitchen table, Margaret sipped her tea and reflected on her flower garden. Each bloom was a gentle reminder of God's handiwork, from the unique shapes of the petals to the vibrant colors that brought her joy. One day, while pruning the roses, she noticed a tiny ladybug perched on a leaf, and it struck her how even the smallest creatures were crafted with care. In that moment, Margaret realized that God's attentiveness extended to every detail in her life— from the laughter of her grandchildren to the quiet moments alone with her thoughts. It brought her comfort to know that just like the ladybug, she too was seen and cherished.

God's love is woven through the intricate details of our lives, reminding us that we are never overlooked.

DAILY REFLECTION

What small moments in your daily life make you feel God's presence? How can you appreciate the intricate ways He impacts your journey?

PRAYER

Dear God, thank you for the everyday miracles that surround us. Help us to see Your handiwork in the details of our lives, guiding us with Your gentle touch.

"God's grace is woven into the fabric of our daily lives, if only we take a moment to look."

LETTING GO OF THE PAST

"I remember the days of long ago; I meditate on all your works and consider what your hands have done." **Psalm 143:5**

DEVOTIONAL

Mabel found herself surrounded by boxes filled with memories—old photographs, letters from loved ones, and trinkets from adventures long past. Each item told a story, reminding her of joyful days and cherished voices. But as she watched her grandchildren play in the backyard, she began to feel the weight of those memories holding her back. She realized that while the past shaped her, it didn't have to define her future. With a deep breath, she began to sort through the boxes, keeping only what truly brought her joy and letting go of the rest with a grateful heart.

Letting go of the past isn't forgetting; it's freeing yourself to embrace the beautiful moments yet to come.

DAILY REFLECTION

What memories or experiences from your past are you holding onto tightly? How might your life be different if you allowed yourself to let go of these burdens and embrace the present?

PRAYER

Dear Lord, help me to release the weight of my past, trusting in Your love and guidance. May I find peace in the present and joy in the days ahead, with Your gentle support by my side.

"Embracing the present opens the door to future joys."

CHOOSING FAITH IN UNCERTAINTY

"When I am afraid, I put my trust in you, in God, whose word I praise; in God I trust and am not afraid. What can mere mortals do to me?" **Psalm 56:3-4**

DEVOTIONAL

In the quiet of her home, Martha often reflected on her life as she brewed her favorite cup of chamomile tea. After years of bustling around as a teacher, she now found herself in a season of uncertainty, with health concerns and the loss of friends weighing heavily on her heart. One afternoon, while watching the sunlight dance through the leaves outside, she recalled the many challenges she faced during her teaching years. Each time a student struggled, she reminded them that their potential was far greater than their doubts. Now, as she faced her own uncertainties, she decided to lean into her faith, choosing to trust that God was still at work in her life, even when the path ahead seemed unclear.

In a world filled with uncertainties, choosing to trust God's plan can bring peace and renewed strength.

DAILY REFLECTION

What uncertainties are you facing right now, and how might choosing faith change your perspective on them?

PRAYER

Dear God, in this season of life filled with unknowns, help me to lean on Your promises and trust in Your guidance. Surround me with Your peace as I navigate through the moments that feel uncertain.

"Faith is the anchor that holds us steady amid the waves of life's uncertainties."

YOU ARE SEEN AND KNOWN

"You have searched me, Lord, and you know me. You know when I sit and when I rise; you perceive my thoughts from afar. You discern my going out and my lying down; you are familiar with all my ways. Before a word is on my tongue you, Lord, know it completely."
Psalm 139:1-4

DEVOTIONAL

Mabel spent many afternoons in her garden, tending to her flowers. One day, while pruning a stubborn rose bush, she was reminded of how every petal, every thorn, and every budding bloom was known to her. Each flower had a unique story that unfolded with time, and she found joy in nurturing them. It comforted her to realize that just as she tended to her garden, God tended to her heart, knowing her joys, sorrows, and every thought hidden beneath the surface. In that moment, she felt truly seen and cherished, not just as a retiree but as a beloved daughter of God.

You are never forgotten; your story is known and cherished by the One who created you.

DAILY REFLECTION

What are the ways you've seen God's presence in your life recently, and how has He reminded you that you are known and cherished?

PRAYER

Dear Lord, thank You for seeing me in all my seasons of life. Help me to embrace Your love and the unique story You've written for me. May I find comfort in knowing I am cherished just as I am.

"Even in the quietest moments, His love whispers, 'You are seen and known.'"

THE STRENGTH OF QUIET OBEDIENCE

*"Be still before the Lord and wait patiently for him; do not fret when people succeed in their ways, when they carry out their wicked schemes." **Psalm 37:7***

DEVOTIONAL

Mabel spent her mornings in quiet devotion, sipping tea while reading her favorite Bible passages. Though her days had slowed down in retirement, she found solace in small acts of service—whether it was baking cookies for a neighbor or sending notes to old friends. One day, after a brief conversation with a newcomer in church, she discovered her quiet encouragement had made a significant difference in that person's life. Mabel realized that her gentle, routine acts of love were powerful offerings of obedience that reflected God's grace to those around her.

Embrace the strength found in quiet obedience, for your small acts of faith can have a profound impact on those you touch.

DAILY REFLECTION

What does it mean for you to practice quiet obedience in your daily life, and how might it change your perspective on the small tasks you embrace?

PRAYER

Dear Lord, help me to embrace the beauty of quiet obedience in my life, trusting that even the small acts can reflect Your love. May my heart be open to Your guidance in all I do.

"True strength often lies in the gentle embrace of obedience, where love and trust guide each step."

REFINED BY FIRE

*"In this you greatly rejoice, though now for a little while you may have had to suffer grief in all kinds of trials. These have come so that the proven genuineness of your faith—of greater worth than gold, which perishes even though refined by fire—may result in praise, glory and honor when Jesus Christ is revealed." **1 Peter 1:6-7***

DEVOTIONAL

Once, a beloved grandmother shared her experience of watching her garden flourish after a harsh winter. The frost had nipped at her tender blooms, leaving behind branches that looked bare and lifeless. Yet, when spring arrived, she noticed that those very plants were stronger, their colors brighter, and their roots deeper. With loving care, she had fertilized and pruned away the dead parts, nurturing them back to health. Much like her garden, we too must sometimes endure seasons of hardship to grow and blossom into the fullness of life that God intended for us.

Just as a garden thrives after being pruned, embracing the challenges of life can lead to our greatest growth.

DAILY REFLECTION

What challenges or trials have you faced in your life that have helped shape your character and faith? How can you embrace these experiences as a part of your journey?

PRAYER

Dear God, thank you for being with me through every trial and triumph. Help me to embrace the refining process of my life and draw closer to You in my moments of need.

"Through the fire, we discover our true strength and the treasures hidden within us."

GOD'S GRACE IN YOUR WEAKNESS

"My flesh and my heart may fail, but God is the strength of my heart and my portion forever." **Psalm 73:26**

DEVOTIONAL

As she sat on her front porch, sipping tea and watching the seasons change, Helen reflected on her recent struggles. The bustling days of her youth had given way to quiet moments filled with memories and some aches she hadn't anticipated. It was during one of those moments of vulnerability that she picked up her Bible and felt an overwhelming sense of peace wash over her. In her limitations, she realized, God's grace was there to uplift her, reminding her that even in her weaknesses, she was incredibly cherished and never alone.

In those quiet moments of reflection, remember that even when you feel fragile, God's strength is more than sufficient to carry you through.

DAILY REFLECTION

What areas of your life feel heavy with weakness, and how might you invite God's grace into those spaces?

PRAYER

Dear God, thank You for Your unending grace that carries me in my moments of weakness. Help me to lean into Your strength and find comfort in Your loving embrace.

"In our frailty, God's grace shines the brightest."

LIVING INTENTIONALLY

"And this is my prayer: that your love may abound more and more in knowledge and depth of insight, so that you may be able to discern what is best and may be pure and blameless for the day of Christ," **Philippians 1:9-10**

DEVOTIONAL

As Mary sat on her porch, sipping tea and watching the world go by, she reflected on how her life had shifted since retirement. No longer defined by her job, she searched for new moments of joy and purpose. One day, she decided to volunteer at a local shelter, helping to serve meals. The smiles and gratitude from those she served filled her heart with warmth. It was in these small, intentional acts that she discovered a deeper fulfillment and connection with her community. Each day became an opportunity to touch lives in meaningful ways.

Living intentionally means embracing each day as a gift, seeking ways to share love and wisdom with those around you.

DAILY REFLECTION

What does it truly mean for you to live intentionally in this season of your life? How can you bring more purpose to your daily activities, and what passions have you yet to explore?

PRAYER

Gracious God, thank you for this beautiful chapter of life. Help me to embrace each day with intention and purpose, guided by Your love and wisdom.

"Intentional living is choosing to create a life that reflects your deepest values and dreams."

THE JOY OF THE LORD IS YOUR STRENGTH

"Nehemiah said, 'Go and enjoy choice food and sweet drinks, and send some to those who have nothing prepared. This day is holy to our Lord. Do not grieve, for the joy of the Lord is your strength.'" **Nehemiah 8:10**

DEVOTIONAL

One sunny morning, Mary decided to visit her local garden club instead of staying at home. As she joined a group of fellow enthusiasts, she discovered an overwhelming sense of joy among women sharing their gardening experiences, tips, and laughter. They helped each other plant new flowers and shared stories of their personal journeys. In that moment, Mary realized that joy was rooted in connection with others and nurturing what God had placed in her heart. It was a day that transformed her perspective on retirement from one of solitude to a season rich with potential for fellowship and growth.

You are never too old to cultivate joy in your life; it is often found in the relationships you nurture and the passions you pursue.

DAILY REFLECTION

What brings you joy in your daily life, and how can you invite more of the Lord's presence into those moments?

PRAYER

Dear Lord, as we embrace this season of life, may Your joy fill our hearts and strengthen our spirits. Help us to seek Your presence in our daily activities and remind us of the beauty surrounding us.

"In every moment of joy, we find a hint of God's grace."

CLINGING TO WHAT IS GOOD

"Love must be sincere. Hate what is evil; cling to what is good."
Romans 12:9

DEVOTIONAL

As she settled into her favorite armchair, Margaret looked around her living room filled with memories—family photos, handmade gifts from her grandchildren, and the quilt she and her late husband crafted together. Every piece spoke of love, laughter, and moments that were truly good, reminding her of the beauty she had shared throughout her life. In the quiet, she reflected on how easy it had been to focus on losses and the changes of this new chapter. Yet, by anchoring herself in these tangible reminders of goodness, she felt a warmth fill her heart, allowing her to embrace gratitude and joy once more.

In every season of life, it's vital to cling to what brings you joy and goodness, allowing those memories and connections to light the way forward. Seek out and cherish the goodness in your life, for it is a wellspring of joy that sustains you through every change.

DAILY REFLECTION

What brings you joy and comfort in your daily life? How can you hold onto those good things as you navigate the changes of this season?

PRAYER

Dear God, thank you for the blessings you have surrounded me with. Help me to remain aware of the good in my life and to cherish those moments of joy and gratitude.

"Embrace the beauty of each day, for in every moment lies a gift waiting to be discovered."

FAITHFUL IN THE SMALL THINGS

"The one who calls you is faithful, and he will do it."
1 Thessalonians 5:24

DEVOTIONAL

Once, a retired woman named Mary found joy in the small rituals of her daily life. Each morning, she would tend to her modest garden, nurturing each flower and vegetable with love. As she watered the plants and pulled out the weeds, she realized that these small acts brought her immense peace and fulfillment. One day, as she shared her homegrown vegetables with her neighbors, she discovered that her simple gestures brought smiles and connections that enriched her community. It wasn't the grand things that made her life bright, but the little moments of care and kindness that truly blossomed.

Remember that even in this season of life, your small acts of faithfulness can nourish not just your soul, but the souls of those around you.

DAILY REFLECTION

What small ways has God been calling you to serve or show kindness in your daily life? How might embracing these moments deepen your faith?

PRAYER

Dear Lord, thank You for the daily opportunities to serve and love others in small ways. Help me to remain attentive to these moments and to trust that You multiply each act of kindness.

"Even the smallest kindness can echo in eternity."

RENEWING YOUR MIND

"We demolish arguments and every pretension that sets itself up against the knowledge of God, and we take captive every thought to make it obedient to Christ."
2 Corinthians 10:5

DEVOTIONAL

Mary, a retired teacher, found herself frequently replaying old narratives in her mind—thoughts of missed opportunities and unfulfilled dreams. One day, while sipping tea on her porch, she picked up her well-worn Bible and began to read Psalm 139. As she reflected on how fearfully and wonderfully she was made, she felt a gentle nudge from the Holy Spirit to let go of her past regrets. Inspired, she began journaling her blessings instead of her burdens, slowly renewing her perspective and embracing the joy that each day brings.

Our thoughts shape our world; by intentionally focusing on the beauty of today, we can transform our hearts and minds for the better.

DAILY REFLECTION

What thoughts or beliefs are you nurturing in your mind today that could benefit from a fresh perspective?

PRAYER

Dear Lord, help me to open my heart and mind to Your truth, guiding me toward renewal and peace. May Your wisdom transform my thoughts, illuminating my path with grace.

"Renewed thoughts lead to renewed lives; let your mind be a garden of hope."

THE BEAUTY OF SURRENDER

"Oh, the depth of the riches of the wisdom and[a] knowledge of God! How unsearchable his judgments, and his paths beyond tracing out!" **Romans 11:33**

DEVOTIONAL

In her cozy armchair, Margaret gazed out the window at the changing leaves, reflecting on the many seasons she had experienced in her life. After retiring, she found herself grappling with who she was without the structure of a job. One afternoon, while tending to her garden, she noticed how the flowers seemed to thrive best when she allowed them to grow freely, unencumbered by her attempts to control every aspect of their development. Surrendering to the natural ebb and flow—trusting in the wisdom of nature—she began to see how this mirrored her own journey of letting go. In that moment, she realized that her life's true beauty blossomed when she allowed God to be in charge, nurturing her spirit just like the flowers she loved.

Surrendering often gives us the freedom to grow and discover joys we never anticipated.

DAILY REFLECTION

What does it mean for you to surrender control and embrace the beauty of trust in this season of your life?

PRAYER

Dear Lord, help me to let go of my worries and fears. May I find peace in the act of surrendering to Your will and embracing the beauty that comes with it.

"Surrendering is not giving up; it is opening up to the divine possibilities that await us."

HE WORKS ALL THINGS FOR GOOD

"For his anger lasts only a moment, but his favor lasts a lifetime; weeping may stay for the night, but rejoicing comes in the morning." **Psalm 30:5**

DEVOTIONAL

Once there was a retired schoolteacher named Margaret who found herself feeling lost after leaving the classroom she loved for many years. As she navigated her new life, she decided to take up knitting, a craft she'd always admired but never pursued. As she knitted, she reflected on her days as an educator, and soon, her knitting group blossomed into a vibrant community of women who supported each other's dreams and struggles. What began as an uncertain retirement transformed into a beautiful tapestry of friendships, demonstrating how God can weave joy into our lives even when we least expect it.

Every twist and turn in your life can lead you to new beginnings and treasured moments, reminding you that God is always working for your good.

DAILY REFLECTION

What experiences in your life have challenged you, yet ultimately led to unexpected blessings or growth? How can you view your current circumstances through the lens of God's promise to work all things for good?

PRAYER

Dear Lord, thank you for your unwavering promise to bring goodness out of every situation in our lives. Help us to trust in your plan and find peace in knowing that you are always at work for our benefit.

"In every season of life, God weaves threads of purpose into our story."

A STEADFAST SPIRIT

"Create in me a clean heart, O God, and renew a right spirit within me."
Psalms 51:10

DEVOTIONAL

In a cozy little home filled with trinkets from years gone by, Mary spent her afternoons reminiscing about the adventures she had experienced throughout her life. She often sat at her window, gazing out at the garden she had nurtured, each flower a testament to her care and resilience. One day, as she tugged at a stubborn weed, it struck her how just as she tended her garden, she needed to nurture her own spirit. There were days when loneliness crept in, but she found solace in her faith, reminding herself that like those flowers, she too could bloom again with a steadfast spirit anchored in God's love.

As time moves forward, it is vital to cultivate a spirit of unwavering hope and positivity, just as we nurture the flowers in our gardens.

DAILY REFLECTION

What does it mean for you to cultivate a steadfast spirit in this season of your life? How can you lean into faith during moments of uncertainty or change?

PRAYER

Dear Lord, thank you for the gift of this new season in life. Help me to embrace peace and strength as I trust in Your steadfast love.

"Faith, like a sturdy tree, is rooted deep and sways gently in the winds of change."

HOPE THAT HOLDS

"But now, Lord, what do I look for? My hope is in you."
Psalm 39:7

DEVOTIONAL

Once there was a retired teacher named Margaret, who spent her days tending to her garden and volunteering at the local library. After years of nurturing young minds in the classroom, she found herself in a new season of life, filled with both joy and uncertainty. One day, while pruning her roses, she noticed a tiny bud peeking through the soil, a delicate promise that bright blooms were on the way. It reminded her that, just like in life, we often must wait for our hopes to blossom, trusting that the Lord is at work even when we can't see it. In that moment, Margaret realized that hope is not just a feeling; it's a quiet assurance that something beautiful is coming, just around the corner.

Hope is a quiet assurance that what lies ahead is filled with promise, waiting for the right moment to bloom.

DAILY REFLECTION

What does hope mean to you in this season of your life, and how can you nurture that hope each day?

PRAYER

Dear God, thank You for the gift of hope that surrounds us and upholds us. May we find reassurance in Your promises and a deep peace in the journey ahead.

"Hope is the anchor for our souls, steadying us through life's waves."

CASTING YOUR CARES

This is the confidence we have in approaching God: that if we ask anything according to his will, he hears us. **1 John 5:14**

DEVOTIONAL

In her retirement, Helen found herself overwhelmed with the small worries of daily life. One sunny afternoon, while tending to her garden, she noticed how effortlessly the flowers leaned towards the sun, soaking in its warmth and light. It struck her that just like those flowers, she too could turn her heart toward the One who cares for her, releasing her burdens and anxieties. As she whispered her worries into the gentle breeze, she felt lighter, as if the weight of them was carried away. With every petal she tended, she began to understand the beauty of trust, realizing that she didn't have to hold on to every concern.

When you lean into faith, you discover that letting go of your cares invites peace to blossom in your heart.

DAILY REFLECTION

What is one worry that has been weighing on your heart lately? How might you be able to release it into God's hands today?

PRAYER

Dear Lord, thank You for being a safe place to cast our cares. Help me to trust in Your loving arms as I surrender my worries to You today.

"Letting go allows space for grace to enter."

HE IS WITH YOU ALWAYS

"Where can I go from your Spirit? Where can I flee from your presence? If I go up to the heavens, you are there; if I make my bed in the depths, you are there." **Psalm 139:7-8**

DEVOTIONAL

Once, a retired friend who felt lost after her husband passed shared how she found solace in her garden. Each morning, as she watered her flowers, she would talk to God, pouring out her heart and feeling His presence surrounding her. One day, while pruning a rose bush, she noticed a small bird building a nest nearby. It struck her that just as the bird found a safe haven, so too could she find comfort and companionship in God's unwavering presence each day. Her garden became her sanctuary, reminding her that even in solitude, she was never truly alone.

Even in moments of loneliness, remember that God walks beside you, nurturing your spirit and filling your heart with His love.

DAILY REFLECTION

What does it mean to you to know that God is with you in every moment of your day, even in the quiet of your home?

PRAYER

Dear Lord, thank you for your constant presence in my life. Help me to feel your love surrounding me today and always.

"His presence is the gentle whisper that assures us we are never alone."

WALKING IN THE LIGHT

"But if we walk in the light, as he is in the light, we have fellowship with one another, and the blood of Jesus, his Son, purifies us from all sin." **1 John 1:7**

DEVOTIONAL

After decades of balancing work, family, and countless responsibilities, Clara found herself with more free time during her retirement. One sunny afternoon, she decided to take a stroll through her local park. As she walked, she noticed the vibrant colors of the flowers, the laughter of children playing, and the warmth of the sun on her face. In that moment, she realized that walking in the light wasn't just about the physical space around her; it was also about embracing the joys of each day and sharing her experiences with others. It reminded her of the warmth of fellowship she cherished in her earlier years, bringing hope and light to her heart.

Embrace each moment of the day in the light of fellowship and joy, for it can illuminate the path ahead.

DAILY REFLECTION

What does it mean for you to walk in the light each day, and how can you share that light with those around you?

PRAYER

Dear God, thank you for the gift of your light that guides our paths. Help us to recognize your presence in our daily lives and to shine that light for others.

"Walking in the Light allows us not only to see clearly but also to illuminate the paths of others."

FORGIVENESS IS FREEDOM

"For if you forgive other people when they sin against you, your heavenly Father will also forgive you. But if you do not forgive others their sins, your Father will not forgive your sins." **Matthew 6:14-15**

DEVOTIONAL

Once there was a retired woman named Clara who had carried the weight of an old family rift for many years. Every time she saw an old photograph of family gatherings, a pang of hurt resurfaced in her heart. One day, after attending a forgiveness workshop at her church, she found the courage to reach out to her estranged sister. The conversation brought tears, laughter, and ultimately a deep sense of relief. Letting go set Clara free, reminding her that love and connection can flourish again, even if time has passed.

Forgiveness is not just a gift to others; it is a liberating act of self-love and healing.

DAILY REFLECTION

What burdens or resentments are you carrying that you could release for your own peace and freedom?

PRAYER

Dear God, help me to find the strength to let go of any hurt and embrace the peace that comes with forgiveness. Teach me to extend grace, both to others and to myself.

"Forgiveness is not just a gift to others; it is a liberation for yourself."

BEARING SPIRITUAL FRUIT

*"Filled with the fruit of righteousness that comes through Jesus Christ—to the glory and praise of God." **Philippians 1:11***

DEVOTIONAL

In her quiet moments after years of a bustling career and family life, Margaret discovered the joys of gardening. She filled her mornings with the soothing act of tending to her flowers, watching them bloom and flourish under her care. With each vibrant petal that opened, she found parallels to her own life—each day an opportunity to cultivate kindness, patience, and joy in her interactions. Just as her garden needed nourishment and light, she realized that her spirit thrived on prayer and reflection, leading her to deepen her relationships with family and friends, and ultimately giving her a sense of purpose she hadn't anticipated in her retirement.

As you nurture your spirit and the lives around you, remember that just like a garden flourishes with love and attention, so too will your heart bear the fruits of joy, peace, and love in this cherished season of your life.

DAILY REFLECTION

What spiritual fruit are you being called to nurture in this season of your life? How can you share those gifts with others in your community?

PRAYER

Dear Lord, thank you for the seasons of life that allow us to grow and bear fruit. Help us to nurture the gifts you have given us, and guide us as we live out our purpose in love and service.

"In the quiet of retirement, the fruits of the Spirit blossom brightest."

DISCOVERING YOUR SPIRITUAL GIFTS

*"There are different kinds of gifts, but the same Spirit distributes them. There are different kinds of service, but the same Lord. There are different kinds of working, but in all of them and in everyone it is the same God at work." **1 Corinthians 12:4-6***

DEVOTIONAL

Margaret had spent a lifetime caring for others, first as a teacher and later as a devoted volunteer at her local community center. With retirement came some quiet moments that felt foreign to her, but it was during these still times that she began to explore her talents. She took a knitting class, rekindled her love for music by joining a choir, and started a book club for her neighbors. One day, she discovered that the laughter and joy she spread through her hobbies were her true gifts.

You are never too old to discover and share the unique gifts God has placed within you.

DAILY REFLECTION

What unique talents and experiences do you possess that could be used to inspire and uplift those around you? How might God be inviting you to share these gifts in new ways during this season of your life?

PRAYER

Dear Lord. thank You for the gifts You have so lovingly bestowed upon me. Help me to recognize and embrace my spiritual gifts, and guide me on how to use them to serve others with joy and love.

"Your golden years are not just a time to rest,
but a season to rediscover and share the treasures within you."

LIVING OUT YOUR LEGACY

"Even when I am old and gray, do not forsake me, my God, till I declare your power to the next generation, your mighty acts to all who are to come." **Psalm 71:18**

DEVOTIONAL

As Sarah settled into her well-deserved retirement, she found herself often reminiscing about the life she had led. Her hands, once busy with work and responsibilities, now had the time to nurture her garden and share stories with her grandchildren. One afternoon, as they eagerly listened to tales of her youth, she realized the importance of passing down her wisdom and values. Every laugh, every lesson shared, became a thread connecting her to the future. In that moment, she grasped that her legacy wasn't just what she accumulated but the love and truth she imparted to those who would carry her story forward.

Life is best measured not by accomplishments alone but by the love and wisdom we share through our stories and relationships.

DAILY REFLECTION

What kind of legacy do you wish to leave behind, and how can you embody that legacy in your daily interactions and decisions?

PRAYER

Dear God, thank you for the gift of this season in life. Help me to honor my past while actively building a legacy of love, wisdom, and joy for future generations.

"You are not just a chapter in your family's story; you are the heart that beats throughout."

YOUR LIFE IS A TESTIMONY

"But in your hearts revere Christ as Lord. Always be prepared to give an answer to everyone who asks you to give the reason for the hope that you have. But do this with gentleness and respect." **1 Peter 3:15**

DEVOTIONAL

Once in a quaint little town, there lived a retired woman named Martha who found joy in her garden. Each morning, she would tend to her flowers, speaking tenderly to them as she planted each seed. One day, a neighbor passing by asked her why she seemed so happy and hopeful, even in the simplest of tasks. Martha smiled and shared her faith, explaining how her love for gardening mirrored her relationship with God—each seed a reminder of new beginnings and the beauty that flourishes with patience and care. Her testimony inspired her neighbor, and they began to share coffee and faith stories, cultivating not just gardens, but a blossoming friendship.

Your life, filled with experiences and grace, serves as a powerful testimony to those around you; let it shine brightly.

DAILY REFLECTION

What stories of faith and resilience have shaped your journey, and how might sharing them inspire others in their own lives?

PRAYER

Heavenly Father, thank You for the tapestry of experiences woven into our lives. Help us to recognize and share our stories in ways that glorify You and encourage those around us.

Your life, lived with intention and grace, serves as a beacon of hope and strength for others.

RESTORING JOY

"Those who sow in tears will reap with songs of joy."
Psalm 126:5

DEVOTIONAL

I remember a dear friend of mine who faced a challenging season after her husband passed away. For months, she kept herself busy, thinking that avoiding her sorrow would bring her peace. It wasn't until a gentle summer afternoon, surrounded by blooming flowers, that she allowed herself to grieve. The tears stained her cheeks, yet after embracing her grief, joy began to seep back into her heart. She found herself gardening again, laughing with her grandchildren, and rediscovering the simple joys of life. Each moment of joy felt like a tribute to the love she had shared, a reminder that it's okay to feel both sorrow and joy.

Embrace your grief, for in acknowledging it, you allow room for joy to blossom anew.

DAILY REFLECTION

What brings you joy these days, and how can you invite more of it into your life?

PRAYER

Dear Lord, thank you for the gift of this season in my life. Help me to gently uncover the joys that still linger within, and guide me towards embracing them fully.

"Joy is not found in the absence of struggles, but in the presence of gratitude and grace."

August 30

GOD'S POWER IN YOUR STORY

*"But God chose the foolish things of the world to shame the wise; God chose the weak things of the world to shame the strong. God chose the lowly things of this world and the despised things—and the things that are not—to nullify the things that are, so that no one may boast before him." **1 Corinthians 1:27-29***

DEVOTIONAL

Once, after years of pouring into her family's needs, a retired woman named Clara discovered the joy of writing. She began penning her life stories, reflecting the trials and triumphs she had navigated. Each page brought her healing, not just for herself but also for readers who found comfort and inspiration in her words. As her stories circulated, Clara realized God had used her life experiences—often perceived as mundane—to touch many hearts, reminding her that every chapter of her story held immeasurable value.

Your experiences, both large and small, are woven together by God's hand to create a tapestry of strength and love that can inspire others.

DAILY REFLECTION

What parts of your life story have you seen God's power at work, and how can you share those moments with others to inspire them?

PRAYER

Dear Lord, thank You for weaving Your strength through the tapestry of our lives. Help us to recognize and embrace the moments when we have felt Your guiding hand, and may our stories uplift others in their journeys.

"Even in the quietest moments of our lives, God's power writes new chapters filled with hope and grace."

THE JOY OF GIVING BACK

"And if you spend yourselves in behalf of the hungry and satisfy the needs of the oppressed, then your light will rise in the darkness, and your night will become like the noonday."
- Isaiah 58:10

DEVOTIONAL

Mabel had always enjoyed her time knitting. As a retired schoolteacher, she found solace in creating colorful hats and scarves. One chilly December afternoon, she decided to donate her handmade creations to a local shelter. When she arrived, the smiling faces of those who received her gifts filled her heart with warmth. It was a simple act, but it blossomed into something far greater; the joy she felt from giving back brightly lit her own spirit, reminding her that though she had stepped away from her career, she still had so much to offer.

True fulfillment often comes when we extend our hands to lift others up.

DAILY REFLECTION

What are some ways you have experienced joy in giving back to others, and how can you encourage that joy in your daily life now?

PRAYER

Dear Lord, thank you for the gift of generosity. Help me find new ways to share my love and time with those around me. May my heart be open to the joy that comes from giving.

"In the act of giving, we often receive more than we could ever give."

LIVING WITH HOPE AND EXPECTATION

"Praise be to the God and Father of our Lord Jesus Christ! In his great mercy, he has given us new birth into a living hope through the resurrection of Jesus Christ from the dead."
1 Peter 1:3

DEVOTIONAL

Margaret had spent her entire working life as a schoolteacher, nurturing countless young minds and watching them blossom. Now, in retirement, she found joy in gardening, spending her days digging in the soil, planting seeds, and patiently waiting for blooms to appear. One morning, she discovered the first tender shoots breaking through the earth, a beautiful reminder that just as she had nurtured her students, she could now nurture her passions and dreams. Each day, she tended to her garden with hope, knowing that, like her plants, her own life would continue to grow and flourish in ways she had yet to imagine.

Keep nurturing the seeds of hope in your life, for the best blooms are often yet to come.

DAILY REFLECTION

What dreams or hopes do you carry in your heart, and how can you nurture them in this season of your life? Reflect on the blessings that await you each day.

PRAYER

Dear God, thank you for the gift of this day and the hope it brings. Fill our hearts with Your joy and remind us of the beautiful plans You have for our lives.

"Hope is the gentle light that guides us through each new day, illuminating the path ahead with promise and possibility."

THE IMPORTANCE OF SELF-CARE

"Do you not know that your bodies are temples of the Holy Spirit, who is in you, whom you have received from God? You are not your own; you were bought at a price. Therefore honor God with your bodies." **1 Corinthians 6:19-20**

DEVOTIONAL

Once upon a time, there was a lovely retired woman named Eleanor who had spent decades nurturing her family and volunteering in her community. One day, as she sat in her garden, she noticed how the flowers thrived when given water, sunlight, and attention. Inspired by this, Eleanor realized that just as her garden needed care to flourish, so did she. She decided to take time each week for herself—whether it was reading a book, taking long walks, or practicing yoga. With every moment dedicated to self-care, she felt revitalized and full of joy, which in turn allowed her to give even more to those she loved.

Self-care is not a luxury, but a vital investment in your well-being that empowers you to bless others even more abundantly.

DAILY REFLECTION

What are some ways you can nurture your body, mind, and spirit today to honor your own needs and happiness?

PRAYER

Dear Lord, thank You for the gift of this day. Help me to embrace the importance of self-care, reminding me that by taking care of myself, I can better serve those I love.

"Taking time for yourself is not a luxury; it is a necessity for a joyful life."

EMBRACING CHANGE WITH GRACE

"My times are in Your hands; deliver me from the hands of my enemies, from those who pursue me." Psalm 31:15

DEVOTIONAL

After decades devoted to work, family, and community, Helen found herself in a quiet home instead of a bustling workplace. The morning coffee routine transformed from hurried sips to leisurely moments on the porch, watching the seasons change. Initially, she grappled with feelings of loss, missing the busyness of her former life. But slowly, she began to embrace the stillness, discovering new hobbies, rekindling old friendships, and nurturing her garden. Each blooming flower became a symbol of the vibrant possibilities that change can bring. In this new chapter, she learned to dance with change rather than resist it.

Embracing change means recognizing that every season of life brings its own gifts and opportunities for growth.

DAILY REFLECTION

What changes are you currently facing in your life, and how can you embrace them with an open heart and mind?

PRAYER

Dear God, thank You for the new seasons in our lives. Help us to embrace change with grace and trust in Your plan. Fill our hearts with peace and joy as we navigate these transformations.

"Embracing change opens the door to new blessings and beautiful surprises."

THE BEAUTY OF SIMPLICITY

"Better a little with the fear of the Lord than great wealth with turmoil."
Proverbs 15:16

DEVOTIONAL

In her cozy sunlit kitchen, Margaret often found joy in the daily ritual of brewing a simple cup of tea. As the steam swirled and danced in the morning light, she reflected on the beauty of life's uncomplicated moments. One day, a neighborhood child stopped by during her tea time, curious about the fragrant aroma. Margaret invited him in, and they shared stories and laughter over cookies and tea. In that moment, she realized that the little joys, like friendship and connection, often held more value than the grand pursuits she once chased in her busy working years.

Finding joy in life's simple pleasures can illuminate your days and enrich your heart.

DAILY REFLECTION

What simple joys bring a smile to your face today, and how can you intentionally embrace them in your daily life?

PRAYER

Dear Lord, thank you for the beauty of simplicity that surrounds us each day. Help us to cherish these little moments and find joy in the ordinary with a grateful heart.

"True beauty often lies in the simple pleasures of life, waiting for us to pause and appreciate them."

SEEKING GOD FIRST

"Love the Lord your God with all your heart and with all your soul and with all your mind and with all your strength." **Mark 12:30**

DEVOTIONAL

Mabel had spent her life dedicated to her family and career, often putting her own dreams and desires on the back burner. Now in retirement, she found herself with time to pursue the hobbies she had once cherished. One sunny afternoon, she decided to join a local prayer group at her church. As she gathered with other women, they shared stories of faith, gratitude, and the joy of seeking God together. Mabel felt a renewed purpose as she listened to their testimonies, realizing that investing in her spiritual life brought her the peace and fulfillment she had long sought.

When you prioritize your relationship with God, you'll find a deeper joy and purpose in this season of life.

DAILY REFLECTION

What does it mean for you to seek God first in your daily life, especially as you embrace this new season of your journey?

PRAYER

Dear Lord, thank You for the gift of this day. Help me to center my heart on You first in all I do, so that Your peace and wisdom guide my steps.

"Seeking God first opens the door to a life filled with purpose and joy."

YOU ARE NEVER ALONE

"I will not leave you as orphans; I will come to you."
John 14:18

DEVOTIONAL

Once, there was a retired woman named Mary who found herself feeling more lonely than she had expected in this new season of life. After her husband passed away, the silence in her home often felt overwhelming, making her question her sense of purpose and connection. One day, while sorting through old photographs, she stumbled upon a picture of her with friends from a community group she hadn't attended in ages. Inspired by the joyful memories they shared, Mary decided to reach out and reconnect with those cherished friends. What started as a simple phone call blossomed into regular gatherings, transforming her loneliness into a circle of love and companionship.

You are never alone; you are surrounded by the love and memories of those who care for you, and sometimes, reaching out can reveal the connection you long for.

DAILY REFLECTION

What are some moments in your life when you felt truly supported by others or by your faith, reminding you that you are never alone?

PRAYER

Dear God, thank you for your constant presence in our lives. Help us to see your support in everyday moments and to feel your love wrapping around us like a warm blanket.

"You are surrounded by love, both seen and unseen, in every step you take."

EMBRACING SOLITUDE

"A heart at peace gives life to the body,
*but envy rots the bones." **Proverbs 14:30***

DEVOTIONAL

In her quiet home, Margaret found herself enveloped in silence for the first time in years. With her children grown and life moving at a gentler pace, she began to explore the beauty of solitude. Each morning, she would sit by her window with a steaming cup of tea, admiring the blooming garden she had nurtured during her retirement. In those still moments, she discovered the whispers of her heart – dreams long forgotten and passions she had set aside for others. It became clear to her that solitude was not loneliness; it was a sacred space where she could reconnect with her true self.

Embracing solitude can lead to profound self-discovery, allowing you to explore the dreams waiting to bloom within your heart.

DAILY REFLECTION

What does solitude mean to you in this season of your life, and how might embracing it lead you to deeper peace and understanding?

PRAYER

Dear Lord, thank you for the gift of quiet moments. Help me to find joy and solace in solitude, and may it draw me closer to You and to my true self.

"Solitude is not a void to be filled, but a sacred space where the soul can breathe."

THE JOURNEY OF FORGIVENESS

*"Be kind and compassionate to one another, forgiving each other, just as in Christ God forgave you." **Ephesians 4:32***

DEVOTIONAL

As Sarah sat on her porch, sipping her afternoon tea, she thought about her life. The years had brought both joy and heartache. A friendship of many years had ended bitterly, leaving her with a heavy heart. One day, while reminiscing over fond memories, she felt a gentle nudge in her spirit to reach out to her former friend. With a hesitant yet hopeful heart, Sarah picked up the phone. Hearing her friend's voice brought back warmth, and they shared tears of forgiveness, opening a new chapter in their relationship.

Forgiveness is a powerful gift we give to ourselves, allowing the past to flow into the present with grace and peace.

DAILY REFLECTION

What does forgiveness mean to you, and are there areas in your life where you feel ready to let go and embrace peace?

PRAYER

Dear Lord, help us to find the courage to forgive ourselves and others. May your love fill our hearts with peace as we journey toward healing.

"Forgiveness is a gift we give ourselves, allowing our hearts to breathe free."

THE FRUIT OF THE SPIRIT

*"This is to my Father's glory, that you bear much fruit, showing yourselves to be my disciples." **John 15:8***

DEVOTIONAL

In her charming garden, Anne found joy in nurturing her vibrant flowers and fresh vegetables. Each morning, she tended to her plants, speaking softly to them as if they could understand her love and care. Over the years, she noticed how the time spent cultivating her garden mirrored her spiritual journey. Just like her flowers blossomed with the right balance of water and sunlight, she recognized that her life flourished when she allowed the Holy Spirit to guide her, bringing forth qualities like kindness, patience, and love in her interactions with others.

Just as a garden needs attention and care to thrive, so too does our spirit require pruning and refreshing to bear the beautiful fruit of love and joy in our daily lives.

DAILY REFLECTION

What aspects of the Fruit of the Spirit do you see blossoming in your life today, and how can you nurture them further in your daily interactions with others?

PRAYER

Dear Heavenly Father, thank you for the gift of Your Spirit in our lives. May we grow in love, joy, and peace as we navigate this beautiful season of life.

"Like a well-tended garden, the Fruit of the Spirit flourishes when we invest time and care into our hearts."

A FAITH THAT GROWS

*"But grow in the grace and knowledge of our Lord and Savior Jesus Christ. To him be glory both now and forever! Amen." **2 Peter 3:18***

DEVOTIONAL

As a retired woman, you may find yourself surrounded by the quietness of life, often reflecting on the vibrant past filled with family gatherings and social events. One summer, a neighbor introduced you to gardening, and you were amazed at how the smallest seeds could transform into beautiful blooms over time with just a little care. As you nurtured those plants, you realized that just like the garden flourished, your faith too could grow with intentional attention. Each day spent in prayer and reading the Word fed your spirit, much like watering those precious flowers.

Even in retirement, there are always opportunities to cultivate your faith, allowing it to blossom beautifully into new seasons of life.

DAILY REFLECTION

What areas in your life are inviting you to trust God more deeply as you seek to grow in faith?

PRAYER

Dear Lord, thank You for the gift of faith that continues to bloom within us. Open our hearts to new experiences and deeper understanding, guiding us gently along this journey of growth.

"Faith is a journey, not just a destination; it flourishes with every step we take."

FINDING JOY IN SERVING

"Truly I tell you, whatever you did for one of the least of these brothers and sisters of mine, you did for me." **Matthew 25:40**

DEVOTIONAL

There once was a retired schoolteacher named Martha, who after years in the classroom found herself at a crossroads. One day, she decided to volunteer at a local food bank. As she unpacked boxes of donations, she began to chat with those who came for assistance, learning their stories and sharing laughter even in moments of difficulty. With each smile she received in return, Martha felt a warmth grow within her heart, an unexpected joy that filled her days with purpose. Through her service, she discovered a renewed sense of community and connection, realizing that her experiences and kindness still had the power to uplift the lives of others.

Serving others brings unexpected joy and fulfillment, rekindling a sense of purpose and connection that enriches both the giver and the receiver.

DAILY REFLECTION

What brings you joy when you serve others, and how can you embrace those moments more fully in your daily life? Consider the times when you felt most fulfilled and how those experiences can guide your path forward.

PRAYER

Dear Lord, thank You for the gift of service and the joy it brings to our hearts. Help us to find opportunities to serve in our communities and let Your love shine through our actions. Amen.

"True joy blossoms when we share our gifts with those around us."

GOD IS YOUR SHELTER

"You have been a refuge for the poor, a refuge for the needy in their distress, a shelter from the storm and a shade from the heat. For the breath of the ruthless is like a storm driving against a wall" **Isaiah 25:4**

DEVOTIONAL

In her cozy home, Margaret sat by the window, sipping her tea as the storm raged outside. She watched the rain drench the garden she had lovingly tended over the years, and it brought back memories of other storms—both physical and emotional. There were times when life felt overwhelming, when she faced health issues and personal losses. Each time, just like that storm outside, she found herself turning to God for comfort. She recalled how prayer had been her refuge, providing her with strength and peace, a gentle reminder that she was not facing the storm alone, but under the protective shelter of God's love.

In moments of turmoil, remember that God is your everlasting refuge, offering you safety and solace amidst life's storms.

DAILY REFLECTION

What does it mean for you to find shelter in God during this season of your life? How can you invite His comforting presence into your daily routine?

PRAYER

Dear God, thank You for being our ever-present shelter. Help us to recognize Your loving embrace and to trust in Your guidance as we navigate this new chapter of life.

"In the quiet moments, God's sheltering love wraps around you like a warm blanket."

THE POWER OF YOUR WORDS

"Let your conversation be always full of grace, seasoned with salt, so that you may know how to answer everyone." **Colossians 4:6**

DEVOTIONAL

Mabel, a retired teacher, spent her afternoons volunteering at a local community center. One day, as she listened to a young single mother share her struggles, Mabel decided to offer her heartfelt encouragement. She shared a simple truth: "You are doing better than you think. Your love shines through your challenges." That small moment of grace transformed the young woman's day and fostered a beautiful friendship between them.

Your words hold the incredible power to bring healing and hope to others, so choose them wisely and generously.

DAILY REFLECTION

What words have you spoken recently that have lifted someone's spirit or deepened a connection? How can you use your voice today to spread kindness and encouragement?

PRAYER

Dear Lord, help me to remember the power in my words. May I speak with grace and love, sharing your light with everyone I meet today. Thank you for the gift of communication and connection.

"Your words can bring healing, joy, and inspiration to those around you."

RETURNING TO GOD'S HEART

"But you, Lord, are a compassionate and gracious God, slow to anger, abounding in love and faithfulness." **Psalm 86:15**

DEVOTIONAL

Once there was a woman named Ruth, who after decades of serving her community and raising her family, found herself alone in her quiet home. One sunny afternoon, while tending to her garden, she felt a stirring in her heart, an inner nudge to reconnect with her faith. With each flower she tended, she began to talk to God, sharing her joys and fears. As the blooms flourished, so did her spirit, reminding her that God's love had been there all along, patiently waiting for her return.

Remember that no matter what seasons you have faced, returning to God's heart is always possible, and it brings a renewal that can blossom in joy and peace.

DAILY REFLECTION

What does it mean for you, in this season of your life, to return to the heart of God? How can you draw closer to Him in your daily routine?

PRAYER

Dear God, I come to You with an open heart and a desire to feel Your presence. Help me to sense the warmth of Your love and to return to the comforts of Your embrace.

"Returning to God's heart is not about perfection; it's about the pursuit of His love and grace."

September 15

EVERY SEASON HAS PURPOSE

*"For the Spirit God gave us does not make us timid, but gives us power, love and self-discipline." **2 Timothy 1:7***

DEVOTIONAL

Once, a retired teacher named Evelyn found herself feeling lost after leaving her career behind. Initially, she struggled to find joy in her newfound freedom. One day, while tending to her garden, she realized that each flower bloomed in its own time, some needing sunlight, others shade. Inspired, she began volunteering at a local school, sharing her love for learning and nurturing the next generation. In that effort, she discovered her season of retirement was not an end, but rather a beautiful beginning filled with purpose.

As you embrace each season of your life, remember that God has a unique purpose waiting for you in every chapter.

DAILY REFLECTION

What are the unique gifts and experiences you've gathered throughout your life that you can share in this season? How might they be used to nurture those around you?

PRAYER

Dear God, thank you for this beautiful season of life filled with purpose. Help me to embrace each moment and to reveal your love through my actions towards others.

"Every season of our lives is wrapped in purpose, blooming in its own time."

September 16

LIVING WITH SPIRITUAL CLARITY

*"For God is not a God of disorder but of peace—as in all the congregations of the Lord's people." **1 Corinthians 14:33***

DEVOTIONAL

Once, a retired teacher named Evelyn found herself overwhelmed after leaving her career. With so much time on her hands, she felt lost, much like a book with pages turned but no clear narrative. One afternoon, she decided to take a nature walk, and as the gentle breeze caressed her face, she became aware of the simple beauty around her. That day, she reflected on her life's purpose, realizing it's not just about moving from one task to another, but embracing the moments God provides to bring others joy and love. Through this, she began volunteering at a local community center, finding renewed purpose and clarity in the service of others.

Life is a journey of rediscovery; embrace this season by seeking to serve and uplift those around you.

DAILY REFLECTION

What does spiritual clarity mean to you in this stage of your life, and how can you seek it each day?

PRAYER

Dear God, help me to find clarity in my thoughts and purpose. May Your light guide me through the moments of uncertainty, leading me to a deeper understanding of Your love and plan for my life.

"Clarity is not about seeing everything perfectly; it's about recognizing the beauty in the journey of faith."

CELEBRATING YOUR UNIQUE STORY

"Just as a body, though one, has many parts, but all its many parts form one body, so it is with Christ. For we were all baptized by one Spirit so as to form one body—whether Jews or Gentiles, slave or free—and we were all given the one Spirit to drink. Even so the body is not made up of one part but of many." **1 Corinthians 12:12-14**

DEVOTIONAL

Evelyn sat on her porch, a cup of herbal tea warming her hands as she gazed out at the blossoming garden she had nurtured for years. Each flower held a memory—her children's laughter, her late husband's smile, and the friends who had come and gone. She chuckled, recalling the mishaps of her previous attempts at gardening, where rogue weeds would suddenly invade or a wrong seed would sprout wildly. Yet, she realized that every bloom, every unique twist and turn in her garden mirrored her life story, made beautiful through its uniqueness and imperfections.

Embrace the beauty of your journey, for every twist and turn has added richness to the masterpiece that is your life.

DAILY REFLECTION

What unique chapters in your life have shaped who you are today, and how can you share them to inspire others?

PRAYER

Dear God, thank you for the beautiful tapestry of experiences that make up our lives. Help us to embrace our unique stories and share them with others, allowing Your light to shine through us.

"Every wrinkle and laugh line tells a story of love, courage, and resilience."

HOPE IN THE HIDDEN PLACES

"I wait for the Lord, my whole being waits, and in his word I put my hope."
Psalm 130:5

DEVOTIONAL

In her quiet garden, Margaret spent many hours tending to flowers that sometimes seemed to struggle amidst the weeds and shadows. After a long winter, she noticed a little patch of daisies emerging right where she had almost given up hope. It reminded her of the seasons of her own life, when she felt invisible and forgotten. Just like the flowers had flourished in unexpected places, she began to see how her experiences—in joy and in sorrow—cultivated resilience and beauty that could bless others in their hidden struggles.

Even in times of solitude or uncertainty, we can trust that hope will blossom in the most unexpected places of our lives.

DAILY REFLECTION

What hidden places in your life are you overlooking where hope can be found? How might you invite God into those spaces to bring light and renewal?

PRAYER

Dear Lord, thank You for the hope You provide, even in the unseen corners of our lives. Help me to embrace Your presence and discover the beauty hidden beneath the surface.

"Hope often blooms where we least expect it, in the quiet moments of our days."

OBEDIENT IN THE UNKNOWN

"However, as it is written: 'What no eye has seen, what no ear has heard, and what no human mind has conceived'—the things God has prepared for those who love him—"
1 Corinthians 2:9

DEVOTIONAL

When Eleanor retired, she envisioned long days filled with hobbies and time with family, but the realities of life took unexpected turns. Her husband fell ill, and her plans shifted dramatically. At first, she felt overwhelmed, struggling to navigate doctor visits and manage her own emotions. But as she leaned into her faith and remained obedient to God's gentle nudges, Eleanor found joy in the small moments—a warm smile from her husband, an unexpected visit from a friend, or a quiet evening of reflection. These seemingly mundane days turned out to be richly rewarding, illustrating how God's purpose often shines brightest in our uncharted journeys.

Even in the face of uncertainty, being faithful to God's calling can lead to unexpected blessings and profound peace.

DAILY REFLECTION

What areas of your life are calling you to step out in faith, trusting God's plan even when the path is unclear?

PRAYER

Dear God, thank you for guiding me through the uncertainties of life. Help me to embrace obedience in every new season and trust that you are by my side.

"Faith is not knowing what the future holds but knowing Who holds the future."

HE REDEEMS EVERY CHAPTER

"Do not cast me away when I am old; do not forsake me when my strength is gone."
Psalm 71:9

DEVOTIONAL

Once upon a time, in a charming little village, there lived a wise woman named Clara. In her retirement, she often reflected on the various seasons of her life—raising children, cultivating friendships, and finding joy in unexpected places. One day, while tending to her garden, she discovered that the oldest tree, which appeared dead, had begun to sprout fresh buds. This moment reminded her that even when she felt spent and unseen, God was still nurturing new beginnings and fresh chapters, showing her life never truly ends; it merely transforms. Clara learned to embrace each new day with hope and gratitude, recognizing that her journey continued to unfold beautifully.

Every chapter of your life brings the promise of new growth, reminding you that redemption and renewal are always within reach.

DAILY REFLECTION

What chapters in your life have felt difficult to understand? How can you invite God into those memories to bring healing and redemption?

PRAYER

Dear Lord, thank you for the journey of life and for the promise that You redeem every chapter. Please help us to see Your hand at work in our past and to trust in Your plan for our future.

"Every season of life holds an invitation to discover God's greater purpose."

YOU ARE FULLY KNOWN AND LOVED

*"I am the good shepherd; I know my sheep and my sheep know me—just as the Father knows me and I know the Father—and I lay down my life for the sheep." **John 10:14-15***

DEVOTIONAL

After decades of caring for others and nurturing her family, Clara found herself in a quiet house, the laughter of grandchildren replaced by a soothing silence. While she enjoyed the peaceful moments, there was a tug at her heart—a yearning for connection and understanding. One afternoon, as she sat in her garden, she reflected on the years filled with nurturing others and realized that beyond all those roles, she was still the same precious daughter of God who had dreams and passions. In that stillness, she felt a whisper of affirmation, reminding her that she was fully known by her Creator, who cherished her deeply, just as she was.

You are never alone; in every season of life, God knows you intimately and loves you unconditionally.

DAILY REFLECTION

What does it feel like to know that you are fully known, with all your strengths and imperfections, yet still deeply loved by God?

PRAYER

Dear Lord, thank You for knowing every part of me and loving me just as I am. Help me embrace this truth and share Your love with those around me. Amen.

In God's eyes, you are not just seen; you are cherished beyond measure.

PRAISE AS A WEAPON

*"'no weapon forged against you will prevail, and you will refute every tongue that accuses you. This is the heritage of the servants of the Lord, and this is their vindication from me,' declares the Lord." **Isaiah 54:17***

DEVOTIONAL

Once, a beloved grandmother in her community faced the daunting challenge of her husband's declining health. Every day, she would rise early and sing praises to God in the quiet of her home. Her voice filled the air with joy, transforming her worry into gratitude, and her fear into faith. Friends noticed her positive spirit, and soon, they began to gather in her living room, joining her in song. Together, they created a powerful atmosphere of worship that inspired not just themselves, but also others hastily seeking comfort and hope during trying times.

Even in retirement, your voice can be a powerful tool; through praise, you can uplift not only your spirit but also the spirits of those around you.

DAILY REFLECTION

What battles in your life could be transformed through the power of praise? How can you incorporate moments of gratitude into your daily routine to uplift your spirit?

PRAYER

Dear God, thank You for the gift of praise and worship. Help me to embrace every moment with a heart full of gratitude, using praise as a source of strength in my life.

"Praise shifts our focus from the problem to the Provider."

UNSHAKEN IN THE STORM

"When the storm has swept by, the wicked are gone, but the righteous stand firm forever."
Proverbs 10:25

DEVOTIONAL

Mabel, a retired schoolteacher, often reminisced about the storms of her life. She recalled the winter when her husband fell ill, and the world seemed to tilt on its axis. Despite the fierce winds of uncertainty and fear, she found strength in her faith and the love of her community. Friends rallied around her, delivering meals and sharing prayers, reminding her that she was never alone. With every thunderous night, she learned to lean into the support she was offered and trust that calmer days would follow. Now, she shares her story with others going through similar storms, encouraging them to hold firm.

In every storm you face, know that your faith and the support of loved ones can anchor you, helping you emerge stronger on the other side.

DAILY REFLECTION

What storm in your life feels overwhelming right now, and how can you lean on your faith to find peace and strength amidst it?

PRAYER

Dear Lord, thank You for being our anchor in life's storms. Help us to remember Your presence and to trust in Your loving guidance as we navigate through difficult times.

"Even the fiercest storms cannot shake the spirit anchored in faith."

THE POWER OF LISTENING

"My dear brothers and sisters, take note of this: Everyone should be quick to listen, slow to speak and slow to become angry," **James 1:19**

DEVOTIONAL

Just the other day, Clara, a retired schoolteacher, found herself chatting with a young neighbor who was feeling overwhelmed with life's demands. Instead of offering uninvited advice or trying to share her own stories, Clara simply sat with her, listening intently. The more she listened, the more the young woman opened up, revealing her fears and hopes. Clara felt a profound connection form, realizing that sometimes all we need to do is offer our ears and heart, allowing others to feel heard and understood.

In this season of life, the simple act of listening can nurture relationships and bring comfort to those around us.

DAILY REFLECTION

What does it feel like when you truly listen to someone? How can you create more space in your heart and mind for the voices of those around you?

PRAYER

Dear Lord, help me to embrace the quiet moments and truly listen to those you place in my path. May my heart be open and my ears be attentive, that I may reflect your love through the gift of listening.

"Listening is not just hearing; it's the art of understanding the soul behind the words."

WALKING IN SPIRITUAL WISDOM

*"If any of you lacks wisdom, you should ask God, who gives generously to all without finding fault, and it will be given to you." **James 1:5***

DEVOTIONAL

When Clara retired, she looked forward to enjoying more time in her garden. One sunny afternoon, she noticed her neighbors always hurried past without admiring her blooms. Encouraged by a whisper in her heart, Clara decided to invite them over for tea and a stroll through her garden. As her friends admired the flowers, they began to share their own life stories, creating bonds of friendship that blossomed into a close-knit community. Clara learned that sometimes the simplest acts of kindness can yield the richest rewards, bringing people together in unexpected ways.

The wisdom we cultivate by sharing our lives can bloom into beautiful connections that uplift not only ourselves but also those around us.

DAILY REFLECTION

What does walking in spiritual wisdom look like for you in this new season of life? How can you seek to deepen your understanding and application of God's guidance each day?

PRAYER

Dear Lord, thank You for the gift of this season, where we have more time to seek Your wisdom. Help us to listen and learn from You as we navigate our days, filling our hearts with Your love and grace.

"Spiritual wisdom is not just knowledge; it's an invitation to live lovingly and intentionally."

NURTURING RELATIONSHIPS

"We love because he first loved us."
1 John 4:19

DEVOTIONAL

In her new life of retirement, Grace found herself with more time than she had ever known. She took joy in inviting her neighbors over for coffee, sharing stories and laughter. One afternoon, as they reminisced about their youth, she realized these small moments of connection brought warmth and joy into her heart. Each cup of coffee wasn't just a drink; it was a thread weaving their lives together, nurturing friendships that had been dormant in the hustle of life. Grace discovered that with every shared laugh and heartfelt conversation, she was watering the seeds of love that the Lord had planted in her life.

Nurturing relationships isn't just about spending time together; it's about cultivating love and joy in the little moments.

DAILY REFLECTION

What relationships in your life need a little more nurturing today? How can you show love and support to those around you in simple yet meaningful ways?

PRAYER

Dear God, thank you for the gift of relationships in our lives. Help us to cultivate love and kindness, nurturing connections that bring joy and fulfillment in this season of our life.

"Relationships are like gardens; they flourish with care, attention, and love."

YOUR LIFE IS A LIGHT

*"Jesus spoke to them, saying, 'I am the light of the world. Whoever follows me will never walk in darkness but will have the light of life.'" **John 8:12***

DEVOTIONAL

As a retiree, you may find yourself reflecting on the many seasons of your life. Think about the times you've been a guiding light for family and friends. Perhaps it was during a challenging moment when you shared your wisdom over a cup of tea, or it was a simple act of kindness that brightened someone's day. Even in your retirement, the ways you touch lives can be profound, just like the small rays of sunlight that can brighten even the cloudiest day.

Your life has been adorned with countless experiences. Each one has prepared you to shine in your own unique way, offering warmth and clarity to those who may feel lost. Remember, your story doesn't end here; it continues to illuminate the paths of those around you, encouraging them to seek their light. Embrace the truth that your life is a light, illuminating not just your own path but also guiding others through their darkest times.

DAILY REFLECTION

What are some ways you can let your light shine in the lives of those around you today?

PRAYER

Dear God, thank you for the unique light you have placed within me. Help me to share this light with others and embrace the moments where I can bring joy and kindness into their lives.

"Your light doesn't diminish by being shared; it only grows brighter."

THE BLESSING OF NEW FRIENDSHIPS

*"My command is this: Love each other as I have loved you. Greater love has no one than this: to lay down one's life for one's friends." **John 15:12-13***

DEVOTIONAL

After years of dedicated service in her career, Margaret found herself with ample time on her hands. While she cherished her solitude, she often reminisced about the warmth of close friendships that once filled her days. One rainy afternoon, she attended a local community class, hoping to pass the time. Much to her delight, she connected with several women who shared her passions for gardening and reading. As they exchanged stories over cups of warm tea, Margaret felt a sense of joy reminding her that friendship can blossom at any age, nurturing her spirit in ways she hadn't anticipated.

The beauty of new friendships lies in their ability to enrich our lives with shared experiences and laughter, no matter our age.

DAILY REFLECTION

What new friendships have you been cultivating in this season of your life, and how have they enriched your journey?

PRAYER

Dear Lord, thank You for the gift of companionship. May I be open to new friendships, trusting that each connection can bring joy and support along this path of life.

"Every new friend brings a new blessing to the heart."

EMBRACING SPIRITUAL GROWTH

"Instead, speaking the truth in love, we will grow to become in every respect the mature body of him who is the head, that is, Christ." **Ephesians 4:15**

DEVOTIONAL

Once upon a time in a small town, a retired teacher named Margaret found herself immersed in her newfound freedom. She decided to join a local book club, where the discussions often led her to reflect on her life and values. As they delved into stories of resilience and growth, Margaret realized that each chapter was an opportunity to not only share her wisdom but to also embrace new ideas and perspectives. By opening her heart and mind to different viewpoints, she discovered that her spiritual journey was just as dynamic as the pages she turned.

Always be willing to learn and share, for spiritual growth thrives in the fertile soil of openness and community.

DAILY REFLECTION

What does spiritual growth mean to you in this new chapter of your life, and how can you actively seek ways to nurture it each day?

PRAYER

Dear Lord, thank you for the journey of life and the wisdom it brings. Help me, as I embrace this period of growth, to draw closer to You and find joy in the discoveries that await.

"Embrace this beautiful season of life as a canvas for your spiritual growth; each day holds a new brushstroke of wisdom."

GRACE FOR THE PROCESS

"For the grace of God has appeared that offers salvation to all people. It teaches us to say 'No' to ungodliness and worldly passions, and to live self-controlled, upright and godly lives in this present age." **Titus 2:11-12**

DEVOTIONAL

Mabel, a recently retired school teacher, found herself overwhelmed adjusting to the slower pace of life. Every day felt like an endless stretch of hours, and she struggled to find purpose in her new routine. One evening, as she was sorting through old photographs, she stumbled upon a picture of her younger self, laughing with her class. It struck her how each phase of life has its beauty and challenges, and that grace was present in both. Remembering the joy she brought to her students reminded her that life was about embracing each season, trusting that God's grace would guide her through this transitional time.

Life is a journey, not a race; embrace each phase with grace, knowing that every process has its purpose.

DAILY REFLECTION

What areas of your life are you currently navigating, and how can you invite God's grace into each step of the process?

PRAYER

Dear Lord, thank you for your unwavering grace that guides us through every season of life. Help us to rest in your presence as we embrace the beauty of the process, trusting that you are working all things for our good.

"Embrace the journey; each step is a testament to God's grace in your life."

A Moment of Gratitude

If this devotional has brought moments of peace, strength, or reflection into your life, a short review on Amazon can help others discover it too.

devo.anchoredgraces.com/retired

Even a few words about your experience can make a meaningful difference.

Thank you for continuing this journey.

CELEBRATING GOD'S FAITHFULNESS

"For the Lord is good and his love endures forever; his faithfulness continues through all generations." **Psalm 100:5**

DEVOTIONAL

Mabel sat on her porch, sipping tea and watching the sun set over the garden she had lovingly tended for decades. As she reflected on her life, moments of joy and sorrow danced before her like the soft sway of the flowers in the breeze. She recalled how God had been her anchor through the challenges — from raising her children to navigating the loss of loved ones. Each season of her life, while painted with different hues, had revealed God's faithfulness in ways she could never have anticipated. Now, in her golden years, she found comfort in knowing that the same God who guided her in the past was still weaving His goodness into her present and future.

In every season, trust that God's faithfulness is a promise that undergirds your journey, reminding you that each day is a gift filled with grace.

DAILY REFLECTION

What moments in your life have you seen God's faithfulness? How can you celebrate those times today?

PRAYER

Dear God, thank You for the myriad of ways You've shown Your faithfulness in my life. Help me to recognize and celebrate those moments with joy and gratitude.

"Every wrinkle tells a story of faithfulness, every silver strand is a reminder of God's enduring grace."

THE ADVENTURE OF LIFELONG LEARNING

"Let the wise listen and add to their learning, and let the discerning get guidance—" **Proverbs 1:5**

DEVOTIONAL

Once upon a time, in a quaint little town, there lived a retired schoolteacher named Margaret. Though her days of teaching were behind her, she found immense joy in exploring new hobbies every week—be it painting, gardening, or learning to play the ukulele. Each new challenge sparked joy in her heart and brought her closer to her neighbors who shared her love for learning. One summer evening, as she strummed her ukulele under the twinkling stars with friends, Margaret realized that life doesn't end at retirement; it becomes a canvas for endless discovery.

Embrace every opportunity to learn something new, for each adventure adds richness to your golden years.

DAILY REFLECTION

What new skill or knowledge are you curious about exploring in this beautiful season of your life? How can you take a small step today to ignite that curiosity?

PRAYER

Dear God, thank you for the gift of life and the opportunity to learn. Help me to embrace each day with an open heart and an eager mind, ready to discover the wonders that await.

"Every day is a new page in the story of your life; make it a chapter worth reading."

YOU ARE CHOSEN

*"You did not choose me, but I chose you and appointed you so that you might go and bear fruit—fruit that will last—and so that whatever you ask in my name the Father will give you." **John 15:16***

DEVOTIONAL

When Elaine retired, she found herself contemplating her new chapter in life. After years of caring for others, she felt a sense of uncertainty about her purpose. One afternoon, as she sifted through old photographs, she stumbled upon a box of letters exchanged with friends over the years. Each letter contained memories of laughter, support, and deep connection. It became clear to Elaine that her relationships were not just a part of her past; they were a calling for her present. She decided to organize weekly coffee meet-ups, creating a community where friends could share their stories, encourage one another, and cultivate joy. In this simple act of connection, Elaine realized she was chosen to spread love and companionship in a world that sometimes felt lonely.

You are chosen to nurture the bonds that uplift and inspire others, reflecting God's love through your presence and kindness.

DAILY REFLECTION

What does it mean to you to know that you are chosen by God, and how can this truth shape your everyday life?

PRAYER

Dear Lord, thank You for choosing me and embracing me with Your love. Help me to understand the significance of my value in Your eyes and guide me to share this love with others around me.

"You are not just a participant but a beloved daughter in the grand story of God's unfolding grace."

WHEN YOU NEED DIRECTION

*"I will instruct you and teach you in the way you should go; I will counsel you with my loving eye on you." **Psalm 32:8***

DEVOTIONAL

After years of nurturing her family and building her career, Margaret found herself facing the wide-open days of retirement. Initially, she felt a sense of freedom, but soon it was replaced by a gentle nagging—what was her purpose now? One quiet morning, she decided to take a walk in her favorite park, where she often found solace. As she strolled by the familiar paths, she noticed a bench where she had shared countless conversations with friends over the years. Sitting there, she reflected on her life's seasons and felt a tug in her heart; it was time to use her gifts in new ways. With each moment spent in contemplation, Margaret realized that volunteering at the local library could bring joy not only to her but also to the community.

Even in transitions, God's guidance is present, waiting to illuminate the path forward.

DAILY REFLECTION

When you find yourself at a crossroads or feeling uncertain about the path ahead, where do you turn for guidance?

PRAYER

Dear Lord, as I seek direction in this season of my life, please grant me clarity and peace. Help me to trust in Your wisdom and embrace the journey ahead.

"Even in the quiet moments, God is whispering the next steps for our journey."

HOPE BEYOND THE RETIREMENT YEARS

*"So with you: Now is your time of grief, but I will see you again and you will rejoice, and no one will take away your joy." **John 16:22***

DEVOTIONAL

Mabel spent the first few years of her retirement feeling adrift, missing the routine and purpose of her career. One sunny afternoon, she sat on her porch, reflecting on what truly brought her joy. As she watched her grandchildren play in the yard, she realized that her life was far from over; instead, it was a new chapter filled with opportunities for love and legacy. Inspired, she began volunteering at a local community center, where she quickly became a beloved figure, sharing her wisdom and warmth with both young and old. Mabel discovered that her heart was now fuller than ever, not just from her family but from the connections she was building in her community.

Apprecicte that even in the twilight years, there are new paths and joys waiting to be discovered.

DAILY REFLECTION

What dreams or passions have you set aside in this season of your life that might still hold a spark of joy?

PRAYER

Dear God, thank you for the gift of this season. Help me to embrace new opportunities and to be open to your guidance in pursuing the dreams you still place in my heart.

"Each new chapter is an invitation to discover the beauty that still awaits us."

THE STRENGTH TO SAY YES

*"Commit to the Lord whatever you do, and he will establish your plans." **Proverbs 16:3***

DEVOTIONAL

Once a devoted caregiver for her family, Sarah found herself at a crossroads after retiring. With her children grown and her time now her own, she hesitated to embrace new opportunities, wondering if she had the strength to try new things. One day, a friend invited her to join a local book club. Initially reluctant, Sarah remembered the joy of shared stories and laughter. She said yes, and as the months passed, her world opened to new friendships, hobbies, and even a hidden talent for writing. Each meeting was a reminder that sometimes, the most fulfilling moments come from embracing the unexpected.

Saying yes to new experiences can lead to moments that enrich our lives in ways we never imagined.

DAILY REFLECTION

What is one opportunity or calling in your life that you feel stirred to embrace, and what is holding you back from saying yes?

PRAYER

Dear Lord, thank You for the gifts of wisdom and experience that come with each moment of our lives. Help me to trust in Your strength, as I step boldly into the blessings You have waiting for me.

"Every 'yes' to God is a step into the abundant life He has prepared for us."

GOD'S LOVE NEVER CHANGES

*"Though the mountains be shaken and the hills be removed, yet my unfailing love for you will not be shaken nor my covenant of peace be removed,' says the Lord, who has compassion on you." **Isaiah 54:10***

DEVOTIONAL

Maggie often reminisces about her younger days, a time when the world felt vibrant and full of promise. As she sifts through old photographs, she stumbles upon memories of her late husband, family gatherings, and cherished friendships. Life has brought its fair share of changes—seasons of loss, solitude, and shifting roles. Yet, in the quiet moments of reflection, Maggie feels a profound sense of peace. She understands that while everything around her may alter, the love she has always experienced from God remains a steadfast anchor. It is a love that has cradled her through every trial and celebration, reminding her that she is never alone.

God's love is a constant presence, unwavering even in the face of life's uncertainties.

DAILY REFLECTION

What experiences in your life remind you that God's love has remained constant, even through change?

PRAYER

Dear God, thank you for your unwavering love that surrounds me each day. Help me to rest in your embrace and feel the comfort of your presence as I journey through this season of life.

In the midst of life's transitions, God's love remains a steadfast anchor for our souls.

HE SEES THE WHOLE PICTURE

*"The eyes of the Lord are everywhere, keeping watch on the wicked and the good." **Proverbs 15:3***

DEVOTIONAL

Margaret had always found joy in piecing together jigsaw puzzles. As she sat with the last piece in her hand, a memory struck her—how often she had looked at her life like a puzzle missing some vital pieces. In her retirement, she reflected on the times she felt lost or uncertain, wondering how her past choices fit into God's grand design. One afternoon, while working on a particularly challenging puzzle, she noticed how, even without knowing where each piece belonged at first, the image gradually formed beautifully in front of her. It dawned on her that just like the puzzle, God sees the entire picture of her life, and every experience—joyful or heartbreaking—was contributing to a masterpiece only He could understand fully.

Trust that God sees the whole picture of your life, weaving together each experience into His perfect plan.

DAILY REFLECTION

What parts of your life do you feel uncertain about right now, and how can you trust that God sees the whole picture in those moments?

PRAYER

Dear Lord, thank you for guiding us through every season of our lives. Help us to trust in Your infinite wisdom, knowing that You see the entire tapestry we've woven with our experiences.

"God's perspective encompasses all of our past, present, and future, reminding us that every thread of our life has purpose."

A HEART ALIGNED WITH HIS

"In your relationships with one another, have the same mindset as Christ Jesus."
Philippians 2:5

DEVOTIONAL

Mabel had always poured her heart into her family, friends, and community during her busy years of motherhood and work. Now, in retirement, she found herself sitting alone on her porch, reflecting on the seasons of life she had lived. One morning, she noticed a small bird feeding its young from a nearby tree, tirelessly providing for them without thought of her own need for rest. In that moment, Mabel felt a gentle whisper of contentment, reminding her that aligning her heart with Christ meant serving those around her, just like the bird—finding joy in nurturing others and seeking a purpose that extended beyond her own comfort.

True fulfillment often springs from a heart that seeks to serve others with love and compassion, creating a beautiful alignment with His purpose.

DAILY REFLECTION

When you consider the busy seasons of your life, how has God aligned your heart with His purpose, and how can you continue to seek that alignment in your everyday moments?

PRAYER

Dear Lord, thank you for the grace you extend to us each day. Help us to draw nearer to You, cultivating a heart that reflects Your love and wisdom. May our thoughts and actions align more closely with Your will.

"An aligned heart finds joy in the simplicity of God's presence."

MENTORING THE NEXT GENERATION

"As iron sharpens iron, so one person sharpens another."
Proverbs 27:17

DEVOTIONAL

A lovely neighbor of mine, Mrs. Thompson, spent her retirement volunteering at the local school, helping children learn to read. One day, she met a young girl who struggled with her confidence and often felt left behind. With patience and encouragement, Mrs. Thompson not only improved the girl's reading skills but also nurtured her spirit, inspiring her to believe in herself. This connection blossomed into a heartfelt friendship, showing how sharing our time and knowledge can light the way for those who are just beginning their journeys.

In mentoring the next generation, remember that your wisdom and gentle guidance can be a beacon of hope and strength for others starting their paths in life.

DAILY REFLECTION

What wisdom do you wish to pass on to the younger women in your life, and how can you begin to share it today?

PRAYER

Dear Lord, thank You for the experiences and lessons that come with age. Guide me in sharing my journey with the next generation, and may my words inspire them to grow in faith and purpose.

"Your life is a legacy; let it shine like a beacon for those who follow."

THE PROMISE OF RENEWAL

"Create in me a pure heart, O God, and renew a steadfast spirit within me."
Psalm 51:10

DEVOTIONAL

As a retired woman, you may find yourself embraced by the stillness of a new chapter, filled with quiet mornings and cherished memories. Yet, amidst this tranquility, the heart may whisper for something fresh, for new purpose and passion. Imagine a garden; as the seasons change, it may appear dormant, but beneath the soil, life is stirring and preparing for a glorious bloom. So too can your spirit flourish, as God gently tends to the places within you longing for renewal.

In every stage of life, there is an opportunity for rebirth, and with faith, we can embrace the promise that each day holds the possibility of renewal.

DAILY REFLECTION

What areas of your life feel tired, and how can you invite the promise of renewal into them?

PRAYER

Dear Lord, thank you for the gift of each day and the promise of renewal that comes with it. Help me to embrace this new season with hope and joy, trusting in your unfailing love.

"Every ending carries the promise of a new beginning."

SLOWING DOWN WITH GRACE

"Let your gentleness be evident to all. The Lord is near."
Philippians 4:5

DEVOTIONAL

Mabel had always been the one who stayed busy: raising children, volunteering, and nurturing friendships. But since retirement, she found herself with an abundance of free time. One rainy afternoon, she decided to take a quiet stroll through her garden, something she'd often rushed past. As she walked slowly, she noticed the colors of the flowers more vividly, the sound of raindrops tapping against the petals. Each step became a moment to breathe and reflect, and she realized that there was a beautiful rhythm in taking her time. It was as though Nature was whispering, "There's grace in slowing down."

Taking time to savor life's simple joys can lead to a deeper understanding of peace and fulfillment.

DAILY REFLECTION

What areas of your life could benefit from a slower, more graceful pace? How might you invite peace and intention into your daily routine?

PRAYER

Dear Lord, help me to embrace this season of life with gentleness and grace. Guide me to find moments of stillness where I can savor your presence and reflect on your goodness.

"Slowing down is not about doing less; it's about making space for what truly matters."

RUNNING THE RACE WELL

*"Do you not know that in a race all the runners run, but only one gets the prize? Run in such a way as to get the prize. Everyone who competes in the games goes into strict training. They do it to get a crown that will not last, but we do it to get a crown that will last forever. Therefore I do not run like someone running aimlessly; I do not fight like a boxer beating the air. No, I strike a blow to my body and make it my slave so that after I have preached to others, I myself will not be disqualified for the prize." **1 Corinthians 9:24-27**

DEVOTIONAL

There was once a retired teacher named Margaret who devoted her afternoons to helping children at the local community center. Every Wednesday, she would spend hours tutoring students struggling in math and reading. One day, a little boy named Lucas, discouraged by his setbacks, noticed her warm smile and asked why she cared so much. Margaret gently replied, "Because every child is a treasure. I'm just here to help you find your value and reach the finish line." That moment sparked a deep bond, energizing both Lucas and Margaret as they celebrated small victories together, proving that even in retirement, life's races can be rich and fulfilling.

In this chapter of your life, remember that running the race well means pouring your energy into nurturing others and seeking fulfillment in relationships.

DAILY REFLECTION

What does running the race well mean to you in this season of life? How can you embrace the journey ahead with grace and purpose?

PRAYER

Dear Lord, thank You for the privilege of running this race of life. Help me to cherish each moment and encourage those around me as I seek to finish strong in faith and love.

"Every day is an opportunity to run towards joy, regardless of the hurdles behind us."

TRUSTING GOD'S TIMING

*"For I know the plans I have for you, declares the Lord, plans to prosper you and not to harm you, plans to give you hope and a future." **Jeremiah 29:11***

DEVOTIONAL

In her garden, Margaret toiled each spring, eagerly planting seeds for blooms she hoped to see right away. Yet, each year was a lesson in patience as she watched those seedlings push through the soil at their own pace. One sunny afternoon, as she sat sipping tea, she noticed the vibrant roses finally bursting forth after weeks of waiting—each petal a testament to the beauty of trusting the process. It dawned on her that just as flowers take time to flourish, so too does God's plan for her life, unfolding with each passing day.

Trusting in God's timing not only nurtures our patience but reveals the beauty of His perfect plans for our lives.

DAILY REFLECTION

What areas of your life do you find it hardest to trust God's timing, and how might surrendering those to Him bring you peace?

PRAYER

Dear God, thank You for the gift of time and the promise of Your perfect plan. Help me to rest in Your timing and to find joy in each moment You provide.

"God's timing is not just about waiting; it's about growing and discovering His purpose in the waiting."

YOUR FAITH CAN MOVE MOUNTAINS

*"Therefore I tell you, whatever you ask for in prayer, believe that you have received it, and it will be yours." **Mark 11:24***

DEVOTIONAL

There once was a woman named Grace, who had dedicated her life to her family and community. After retirement, she often found herself reflecting on dreams left unfulfilled and challenges that seemed insurmountable. One day, she decided to take a leap of faith and join a local garden club, hoping to cultivate both flowers and friendships. As she planted seeds in the rich soil, she realized that just like those seeds, her dreams had potential, waiting patiently for her belief and nurturing to bring them to life. With each blooming flower, she felt a renewed sense of purpose and the joy that arises when faith takes root.

Embrace the belief that your faith, even in the simplest of moments, holds the power to transform your dreams into reality.

DAILY REFLECTION

What mountains in your life feel too large to move? How might your faith be the tool to help you address these challenges?

PRAYER

Dear Lord, thank You for the gift of faith that guides us through life's challenges. Help us to trust in Your power and to lean on You when our burdens feel heavy.

"Sometimes the smallest act of faith can have the greatest impact."

LET GOD REWRITE YOUR STORY

*"Your eyes saw my unformed body; all the days ordained for me were written in your book before one of them came to be." **Psalm 139:16***

DEVOTIONAL

Mabel spent years living within the confines of her family's expectations, prioritizing everyone's needs over her own. Now in her retirement, she felt a longing to discover who she truly was beneath the layers of duty and obligation. One day, she decided to take a watercolor class—a activity she's always dreamt of but never pursued. In the vibrant colors she splashed across the canvas, Mabel found freedom and the joy of self-expression, realizing that her life story was still being written and she had a pen in hand.

Embrace this season of life as an opportunity for new beginnings, allowing God to guide your story in unexpected and beautiful ways.

DAILY REFLECTION

What parts of your life story have been difficult to accept, and how might you invite God to rewrite those chapters with His grace and love?

PRAYER

Dear Lord, thank You for the gift of a new season in my life. Help me to trust in Your guidance as You rewrite my story, filling it with hope and purpose.

"God's hands can craft beauty out of the broken pieces of our past."

COMPASSION IN ACTION

"The Lord is good to all; he has compassion on all he has made."
Psalm 145:9

DEVOTIONAL

In her small, sunlit kitchen, Anna prepared a meal for a neighbor who had recently lost her husband. She stirred the soup slowly, recalling how her own heart had felt heavy when she faced loss. As she delivered the warm bowl to her friend, she saw the tears glistening in her eyes. Anna enveloped her in a comforting hug, and in that moment, both women felt a gentle connection that reminded them they were not alone, bound together by shared experiences and love. Compassion came naturally, like a warm blanket on a chilly day, knitting their hearts closer together.

Acts of kindness, no matter how small, can create profound bonds and heal old wounds. Embrace opportunities to show compassion, for your warmth can light the way for others who are walking through difficult seasons.

DAILY REFLECTION

What does compassion look like in your everyday life, and how can you take small steps to express it more often to those around you?

PRAYER

Dear Lord, help me to open my heart to the needs of others. May my actions reflect Your love and may I find joy in serving those around me.

"Compassion shines brightest in the simple acts of kindness we extend to one another."

THE POWER OF A QUIET YES

"But when you pray, go into your room, close the door and pray to your Father, who is unseen. Then your Father, who sees what is done in secret, will reward you." **Matthew 6:6**

DEVOTIONAL

In her bustling days of raising children and working, Margaret often felt the pressure to say yes to every request, whether it was a volunteering opportunity, a family gathering, or a neighbor in need. Now retired, she discovered the beauty of a quiet yes. One afternoon, nestled in her favorite chair with a cup of tea, she realized the power of taking time to reflect before responding. Rather than quickly acquiescing, she began to weigh her commitments carefully, leading to deeper engagement in activities she truly valued. This newfound approach brought her a sense of peace and fulfillment she had long sought.

The strength of a quiet yes allows you to embrace what truly matters in this season of life, leading to more authentic joy and connection.

DAILY REFLECTION

What does a quiet yes look like in your life, and how can it lead you to deeper peace and fulfillment?

PRAYER

Dear Lord, thank you for the gentle whispers that guide us. Help us embrace the power of a quiet yes, trusting in Your plan as we navigate this season of life.

"In a world filled with noise, the quiet yes speaks volumes of faith and commitment."

CELEBRATING GOD'S GOODNESS

"I thank my God every time I remember you."
Philippians 1:3

DEVOTIONAL

Once, a retired woman named Mary gathered with her old friends for a reunion after many years apart. As they shared their lives, laughter flowed abundantly, and tears of joy mixed with stories of overcoming challenges. Each friend took turns expressing gratitude not just for memories but for the grace that had been present through each season of their lives. Mary realized that even in moments of struggle, God's goodness had been a constant companion, weaving their stories together like a beautiful tapestry of love and resilience.

In celebrating the goodness of God, we embrace the rich tapestry of our lives, recognizing His hand in every joyful and challenging moment.

DAILY REFLECTION

What moments in your life have you cherished that clearly show God's goodness? How can you celebrate those blessings today?

PRAYER

Dear Lord, thank you for the countless ways you show your goodness in our lives. Help us to recognize and celebrate each blessing, big or small, as a reflection of your love.

"God's goodness is woven into the fabric of our everyday lives, waiting for us to notice and celebrate."

YOUR VOICE MATTERS

"She speaks with wisdom, and faithful instruction is on her tongue."
Proverbs 31:26

DEVOTIONAL

Mabel sat in her favorite armchair, sipping tea while she listened to her granddaughter, Lily, excitedly share stories from school. As Lily spoke, Mabel felt a flicker of nostalgia for her own youthful days filled with dreams and aspirations. With each word her granddaughter shared, Mabel realized how often her own voice had been quieted over the years, yet here, in the warmth of their bond, she sensed the power of her presence. Inspired, she decided that it was time to reclaim her stories, sharing tales of love and resilience that might guide Lily in her own journey.

Your voice carries a legacy of wisdom that can light the path for younger generations and remind them of the importance of kindness and strength. Embrace the power of your voice; sharing your experiences can inspire and empower others in ways you may never fully realize.

DAILY REFLECTION

What are the unique experiences and wisdom you've gained over your lifetime that can inspire and uplift others around you?

PRAYER

Dear God, thank you for the gift of voice in our lives. Help us to share our stories and wisdom with courage and love, knowing that each word can make a difference.

"Your voice, borne from years of experience, is a treasure waiting to be shared."

HE DELIGHTS IN YOU

"The Lord delights in those who fear him, who put their hope in his unfailing love."
Psalm 147:11

DEVOTIONAL

Once upon a time in a quaint little town, there lived a retired teacher named Margaret. In her spare time, she devoted herself to gardening, and with each blooming flower, she felt a sense of accomplishment and joy. One day, a neighbor stopped by and commented, "Your garden is a true reflection of your heart; it blossoms with love and care." Margaret realized in that moment that just as she tended to her garden, God delights in nurturing her spirit and watching her flourish in this season of life.

As you tend to the gardens of your life, remember that God delights in you as you bloom in His love.

DAILY REFLECTION

What are the unique qualities and experiences in your life that you believe bring delight to God? How might acknowledging His pleasure in you change the way you see yourself today?

PRAYER

Dear Lord, thank you for creating me with such love and care. Help me to recognize the joy I bring to You just by being myself, and guide me to embrace this gift in my daily life.

"You are a beautiful creation, and His heart sings with joy when He sees you."

PURSUING GOD OVER PERFECTION

"If we claim to be without sin, we deceive ourselves and the truth is not in us. If we confess our sins, he is faithful and just and will forgive us our sins and purify us from all unrighteousness." **1 John 1:8-9**

DEVOTIONAL

Martha had always prided herself on maintaining a perfect garden. Through the years, she'd spent countless hours ensuring each flower bloomed just right and every weed was pulled. However, as she looked around one sunny afternoon, she noticed that the most beautiful moments came not from perfection but from the bees dancing among the wildflowers and the laughter of children running through her garden's maze. She realized that in her pursuit of perfection, she had missed the simple joys and the blessings God placed around her every day.

Life is not about achieving perfection, but about pursuing a deep, loving relationship with God who delights in our authentic selves.

DAILY REFLECTION

What does pursuing a deeper relationship with God look like for you in this season of life? What small steps can you take today to shift your focus from perfection to connection with Him?

PRAYER

Dear Lord thank You for this moment of quiet. Help me to find joy in the journey of seeking You, rather than striving for unattainable perfection. Fill my heart with Your peace as I embrace the beauty of each day.

"God delights in our hearts, not in our flawless performances."

FINANCIAL TRUST IN RETIREMENT

"And my God will meet all your needs according to the riches of his glory in Christ Jesus."
Philippians 4:19

DEVOTIONAL

As Claire settled into her cozy armchair, she took a moment to reflect on her journey through retirement. Initially anxious about her fixed income, she recalled a time when her late husband had surprised her with a number of thoughtful small gifts, even when times were tight. One day, they were short on cash, yet they hosted an impromptu gathering for friends, and laughter filled the room. In hearing her friends' stories and joys, Claire realized that true wealth was not just in financial security but in the abundance of love and joy shared with others. Trusting in God's provision allowed her to focus on what truly mattered.

Trust that your worth and abundance extend far beyond finances; your value is in love, friendship, and faith.

DAILY REFLECTION

What financial worries keep you up at night, and how can you shift your focus to deeper trust in the Lord's provision?

PRAYER

Dear God, thank You for the blessings of this season in life. Help me to rest in your promises and trust that you will provide for each day ahead.

"Trusting God means letting go of anxiety about the future and embracing the peace of His presence."

FAITH THAT OVERFLOWS

"They feast on the abundance of your house; you give them drink from your river of delights." **Psalm 36:8**

DEVOTIONAL

Grace had always been one to extend kindness to others. In her retirement, she began to volunteer at the local food pantry, finding fulfillment in serving those in need. One day, she met a young mother struggling to provide for her children. With a warm smile and open heart, Grace not only offered her assistance but also shared stories of hope and faith that had seen her through life's challenges. The young mother left with a full bag of groceries and a newfound sense of strength, inspired by Grace's faith that overflowed from her heart.

The joy you find in sharing your blessings can create ripples of faith and generosity in the lives of others.

DAILY REFLECTION

What does it mean for your faith to overflow into the lives of those around you? Can you recall a time when your belief in God positive impacted someone else's life?

PRAYER

Dear Lord, thank you for the gift of faith that fills our hearts. Help me to share this overflowing love with others, bringing light and joy into their lives each day.

"Let your faith be a wellspring of hope and love, nurturing those around you."

FINDING COMFORT IN SCRIPTURE

"Blessed are those who mourn, for they will be comforted."
Matthew 5:4

DEVOTIONAL

Once upon a time, there was a retired woman named Evelyn who had recently lost her husband. Each day felt a bit heavier as memories flooded her thoughts. In her quiet moments, she found solace in sitting on her porch with a warm cup of tea. One day, while browsing through an old family Bible, she stumbled upon the verse about comfort in mourning As she read the words aloud, she felt a gentle nudge of peace wash over her, knowing that it was okay to grieve but also to allow herself to be comforted by faith and those around her.

In times of sorrow, turning to Scripture can provide profound comfort and reassurance that you are never alone in your struggles.

DAILY REFLECTION

What scripture have you turned to in times of need, and how did it bring you peace during those moments? Reflect on the verses that have wrapped around your heart like a comforting embrace.

PRAYER

Dear God, thank you for the gift of Your Word, which brings solace and wisdom into our lives. Help me open my heart to the comfort of scripture and let it guide me in times of uncertainty.

"Scripture is the gentle whisper that calms our restless hearts."

FROM ROUTINE TO RENEWAL

"Therefore, if anyone is in Christ, the new creation has come: The old has gone, the new is here!" **2 Corinthians 5:17**

DEVOTIONAL

Devotional Story: Betty had spent decades in a routine of caretaking, homemaking, and volunteering. Yet, as she settled into retirement, she felt a stirring within her—a desire for new adventures and experiences. One crisp autumn morning, she picked up a paintbrush for the first time, letting the colors flow freely, as if each stroke was a step into her rejuvenated self. She laughed with her friends, shared her creations, and discovered a new part of her spirit that had been waiting for the right moment to emerge. In this newfound freedom, Betty found joy that filled her days with purpose.

Life Lesson: Embrace this season of life as an opportunity for renewal and rediscovery, allowing your heart to explore what brings you joy.

DAILY REFLECTION

What small change can you make in your daily routine to invite a sense of renewal and refreshment into your life?

PRAYER

Dear God, thank you for the gift of each new day. As I seek renewal, help me to embrace the changes that lead me closer to you and fill my heart with joy.

"Every day holds the potential for transformation;
all we need is the willingness to explore."

YOU WERE MADE FOR THIS SEASON

"Gray hair is a crown of splendor; it is attained in the way of righteousness."
Proverbs 16:31

DEVOTIONAL

In her cozy living room, Clara sipped her tea and looked out at her garden, a riot of color and life. She often thought about how many seasons she had lived through—springtime joys, summer adventures, autumnal change, and now the serene beauty of winter. One day, a friend visited and remarked how lovely her garden was, and Clara smiled, realizing that it had taken years to cultivate it into something so beautiful. Just as her garden flourished through all the seasons, she too had grown in wisdom and grace, crafting a life filled with purpose and meaning, especially in this, her golden season.

Embrace this time of your life as a season of rich and fulfilling possibilities meant just for you.

DAILY REFLECTION

What unique gifts and experiences has God given you to embrace in this season of your life? How can you use them to bless others around you?

PRAYER

Dear Lord, thank You for this beautiful season of life. Help us to see the purpose in each moment and guide us to share Your love with those we encounter.

"Every season of life is a chapter in your story—
embrace it as the masterpiece it was meant to be."

THE ANCHOR OF GOD'S WORD

"This is what the Lord says— your Redeemer, the Holy One of Israel: 'I am the Lord your God, who teaches you what is best for you, who directs you in the way you should go."
Isaiah 48:17

DEVOTIONAL

When Mary retired, she found herself with more time than she ever imagined. At first, it was a relief, but as weeks turned into months, she began to feel a sense of aimlessness creeping in. One evening, she picked up a well-worn Bible that had been in her family for generations. As she flipped through the pages, she stumbled upon verses promising comfort and guidance. Each line felt like an anchor for her unpredictable days, reminding her that God's word was a steady presence in her life, guiding her choices, big or small. Mary started reading a verse each morning, allowing it to shape her day; soon, she realized that with God's wisdom, even the simplest of decisions brought her joy and peace.

Just as an anchor holds a ship steady amid the waves, God's Word can be your unwavering support in life's seasons of change.

DAILY REFLECTION

What verses in God's Word have served as your anchor during challenging times? How can you allow these scriptures to guide you in your current season of life?

PRAYER

Dear Heavenly Father, thank You for the gift of Your Word that stabilizes our lives. Help us to lean into its truths and find comfort and guidance in every situation we face.

"The promises of God are the steadfast anchors in life's turbulent seas."

FILLING THE CALENDAR WITH MEANING, NOT BUSYNESS

"So whether you eat or drink or whatever you do, do it all for the glory of God."
1 Corinthians 10:31

DEVOTIONAL

Margaret had always filled her calendar with endless appointments and activities, often saying "yes" to everything that came her way. When she retired, she realized that her days were filled with busyness but lacked true meaning. One day, she decided to spend her afternoon volunteering at the local shelter instead of attending yet another social event. As she helped serve meals and talk with those in need, Margaret felt a stirring in her heart that had long been forgotten. The joy and fulfillment from serving others resonated deeply, reminding her that purpose is found in connection, not just in a calendar full of engagements.

Cultivate a life of significance by choosing to fill your days with meaningful connections and acts of service, rather than mere activities.

DAILY REFLECTION

What activities in your life bring you genuine joy and connection, rather than simply filling your time? How can you realign your calendar to reflect your deepest values and passions?

PRAYER

Dear Lord, help me to embrace this season of life with purpose and to prioritize what truly matters. Guide my heart as I make choices that foster fulfillment and joy.

"Purposeful living transforms mere moments into meaningful memories."

THE MINISTRY OF GRANDPARENTING

"Children are a heritage from the Lord, offspring a reward from him. Like arrows in the hands of a warrior are children born in one's youth. Blessed is the man whose quiver is full of them. They will not be put to shame when they contend with their opponents in court."
Psalm 127:3-5

DEVOTIONAL

In the golden years of her retirement, Grace discovered a new chapter she had never fully anticipated: the beautiful ministry of grandparenting. Every week, her grandchildren flocked to her cozy home, giggles and laughter filling the air as they baked cookies and crafted colorful creations. One afternoon, as they gathered around the kitchen table, Grace noticed the sparkle in their eyes, each eager to share stories from their week. In that moment, she realized that these cherished interactions were not merely playdates; rather, they were her sacred opportunity to pour love, wisdom, and faith into the next generation. Each cookie baked and each story told became a thread that wove their hearts closer together, solidifying a legacy of love and grace.

The ministry of grandparenting is a divine calling that allows you to nurture love, wisdom, and faith in the lives of your grandchildren while creating lasting memories that enrich your soul.

DAILY REFLECTION

What joys and lessons have your grandchildren brought into your life, and how can you further nurture their growth in faith?

PRAYER

Dear Lord, thank you for the gift of family and the special bond of grandparenting. Help me to embrace my role with love, wisdom, and patience, nurturing my grandchildren's hearts and minds as they grow.

"Grandparenting is not just an addition to your family;
it's a ministry that can shape the next generation in profound ways."

YOUR STORY REFLECTS HIS GLORY

"Everyone who is called by my name, whom I created for my glory, whom I formed and made."
Isaiah 43:7

DEVOTIONAL

As you sit in your favorite chair, perhaps sipping a warm cup of tea, think about the tapestry of your life. Every thread, from joyful moments spent with family to the challenges that shaped your character, tells a story that reflects God's handiwork. In quiet times, you may remember a particularly trying season—raising children, navigating careers, caring for aging parents. Each experience has been a brushstroke on the canvas of who you are, revealing shades of grace that others see and admire. Like precious pearls, your stories shine, inviting others to witness the beauty of faith lived out in everyday moments.

The life lessons we've gathered over the years serve not just to teach us but also to inspire those around us. Just as a stained glass window catches the light and splashes it in vibrant colors, your unique story adds to the glory of God's creation. Your journey, filled with ups and downs, sickness and health, is woven into the greater narrative of His love and purpose. Remember, it is not only in grand accomplishments but also in humble acts of kindness and perseverance that His glory is reflected through you.

DAILY REFLECTION

What chapters in your life have shown you His grace and love? How have your experiences shaped the woman you are today, reflecting the glory of His story?

PRAYER

Dear Lord, thank You for the beautiful tapestry of life that you have woven in me. Help me to see each moment as a reflection of Your glory, and guide me to share my story with those around me.

Every story, filled with trials and triumphs, paints a unique expression of God's glory in our lives.

WALKING IN THE LIGHT

*"The path of the righteous is like the morning sun,
shining ever brighter till the full light of day."* **Proverbs 4:18**

DEVOTIONAL

As the sun rises each morning, casting its gentle rays on the world, so too does a life walked in faith shine brightly. Imagine a retiree named Clara, who after stepping away from her long career found herself at a crossroads. One morning, as she sipped her tea on the porch, she noticed the way the sunlight danced on the flowers in her garden. That moment sparked a realization: just like those blooms, she too could thrive and share her light with others, whether it was volunteering at a local shelter or simply inviting neighbors over for tea. Through this renewed purpose, Clara discovered that the golden years are an opportunity to illuminate the lives of those around her.

Your journey does not end with retirement; instead, it is a new chance to walk in the light, sharing warmth and love with your community.

DAILY REFLECTION

What areas of your life need more of God's light today, and how can you invite His illumination into those shadows?

PRAYER

Dear Lord, thank you for Your everlasting light that guides us through every season of life. Help us to open our hearts and minds to Your presence, illuminating our paths with hope and wisdom.

"Walking in the light means embracing each new day with faith and gratitude, discovering beauty in the ordinary."

OVERCOMING REGRET IN OLD AGE

"He has made everything beautiful in its time. He has also set eternity in the human heart; yet no one can fathom what God has done from beginning to end." **Ecclesiastes 3:11**

DEVOTIONAL

Lila sat on her porch, sipping tea as she watched the world go by. The memories flowed freely—decisions made, roads not taken, and the life she imagined in her younger years. One afternoon, she noticed a young couple passing by, eagerly making plans and dreaming out loud. Instead of feeling regret, Lila smiled, realizing she had a lifetime of beautiful moments and lessons behind her, each contributing to the woman she is today. She embraced her story, understanding that every chapter led her to this day—a day filled with gratitude and newfound joy.

In every season of our lives, we find beauty, and it's never too late to embrace who we are and the journey we've taken.

DAILY REFLECTION

What are some regrets you hold onto, and how might embracing them as part of your journey help you find peace? How can you turn those lessons into wisdom for yourself and others?

PRAYER

Dear Lord, help me to release the weight of my regrets and embrace the beauty of your grace. Grant me the strength to find peace in my past and the joy of living fully in the present.

"Every regret is a lesson wrapped in love, guiding us toward the fullness of life."

HE IS FAITHFUL STILL

"I will sing of the Lord's great love forever; with my mouth I will make your faithfulness known through all generations." **Psalm 89:1**

DEVOTIONAL

As I settled into my favorite chair one quiet afternoon, I found myself reflecting on decades gone by. The years seem to have flown by, filled with moments of joy and sorrow, grand milestones, and simple pleasures. I remember a time when my children were young and life was brimming with responsibilities and worries. But through every twist and turn, I realized that even in the chaos, God was there, guiding me gently. Now, I witness His faithfulness in the laughter of my grandchildren and the stillness of my mornings—each reminder that His promise endures beyond the seasons of life.

In every chapter, God remains unchanging, His love unyielding. As we embrace this new phase of life, let us acknowledge that His faithfulness does not wane; it only reveals itself in deeper and more profound ways.

Trust that the love and faithfulness of the Lord will always guide you through every season, reminding you that He is with you, always.

DAILY REFLECTION

What moments in your life have shown you His unwavering faithfulness, and how can you carry that assurance into your next chapter?

PRAYER

Dear Lord, thank You for Your steadfast love that carries me through every season of life. Help me to rest in Your faithfulness and trust that You are guiding my steps as I embrace this new journey.

"His faithfulness is like a gentle stream, always flowing, refreshing and renewing our spirits."

THE SACREDNESS OF FREE TIME

"There is a time for everything, and a season for every activity under the heavens."
Ecclesiastes 3:1

DEVOTIONAL

Once upon a time, a retired woman named Ruth discovered the joy of her free days. She filled her mornings with gardening, nurturing her flowers just as she used to nurture her family. One day, as she sat in her garden, a passing neighbor stopped to admire her blooms. This simple exchange blossomed into a friendship that brightened her afternoons. Ruth realized that her free time was not just an empty space to fill, but a sacred opportunity to connect her heart with others and serve her community in ways she had never imagined.

Embrace your free time as a sacred gift, an opportunity to cultivate both beauty in your surroundings and relationships in your life.

DAILY REFLECTION

What does free time mean to you in this season of your life, and how can you use it to nourish your spirit and connect more deeply with God and others?

PRAYER

Dear Lord, thank you for the gift of free time in this season of life. Help me to embrace these moments, finding joy and purpose in the stillness and opportunities to serve others around me.

"Embrace the quiet moments;
they are where God whispers His most profound truths to your heart."

THE POWER OF REMEMBERING

"Praise the Lord, my soul, and forget not all his benefits—"
Psalm 103:2

DEVOTIONAL

In her quiet living room filled with photographs of children and grandchildren, Martha often sat with her cup of tea, reminiscing about the years gone by. She recalled the joy on her daughter's wedding day, when laughter filled the air, and the summer vacations spent at the beach where the sand seemed to swallow up their worries. Each memory was a gift that brought warmth to her heart, reminding her of God's faithfulness through the seasons of her life. One day, while dusting a shelf, she stumbled upon an old journal filled with prayers and praises. As she read her own words, she felt a wave of gratitude wash over her; the act of remembering deepened her faith and revived her spirit.

Remembering the blessings of the past can bring light to the present and hope for the future.

DAILY REFLECTION

What moments from your past bring you joy and strength when you recall them? How can you use those memories to inspire your present and shape your future?

PRAYER

Dear God, thank You for the gift of memory. Help me to cherish the stories of my life and to weave them into my daily walk with You. May I find comfort and inspiration in remembering the blessings of my journey.

"Remembering is not just looking back;
it's a way to honor our journey and celebrate our growth."

WALKING THROUGH GRIEF WITH GOD

"Brothers and sisters, we do not want you to be uninformed about those who sleep in death, so that you do not grieve like the rest of mankind, who have no hope. For we believe that Jesus died and rose again, and so we believe that God will bring with Jesus those who have fallen asleep in him." **1 Thessalonians 4:13-14**

DEVOTIONAL

Once, there was a retired woman named Clara who lost her beloved husband after many years of marriage. In the weeks that followed, grief washed over her like a tide that she couldn't escape. Yet one morning as she sat in her garden, she noticed the flowers pushing through the earth, vibrant and alive despite the cold winter. It was then that she felt God whispering comfort to her heart, reminding her that life continues, and with it, the hope and love that never truly fades. Clara began to spend time in prayer and reflection, discovering that although her heart ached, God was walking beside her, bringing little moments of joy through nature, family, and friends.

As you walk through your own grief, remember that God is present in each step, gently guiding you towards hope and renewal.

DAILY REFLECTION

What memories bring you comfort when you think of your loved one? How can you invite God into your moments of sorrow as you cherish those memories?

PRAYER

Dear Lord, hold my heart in Your gentle hands as I walk through this season of grief. Help me to see the Light even in the shadows, and may Your love surround me in my times of sorrow.

In the embrace of grief, God stands with us, a steadfast companion through every tear.

GOD'S NEW ASSIGNMENTS AT EVERY AGE

"Again Jesus said, 'Peace be with you! As the Father has sent me, I am sending you."
John 20:21

DEVOTIONAL

Mabel had spent years caring for her family, volunteering at church, and contributing to her community. After retiring, she found herself feeling a bit lost, wondering what her purpose would be in this new chapter of her life. One sunny afternoon, she was invited to help lead a women's group at her church, where they focused on sharing stories of faith and support. Initially hesitant, she soon discovered that her life experiences resonated deeply with the younger women in the group, giving them courage and hope. Through this new assignment, Mabel not only found joy in mentoring but also recognized that her wisdom was just as valuable as it had ever been.

Every new age in our lives brings opportunities to share our journeys and inspire others, reminding us that God has purposeful assignments for us at every stage.

DAILY REFLECTION

What new opportunities might God be placing before you in this season of your life? How can you embrace these assignments with an open heart?

PRAYER

Dear God, thank You for the gift of this new season. Help me to see Your plans for me and to courageously step into the new assignments You have for my life.

"Every season of life brings fresh chances to serve and grow in faith."

GOD'S GUIDANCE IN NEW PATHS

"Have I not commanded you? Be strong and courageous. Do not be afraid; do not be discouraged, for the Lord your God will be with you wherever you go." Joshua 1:9

DEVOTIONAL

Once upon a time, there lived a woman named Margaret who had devoted her life to raising her children and supporting her husband. Now in her retirement, she found herself at a crossroads, unsure of what to pursue next. One day, while volunteering at a local community center, she discovered a passion for teaching art to children. What started as a simple act of kindness bloomed into a new chapter filled with joy, creativity, and connection. Margaret learned that even in her later years, God's hand was guiding her toward new paths filled with purpose and excitement.

As you embrace this new season of life, remember that God's guidance is always present, inviting you to explore fresh opportunities and adventures.

DAILY REFLECTION

What new paths in your life is God inviting you to explore, and how can you open your heart to His guidance during this season of change?

PRAYER

Dear Heavenly Father, thank You for the gift of new beginnings. Help me to trust in Your guidance as I navigate this next chapter of my life.

"Embracing the unknown can lead to greater wisdom and deeper joy."

YOU ARE HELD

"Even there your hand will guide me; your right hand will hold me fast."
Psalm 139:10

DEVOTIONAL

After years of dedicated service, Ellen found herself in a new phase of life, rich with freedom but also uncertainty. One crisp autumn afternoon, as she gathered with friends for tea, they shared their dreams and fears about this next chapter. Ellen listened intently, reflecting on how often she had let fear overshadow hope. In that moment, she realized that each of them was held by a loving hand, much greater than their own worries. As laughter filled the room, she felt a wave of warmth wash over her, a comforting reminder that she was supported and carried through both joys and challenges.

Even in retirement, you are beautifully held by a love that knows no boundaries, guiding you toward new and fulfilling adventures.

DAILY REFLECTION

What moments in your life remind you of the ways you have been held by God, and how can you acknowledge those moments today?

PRAYER

Dear Lord, thank You for the gentle reminder that You hold us close, no matter where life takes us. Help us to lean into Your love and find peace in knowing that we are not alone.

"Even in the quiet seasons of our lives, we are cradled in the arms of grace."

A SPIRIT OF THANKSGIVING

"Give thanks to the Lord, for he is good; his love endures forever."
1 Chronicles 16:34

DEVOTIONAL

Imagine a cozy afternoon spent in the garden, where vibrant flowers bloom, and soft breezes carry the scent of fresh earth. As you tend to your plants, you discover how each blossom is a reminder of different seasons of your life, from joy and laughter to challenges faced and overcome. With each gentle touch of a petal, gratitude wells up inside you, revealing God's consistent presence through every chapter. It dawns on you that even the simplest moments—sipping tea or watching the sunset—are profound blessings waiting to be acknowledged.

Cultivating a spirit of thanksgiving can transform ordinary days into extraordinary experiences of grace and joy.

DAILY REFLECTION

What are the little blessings in your daily life that you might overlook, and how can you cultivate a deeper sense of gratitude for them?

PRAYER

Dear Lord, thank you for the countless blessings you provide each day. Open our hearts to recognize and appreciate the beauty and grace that surround us. May we embody a spirit of thanksgiving in all we do.

"Gratitude turns what we have into enough."

WHEN GOD FEELS DISTANT

"The Lord is near to all who call on him, to all who call on him in truth."
Psalm 145:18

DEVOTIONAL

Once, in a quiet neighborhood, a retired woman named Ruth found herself feeling alone as the days turned into a familiar routine. She would sit by the window, watching the world pass by, and sometimes felt God's presence slipping further away during those hours of solitude. One evening, as she poured out her heart in prayer, she felt a gentle nudge to reach out to a friend she hadn't spoken to in months. That simple call led to a joyful reunion, laughter shared, and both women realized how God had been quietly present in their lives, waiting for them to reconnect and share His love through friendship.

When God feels distant, it may be an invitation for you to reach out to others, where His love often shines the brightest.

DAILY REFLECTION

What moments in your life make you feel the farthest from God, and how can you invite Him back into those spaces?

PRAYER

Dear God, help me to feel your presence even when I struggle to see or sense it. Draw near to my heart as I seek to draw near to Yours.

"God's silence does not indicate His absence; it often invites us to deepen our faith."

PEACE THAT PASSES UNDERSTANDING

"In peace I will lie down and sleep, for you alone, Lord, make me dwell in safety."
Psalm 4:8

DEVOTIONAL

The other day, Margaret was sitting on her porch, sipping her evening tea, when she noticed the sun setting behind the trees. It reminded her of how life had its ebbs and flows, just as the day transitioned into night. In her earlier years, she often felt the weight of worries and responsibilities, but now, as she reflected on her journey, she realized that she had learned to let go of many of those burdens. With each passing year, she found a deeper sense of calm that came from trusting in God's plan. That evening, as she watched the colors dance across the sky, Margaret felt a profound peace surround her, the kind that could only come from understanding that she was safe in God's embrace.

Finding peace isn't about eliminating worries, but learning to trust that God's presence offers safety and calm amidst life's uncertainties.

DAILY REFLECTION

What are some moments in your life when you've experienced a sense of peace, even amidst uncertainty or challenges?

PRAYER

Dear Lord, thank you for the peace that envelops us during our most trying times. Help us to embrace this gift and share it with those around us, drawing strength from Your presence.

"True peace blossoms in the heart that trusts in God's perfect plan."

HE RESTORES WHAT WAS BROKEN

"But I will restore you to health and heal your wounds,'declares the Lord, 'because you are called an outcast, Zion for whom no one cares.'" **Jeremiah 30:17**

DEVOTIONAL

When Clara retired, she anticipated days filled with travel and gardening. Instead, she found herself grappling with the loss of close friends and the gradual decline of her health. One rainy afternoon, she revisited an old scrapbook filled with photographs of joyful moments with loved ones, laughter echoing through every page. As she turned each page, she felt a sense of warmth wash over her—a gentle reminder of God's presence in her life, rekindling her spirit. She then took it upon herself to reach out to old friends and reconnect, allowing God to weave new memories into her life. Through this journey, Clara discovered that even in brokenness, God is ever-present, bringing restoration to her heart and relationships.

Embrace the truth that God holds the power to heal and restore every broken piece of your life, no matter how far you feel from joy.

DAILY REFLECTION

What are some areas in your life where you feel God could bring healing and renewal? How can you open your heart to receive His restoration?

PRAYER

Dear Lord. thank You for Your promise to heal and restore our hearts. May we embrace Your gentle touch and allow You to mend what feels broken within us. Guide us in finding peace and joy in the restoration You offer.

"He restores my soul; He leads me in paths of righteousness for His name's sake."

YOU ARE CALLED AND EQUIPPED

"Each of you should use whatever gift you have received to serve others, as faithful stewards of God's grace in its various forms." **1 Peter 4:10**

DEVOTIONAL

Mabel had always seen herself as a caretaker, whether it was nurturing her children or lending a hand to her neighbors. Now in her retirement, she found herself questioning how she could serve in a different season of life. One day, she received a call from her church asking if she could help organize a weekly Bible study for women in her community. Initially hesitant, Mabel recalled all the times she had brought comfort and companionship to those in need and decided to embrace the opportunity. As she led the group, she discovered a renewed sense of purpose, realizing that her experiences and wisdom were invaluable gifts that brought joy and growth to others.

You are never too old to share your gifts and make an impact in the lives of those around you.

DAILY REFLECTION

What unique gifts or talents has God equipped you with that are just waiting to be shared in this season of your life?

PRAYER

Dear God, thank you for the gifts you've bestowed upon me. Help me to see the ways I can use them to serve others and glorify You in my daily life.

You are not just retired; you are refired, ready to shine your light in new and profound ways.

FREEDOM FROM THE PERFORMANCE TRAP

"Therefore, there is now no condemnation for those who are in Christ Jesus."
Romans 8:1

DEVOTIONAL

Mabel spent much of her life juggling family, work, and community responsibilities, often feeling that her worthiness hinged on her achievements. After retiring, she decided to take up painting purely for joy, leaving behind the demands of perfection. At first, the brush felt heavy in her hand, weighed down by the fear of judgment and the desire for validation. However, with each stroke, she began to release the performance-related stress that had held her captive. Mabel discovered that the beauty of painting was not in the end result, but in the freedom of expressive creativity, and for the first time, she felt at peace simply being herself.

You are loved and valued for who you are at your core, not by what you accomplish.

DAILY REFLECTION

What expectations do you place on yourself that might be keeping you from enjoying the freedom God offers?

PRAYER

Dear Lord, thank You for the gift of grace that liberates us from the need to perform. Help us to embrace who we are without striving for perfection, resting in the love You have for each of us.

"True freedom comes when we realize that our worth is not defined by our achievements, but by our identity as beloved daughters of God."

A GRATEFUL HEART IS A STRONG HEART

"Therefore, since we are receiving a kingdom that cannot be shaken, let us be thankful, and so worship God acceptably with reverence and awe." **Hebrews 12:28**

DEVOTIONAL

In her cozy living room, Sarah often found herself reminiscing about her past, filled with barbecues with grandchildren, spontaneous road trips with friends, and long chats over cups of tea. One afternoon, she stumbled upon a box of old photographs, each image a snapshot of rich memories and love. As she sifted through each picture, a smile crept across her face; gratitude filled the room as she gave thanks for a life well-lived and the joys that continued to flow. Inspired, she started a gratitude journal, jotting down moments, big and small, that sparked joy, reminding her daily of the blessings she sometimes overlooked.

A grateful heart nurtures strength in the face of life's challenges and invites joy into our everyday moments.

DAILY REFLECTION

What are three things you are thankful for today, and how can acknowledging these blessings strengthen your heart?

PRAYER

Dear Lord, thank You for the beautiful moments and experiences in life. Help me cultivate a heart full of gratitude, so I can embrace each day with strength and joy.

A heart filled with gratitude is like a fortress;
it brings resilience and peace amidst life's challenges.

USING WISDOM AS A GIFT TO OTHERS

*"But the wisdom that comes from heaven is first of all pure; then peace-loving, considerate, submissive, full of mercy and good fruit, impartial and sincere." **James 3:17***

DEVOTIONAL

At her community center, Martha often volunteered to teach sewing to younger women. One afternoon, she patiently guided a nervous teenager who struggled with her first project. As they worked side by side, Martha shared stories of her own early sewing mishaps, making the young woman laugh. By the end of the session, not only had the teenager finished her project, but she also left with newfound confidence and a warm hug to remind her that mistakes are just steps on the journey towards mastery.

Sharing our wisdom is a beautiful way to sow seeds of confidence and courage in others.

DAILY REFLECTION

What wisdom have you gathered in your life that you can share with those around you to inspire and uplift them? Consider how your experiences can be a light for someone else.

PRAYER

Dear Lord, thank you for the gift of wisdom that comes through our years of living. Help me to share this gift with grace and love, nurturing those around me with understanding and kindness.

"Sharing your wisdom is a way to invest in the hearts of others, allowing your journey to become a guide on their path."

November 18

FAITH IN THE FIRE

"He will sit as a refiner and purifier of silver; he will purify the Levites and refine them like gold and silver. Then the Lord will have men who will bring offerings in righteousness."
Malachi 3:3

DEVOTIONAL

There once was a retired woman named Evelyn who spent much of her time volunteering at a local shelter. One day, she faced a personal challenge when her health began to decline. Initially, she felt overwhelmed and questioned her purpose, wondering how she could still contribute in her weakened state. One afternoon, while reflecting by her garden, she noticed how the new blooms emerged stronger and more vibrant after the harsh winter. It dawned on her that just like those flowers, her faith was being refined through her struggles. She began to find joy in her simple acts of kindness, understanding that even in times of trial, her spirit could shine brightly.

Faith is often forged in the fires of life's challenges, emerging more resilient and beautiful than before.

DAILY REFLECTION

What fires in your life have tested your faith, and how have you seen God's presence through those trials?

PRAYER

Dear Lord, thank You for being our constant companion in every season of life. Help us to trust in Your guidance and find strength in our faith during challenging times.

"Even the fiercest flames cannot consume the love and grace that surround us."

THE BEAUTY OF REFLECTION

*"The beginning of wisdom is this: Get wisdom. Though it cost all you have, get understanding." **Proverbs 4:7***

DEVOTIONAL

As she sat on her porch one warm afternoon, Anna pulled out an old photo album. Flipping through the pages, she marveled at the journey her life had taken—from the laughter of her children's sports days to the quiet moments shared with her husband. Each picture was a doorway to cherished memories and lessons learned. Reflecting on her life brought not just nostalgia, but also clarity and gratitude for the rich tapestry woven by those experiences. It struck her how each season, whether challenging or joyful, had shaped her into the woman she had become.

In the beauty of reflection, we uncover the wisdom that life's moments have to offer, leading us to appreciate the fullness of our journey.

DAILY REFLECTION

What memories from your past bring you the greatest joy, and how can you celebrate those moments in your life today? What lessons have they taught you about love, resilience, and faith?

PRAYER

Dear Lord, thank you for the gift of reflection and the wisdom that comes with age. Help me to embrace my memories and see the beauty they bring to my life today. Amen.

"Every wrinkle on our skin tells a story,
and every gray hair reflects a moment of laughter or sorrow that has shaped who we are."

PREPARING YOUR HEART FOR WORSHIP

*"Consequently, you are no longer foreigners and strangers, but fellow citizens with God's people and also members of his household, built on the foundation of the apostles and prophets, with Christ Jesus himself as the chief cornerstone." **Ephesians 2:19-20***

DEVOTIONAL

Once, a retired woman named Doris began attending a new church after moving to a different town. At first, she felt like an outsider, unsure if she would find her place among the congregation. But as she prepared her heart for worship each week, she found joy in connecting with others over shared stories and prayers. It was during one particular service that she realized she wasn't just a visitor; she belonged. In making space in her heart and mind for connection and community, Doris found not just a church, but a family.

In opening our hearts to worship, we also prepare ourselves to embrace the love and fellowship of those around us.

DAILY REFLECTION

What does it mean for you to prepare your heart for worship each week, and how can you create space for stillness in your life amidst daily distractions?

PRAYER

Dear God, as I come before You today, open my heart and mind to truly receive Your love and grace. Help me to let go of the busyness of life and find peace and joy in worship.

"Preparation is the pathway to connection with the Divine."

LEAVING A SPIRITUAL LEGACY

*"We will not hide them from their descendants; we will tell the next generation
the praiseworthy deeds of the Lord, his power, and the wonders he has done."* **Psalm 78:4**

DEVOTIONAL

Beverly sat on her porch, sipping her afternoon tea, watching her grandchildren play in the yard. With each burst of laughter, she felt a deep sense of gratitude, reflecting on the values and faith she hoped to pass on. Remembering her own grandmother's stories of faith during difficult times, Beverly decided to share her own life lessons with the younger generation. Gathering her grandchildren around her, she began to recount God's faithfulness and the miracles she witnessed throughout her life. Those moments transformed from stories into cherished memories, knitting their hearts together in faith and love.

The beauty of a spiritual legacy lies in our willingness to share our stories and values, creating bonds that can last for generations.

DAILY REFLECTION

What kind of spiritual legacy do you hope to leave behind for your family and friends? How can you nurture the seeds of faith in the lives of those around you today?

PRAYER

Dear Lord help me to embrace this season of my life, using my experiences and wisdom to guide others. May my heart be open to sharing your love, and may my words and actions leave a lasting impact on those I cherish.

"Every life is a book, and each chapter we live is a chance
to pen the story of faith for generations to come."

PRAYER AS YOUR DAILY WORK

"Before they call I will answer; while they are still speaking I will hear."
Isaiah 65:24

DEVOTIONAL

In her small, sunlit kitchen, Grace found herself sipping tea while gazing out at her garden, where flowers bloomed as brightly as her spirit. With her children grown and independent, she often thought about how much quieter her days had become. Yet, this stillness whispered opportunities to pour herself into prayer, a work she hadn't fully embraced until now. Each morning, as she weeded and tended to her plants, she began to offer prayers for her family, friends, and even the world beyond her porch. It seemed that with every whispered intention, God was responding with gentle nudges and surprising blessings in her life.

Prayer isn't just a moment of reflection; it is a vital work that nurtures our souls and shapes the world around us.

DAILY REFLECTION

What does prayer mean to you in this new season of life, and how can you incorporate it into your daily routine as a meaningful act of service?

PRAYER

Dear Heavenly Father, thank you for the gift of prayer. Help me to weave it into the fabric of my day, finding joy and purpose in communicating with you.

"Prayer is not just a ritual; it is the heartbeat of our daily lives."

RELEARNING IDENTITY IN CHRIST

"But our citizenship is in heaven. And we eagerly await a Savior from there, the Lord Jesus Christ." **Philippians 3:20**

DEVOTIONAL

As Helen settled into her new routine of retirement, she found herself grappling with the question of who she really was outside of her roles as a mother and grandmother. One afternoon, while flipping through an old photo album, she stumbled upon pictures of her younger self—bold, adventurous, and filled with dreams. This reflection led her to rediscover pieces of God's unique design woven into her identity, reminding her that her value was never limited to her accomplishments or family ties. With this newfound understanding, she embraced her time to grow in faith, passion, and friendship, realizing that her identity as a beloved daughter of Christ was a constant, regardless of changes in life's circumstances.

In this beautiful season of life, you are reminded that your true identity is rooted in your relationship with Christ, not in your past roles or achievements.

DAILY REFLECTION

What aspects of your identity do you find most challenging to reconcile with your new life in retirement? How can embracing your identity in Christ bring you peace and joy during this season?

PRAYER

Dear Heavenly Father, help me to recognize and embrace my identity in You. As I navigate this new chapter, remind me daily of Your unwavering love and purpose for my life. Amen.

"Your worth is not defined by the roles you once held, but by the love and grace you receive from Christ."

THE SPIRITUAL GIFT OF LISTENING

"To answer before listening— that is folly and shame."
Proverbs 18:13

DEVOTIONAL

Once upon a time in a cozy little town, a grandmother named Ruth often spent her afternoons at the local café, a familiar retreat for many in her community. Over countless cups of tea, she became known for her warm smile and the way she truly listened to those who spoke with her. One day, a young neighbor approached her, overwhelmed with the pressures of life. Instead of offering quick solutions, Ruth simply sat quietly, allowing the young woman to share her burdens. In that safe space, the young mother felt heard, healing began to unfold, and their bond deepened, reminding Ruth of the profound gift that listening can be in a world racing to respond.

Listening isn't just about hearing words; it's a powerful act of love that can transform hearts and relationships.

DAILY REFLECTION

What does it mean for you to truly listen to someone, and how might that deepen your relationships with family and friends?

PRAYER

Dear Lord, help me to cultivate the gift of listening, to hear not only the words but the hearts of those around me. May I create a safe space where others feel valued and understood.

"Listening is a gift we give to others, revealing the depth of our love and care."

HIS MERCY IS NEW TODAY

"Who satisfies your desires with good things so that your youth is renewed like the eagle's." **Psalm 103:5**

DEVOTIONAL

Mabel sat on her porch with a cup of tea, reflecting on the many seasons of her life. As she watched the sun rise, she remembered the trials and joys that had shaped her journey. Each year had its challenges, but there were always moments of grace that reminded her of God's unwavering love and mercy. She thought about how, in her retirement, she had begun to embrace new adventures, whether it was volunteering at the local shelter or picking up painting again. Each day presented a fresh canvas, thanks to God's mercy, and she found joy in the renewal that each morning brought.

Each day is a new opportunity to experience God's grace, reminding us that His mercies are covering and fresh for every chapter of our lives.

DAILY REFLECTION

What new mercy might God be revealing to you today, and how can you embrace it with gratitude? Consider the little moments that bring joy or peace.

PRAYER

Dear Lord, thank You for the gift of today and the fresh mercies it brings. Help me to see Your love in every moment and respond with a grateful heart.

"Every day is an opportunity to experience the tenderness of His grace."

ROOTED IN GRATITUDE

"Always giving thanks to God the Father for everything, in the name of our Lord Jesus Christ." **Ephesians 5:20**

DEVOTIONAL

As Helen settled into her favorite armchair, she gazed out the window to watch the golden leaves dance in the autumn breeze. Retirement had changed her daily rhythm, allowing her to savor moments that had once rushed by in earlier years. She remembered the days spent caring for her family, often feeling overwhelmed, with little time to reflect on the simple joys around her. Now, with every cup of tea and quiet moment with a book, she found herself pausing to appreciate the blessings of each day—her health, friendships, and the warmth of her home. It was in this season of her life that she discovered the power of gratitude, realizing that each thankful thought was a thread weaving into the fabric of her joy.

Gratitude, like a beautiful tapestry, grows richer and more vibrant with each thread of thankfulness we weave into our lives.

DAILY REFLECTION

What are the small, everyday blessings in your life that you might be overlooking? Can you take a moment to recognize and celebrate them today?

PRAYER

Dear God, thank you for the countless gifts you have placed in our lives. Help us to see the beauty in each day and to hold onto a heart full of gratitude.

Gratitude is a gentle reminder that even the simplest moments can hold profound joy.

OVERFLOWING WITH THANKSGIVING

"Rooted and built up in him, strengthened in the faith as you were taught, and overflowing with thankfulness." **Colossians 2:7**

DEVOTIONAL

Mary had always looked forward to her retirement years, dreaming of leisurely mornings and time spent with family. Yet, as the routine settled in, she found herself reflecting more on the challenges of her past rather than the blessings of her present. One afternoon, as she sat on her porch sipping tea, she noticed the beauty of the flowers she had planted years ago—each bloom a reminder of hope and renewal. In that moment, she realized that the joys and struggles of her life had woven together a tapestry of gratitude that enriched her heart. Each day became another opportunity to cultivate thankfulness, filling her life with abundant grace, as she shared stories and laughter with her grandchildren.

In every season of life, cultivating a heart of gratitude transforms our experiences into moments of joy and connection.

DAILY REFLECTION

What are the daily blessings that bring a smile to your heart, and how can you express your gratitude for them today?

PRAYER

Dear Lord, thank You for the gift of today. Help me to notice and appreciate the little things that fill my life with joy, and let my heart overflow with gratitude.

"Gratitude is the gentle reminder that in every season of life, there is always something to cherish."

GOD'S FAITHFULNESS THROUGH GENERATIONS

"Know therefore that the Lord your God is God; he is the faithful God, keeping his covenant of love to a thousand generations of those who love him and keep his commandments." **Deuteronomy 7:9**

DEVOTIONAL

At a family reunion, a retired woman named Sarah gathered her grandchildren around her. As they shared laughter and stories, she pulled out a weathered photo album, filled with pictures of her parents, grandparents, and even great-grandparents. With each page turn, she narrated tales of challenges, joys, and unwavering faith that threaded through her family's history. As she recounted her grandmother's strength during difficult times and her mother's gentle encouragement, Sarah could see how God had woven His faithfulness through the lives of every generation.

Just as Sarah found strength and inspiration in the stories of those who came before her, we too can recognize God's enduring faithfulness that not only shapes our lives but also serves as a reminder for generations to come.

DAILY REFLECTION

What moments in your life have you seen God's faithfulness at work, and how can you pass those stories on to future generations?

PRAYER

Dear Lord, thank You for being a constant presence in our lives. Help us to recognize Your faithfulness and share it with those around us. We are grateful for Your unwavering love and guidance.

"Faithfulness is the thread that weaves together our past, present, and future."

FINDING PURPOSE BEYOND WORK

*"He has saved us and called us to a holy life—not because of anything we have done but because of his own purpose and grace. This grace was given us in Christ Jesus before the beginning of time." **2 Timothy 1:9***

DEVOTIONAL

After decades of pouring herself into her career, Margaret found herself feeling adrift in retirement. Initially, she struggled to fill her days, confused about how to find meaning outside her work. One day, while volunteering at a local food pantry, she connected with a young mother who was facing challenges she once experienced herself. As they shared stories over a cup of tea, Margaret felt a spark of purpose rekindle within her. It became clear: her life experiences could guide and uplift others, turning moments of service into a beautiful journey of giving back.

Even in retirement, you hold within you the power to inspire others and contribute joyfully to your community.

DAILY REFLECTION

What passions have you yet to explore, and how might they bring joy and purpose to this new chapter of your life?

PRAYER

Dear Lord, thank you for the gift of this season. Help me to embrace new opportunities and discover the purpose you have woven into each day.

"Your purpose can flourish even in uncharted territory."

FINDING JOY IN SIMPLICITY

"The Lord has done great things for us, and we are filled with joy."
Psalm 126:3

DEVOTIONAL

Once, in her sunny kitchen, Margaret found delight in the little things—brewing her morning tea, tending to her small garden, and inviting neighbors for simple card games. With each afternoon's golden light, she appreciated how those moments, full of laughter and connection, filled her heart with a deep, lasting happiness. Over time, she realized that joy didn't come from grand adventures but rather from the quiet moments of companionship and gratitude that often went unnoticed.

Seek out the gentle joys in everyday moments, for they are treasures that enrich our lives beyond measure.

DAILY REFLECTION

What small, everyday moments bring you joy, and how can you embrace them more fully in your daily life?

PRAYER

Dear Lord, help me to see the beauty in life's simple pleasures. Thank you for the joy that surrounds me each day, and guide me to embrace it with an open heart.

"Joy often arrives in the quiet moments when we pause to appreciate what is right in front of us."

GRACE TO END THE MONTH WELL

"Therefore, since we have been justified through faith, we have peace with God through our Lord Jesus Christ." **Romans 5:1**

DEVOTIONAL

Once upon a time, in a quiet little town, lived a retired schoolteacher named Agnes. As the month came to an end, she reflected on her journey and the many transitions she had faced —leaving her career, moving to a smaller home, and adjusting to a different rhythm of life. One morning, while sipping tea on her porch, she noticed the vibrant colors of the sunset, reminding her of the beauty in every season. In that moment, she felt a wave of peace wash over her, realizing that each ending is a gracious invitation to rest and embrace the new beginnings that lie ahead.

Let God's grace guide you into this new season, reminding you that every ending is just as important as every beginning.

DAILY REFLECTION

What has this month taught you about God's grace, and how can you carry that lesson into the days ahead? Reflect on the moments of quiet blessing and the challenges that have shaped your journey.

PRAYER

Dear God, thank you for the gift of each new day and the grace that accompanies us. As this month draws to a close, help us to find peace in Your presence and joy in every moment, regardless of the circumstances.

"Grace is not just a moment; it is the thread that weaves through the fabric of our lives."

PREPARING HIM ROOM

"Therefore, my friends, I want you to know that through Jesus the forgiveness of sins is proclaimed to you. Through him everyone who believes is set free from every sin, a justification you were not able to obtain under the law of Moses." **Acts 13:38-3**

DEVOTIONAL

In her cozy living room filled with mementos of a life well-lived, Mary often welcomed friends who needed a listening ear or a warm cup of tea. One afternoon, she noticed that her cherished musical box, which brought delightful memories, was collecting dust on the shelf. Reflecting on her years of nurturing relationships, she realized that the box needed to be opened and shared, just as her heart had always been open to those around her. With a smile, she invited her friends to hear its familiar tunes again, bringing laughter and joy back to her home. It struck her that just as she prepared her space for those beloved moments, she also needed to make room in her heart for new opportunities to share her gifts.

As we navigate retirement, it's vital to remember to create space—both in our homes and our hearts. This preparation allows us to cherish the old while inviting the new, enabling us to continue to serve and bless others in our shining seasons. Prepare your heart and home for the new joys and connections that God is placing in your life; there is always room for more love and grace.

DAILY REFLECTION

What does it mean for you to prepare room in your heart and life for God's presence during this season? Are there distractions or commitments that you can set aside to make space for Him?

PRAYER

Dear Lord, thank you for the quiet moments you offer us, especially in our later years. Help us to choose wisely what we fill our hearts and days with, making room for Your love and guidance.

"Preparing Him room often means clearing out the clutter of our hearts to let the light in."

FINDING JOY IN EVERYDAY MOMENTS

"'Consider how the wild flowers grow. They do not labor or spin. Yet I tell you, not even Solomon in all his splendor was dressed like one of these. If that is how God clothes the grass of the field, which is here today, and tomorrow is thrown into the fire, how much more will he clothe you—you of little faith!'" **Luke 12:27-28**

DEVOTIONAL

One sunny afternoon, Margaret sat on her porch, sipping tea and watching her grandchildren play in the yard. As laughter filled the air, she was reminded of the simple beauty of the moment. The sight of daisies swaying in the breeze drew her attention, and she found herself smiling at how vibrant life could be, even in the smallest details. It dawned on her that joy wasn't reserved for grand occasions; it flourished in everyday moments shared with loved ones.

In the ordinary moments of your day, there's an extraordinary opportunity to embrace joy and gratitude.

DAILY REFLECTION

What small, everyday moment brought a smile to your face today, and how can you cultivate more of these joyful instances in your life?

PRAYER

Dear Lord, thank you for the simple blessings You place in our lives. Help me to open my eyes and heart to recognize and appreciate the joy in each moment today.

Joy often whispers in the quiet corners of our day, inviting us to pause and savor the beauty of the ordinary.

SERVING WITHOUT THE SPOTLIGHT

"She opens her arms to the poor and extends her hands to the needy." **Proverbs 31:20**

DEVOTIONAL

In her years of volunteering at a local food bank, Mary found fulfillment in ensuring that families had meals each week. She never sought recognition or praise but took joy in the smiles of those she helped. Each time she handed out a bag of groceries, she felt a warmth in her heart, knowing she was doing her part in serving others without needing acknowledgment. Over time, she formed bonds with the people she met, realizing that sometimes the most profound connections happen in the shadows of humility.

In the beauty of a quiet heart that serves, we often find our greatest strength.

DAILY REFLECTION

What are some of the unnoticed ways you've served others in your life, and how can you continue to do so in this new season?

PRAYER

Dear Lord, thank you for the opportunities to serve in small and quiet ways. Help me to find joy in loving others without needing recognition, and remind me that each act of kindness is valued in Your eyes.

"True service is often found in the shadows, where love is offered without expectation."

EMMANUEL—GOD WITH US

"'The virgin will conceive and give birth to a son, and they will call him Immanuel' (which means 'God with us')." Matthew 1:23

DEVOTIONAL

In her quiet living room, Margaret often reflected on the seasons of her life. One winter evening, as snowflakes danced outside, she picked up a well-worn photo album filled with memories of family gatherings, travels, and cherished friends. Each page turned was a reminder of love and laughter, but also of times when she felt alone, especially after losing her husband a few years ago. Yet, gazing at those familiar faces, she realized that while some loved ones might not be present, the spirit of their love remained, echoing the presence of Emmanuel—God who walks with us in every chapter, both joyful and heartbreaking.

Remember, dear friend, that in every season of life, God walks beside you, illuminating your path with His eternal presence.

DAILY REFLECTION

What does it mean for you to feel God's presence in your daily life, especially during moments of solitude or reflection?

PRAYER

Dear Lord, thank you for being with us in every season of life. Help us to recognize Your presence as a comforting embrace, guiding us along our journey.

"Emmanuel—God With Us—reminds us that we are never alone, no matter the circumstances of our lives."

LETTING GOD INTERRUPT YOUR PLANS

"For even the Son of Man did not come to be served, but to serve, and to give his life as a ransom for many." Mark 10:45

DEVOTIONAL

Martha, a retired schoolteacher, had meticulously planned her retirement years. She envisioned gardening, traveling, and perhaps volunteering at the local library. One peaceful afternoon, while tending to her roses, a neighbor knocked on her door seeking help with errands and grocery shopping. Initially, Martha felt her plans being interrupted, but as she stepped into service, she found unexpected joy in connecting with her community. That simple act soon evolved into a routine, bringing new friendships and purpose that enriched her retirement in ways she had never imagined.

Sometimes, the interruptions to our carefully laid plans can lead to the most beautiful chapters in our lives.

DAILY REFLECTION

What plans have you held tightly to that you might need to release and allow God to reshape in His perfect timing?

PRAYER

Dear Lord, thank you for reminding me that you hold my future in Your hands. Help me to be open to Your interruptions and to trust in Your plan for my life.

"God's interruptions may lead us to the blessings we never knew we needed."

THE LIGHT HAS COME

"The people walking in darkness have seen a great light; on those living in the land of deep darkness a light has dawned." **Isaiah 9:2**

DEVOTIONAL

As she settled into her favorite armchair with a cup of chamomile tea, Ruth reflected on her life's journey. There were moments that felt heavy with uncertainty and times when darkness seemed to overshadow even the brightest days. Yet, just like the dawn that breaks the night, hope would often arrive unexpectedly—through a phone call from an old friend, a kind word from a grandchild, or a moment of clarity during prayer. Each experience became a gentle reminder that the light of God's love was always nearby, leading her out of the shadows and into a warmth that filled her heart with peace.

In every season of life, remember that God's light shines through even the smallest acts of kindness and love.

DAILY REFLECTION

What areas of your life do you feel the warmth of God's light shining most brightly, and where do you wish to invite more of that light?

PRAYER

Dear God, thank you for the gift of your light that guides us each day. Help us to recognize and embrace it, bringing warmth and joy to our hearts. Amen.

"Even in our golden years, the light of God's love can illuminate paths we've yet to explore."

LIVING LIGHTLY AND LETTING GO

"Let your eyes look straight ahead; fix your gaze directly before you. Give careful thought to the paths for your feet and be steadfast in all your ways. Do not turn to the right or the left; keep your foot from evil. **Proverbs 4:25-27**

DEVOTIONAL

Martha had spent 40 years gathering trinkets, heirlooms, and mementos, believing they held the stories of her life. As she prepared for a downsizing move, she felt overwhelmed by the weight of her possessions. One rainy afternoon, as she sifted through boxes, she picked up a delicate porcelain figurine. It had once been her mother's, but it brought her more stress than joy. With a deep breath, she decided to donate it to a local charity shop. That act of letting go not only lightened her load but also opened her heart to new memories and experiences that awaited her.

Sometimes, letting go of the past can be the key to embracing the future with joy and peace.

DAILY REFLECTION

What are the things you hold onto that no longer serve you, and how might your life change if you let them go?

PRAYER

Dear Lord, help me to embrace the beauty of simplicity in this season of my life. Grant me the wisdom to release what I no longer need and to fill my heart with joy and gratitude.

"Letting go is not losing; it is making room for new blessings to enter."

A SEASON OF SURRENDER

*"Remain in me, as I also remain in you. No branch can bear fruit by itself; it must remain in the vine. Neither can you bear fruit unless you remain in me." **John 15:4***

DEVOTIONAL

As she settled into her favorite armchair with a warm cup of tea, Ruth reflected on this new season of her life. After years of caring for her family and working tirelessly at her job, retirement had brought unexpected quietness. At first, she struggled to find purpose, feeling adrift without the structure of a busy schedule. Yet, in this stillness, she discovered the beauty of surrendering to God's love and direction. She began volunteering at her local community center, nurturing both her spirit and those around her, realizing that her worth was not in how much she did but in how deeply she was connected to the source of true life.

Sometimes, it is in the moments of solitude and surrender that we can best hear the gentle whispers of God guiding our path. Embrace this season of surrender, trusting that even in stillness, you are being woven into a beautiful tapestry of purpose and connection.

DAILY REFLECTION

What does it mean for you to surrender control over the things that weigh heavily on your heart, and how can letting go bring you peace and freedom?

PRAYER

Dear Lord, as I embrace this season of surrender, help me to trust in Your perfect plan for my life. May I find comfort in Your presence and strength in letting go of my worries.

"Surrendering is not giving up; it's giving in to a greater love and purpose."

WELCOMING WONDER

*"And he said: 'Truly I tell you, unless you change and become like little children, you will never enter the kingdom of heaven.'" **Matthew 18:3***

DEVOTIONAL

In her garden, Ellen found herself surrounded by blooms that had burst forth with delightful surprises. Each morning, she would wander through the pathways, marveling at how her once-tamed flowers had twisted and turned in wild directions, creating a tapestry of color to inspire her heart. One morning, she noticed butterflies dancing among the petals and realized she had almost forgotten the simple joy that nature brings. The vibrant colors and gentle sounds awakened an excitement within her that she thought had faded with her youth, reminding her that wonder still existed in the ordinary.

Sometimes, embracing the simple beauty around us can rekindle the wonder we thought had slipped away, inviting joy into our everyday lives.

DAILY REFLECTION

What small wonders have you noticed in your daily life recently, and how can you create space to appreciate them more fully?

PRAYER

Dear God, thank you for the beauty and wonder that surrounds us each day. Open our hearts to recognize and celebrate the small joys in life.

"Each moment is an invitation to see the extraordinary in the ordinary."

FRIENDSHIP IN LATER YEARS

"A friend loves at all times, and a brother is born for a time of adversity."
Proverbs 17:17

DEVOTIONAL

Just the other day, Mary, a 65-year-old retiree, met with her longtime friend, June, for coffee. They had shared countless laughs and tears over the decades, but as they sipped their warm drinks, they spoke of new dreams, fears of loneliness, and the joy in finding new friendships in their retirement community. Both women realized that while their lives had changed, their bond had only grown stronger. Reflecting on how they had weathered life's storms together, they couldn't help but smile, understanding that true friendship remains a cherished gift, no matter the season of life.

In later years, it's never too late to nurture and celebrate the friendships that uplift our spirits and warm our hearts.

DAILY REFLECTION

What new friendships could you nurture in this season of your life, and how might they enrich your experience? Consider what qualities you most appreciate in others and what you can share from your own wisdom.

PRAYER

Dear God, thank You for the gift of friendship in all stages of life. Help me to seek and cherish those connections that bring joy and meaning to my days.

"Friendship is not measured by the years we share, but by the moments that create lasting memories."

THE STRENGTH OF A WILLING HEART

"You, my brothers and sisters, were called to be free. But do not use your freedom to indulge the flesh; rather, serve one another humbly in love." **Galatians 5:13**

DEVOTIONAL

Mabel had always been known for her kind heart. After retiring, she found herself with more time on her hands than ever before. Instead of lounging in her cozy chair, she remembered how she had once loved gardening. This time, however, she decided to share her passion with her neighbors. She organized a community garden where everyone could come together to plant flowers and vegetables. Through her willingness to invest her time and energy into others, not only did the garden bloom, but so did friendships she had long hoped to nurture.

The strength of a willing heart can turn a simple idea into a blossoming community, proving that you can still make a profound impact even in your golden years.

DAILY REFLECTION

What does it mean for you to have a willing heart in this season of your life, and how can you nurture that willingness each day?

PRAYER

Dear Lord, thank You for the gift of this new chapter in life. Open my heart to willingness and strength as I seek to serve and love those around me.

"A willing heart can transform a day, a relationship, and a community."

HEAVEN'S PERSPECTIVE

"For here we do not have an enduring city, but we are looking for the city that is to come."
Hebrews 13:14

DEVOTIONAL

In her small flower garden, Margaret spent countless afternoons tending to her vibrant blooms. One day, as she pruned the wilting petals, she spotted a honeybee busily moving from flower to flower, seemingly unfazed by the chaotic world beyond the garden gate. Margaret realized that just as the bee focused on its task within the beauty surrounding it, she too could cultivate joy and purpose in her retirement. Each moment invested in the garden brought her closer to the beauty of God's creation, reinforcing her understanding that this life is just a glimpse of the everlasting joys awaiting her.

Life is fleeting, so take the time to find beauty in each day, knowing that your true home awaits in Heaven.

DAILY REFLECTION

What does it mean to you to see your life and its changes through Heaven's perspective? How might this shift in view impact your daily thoughts and interactions with others?

PRAYER

Dear God, thank You for the promise of Heaven and for the perspective it brings. Help me to see my life through Your eyes and to embrace each moment as a step toward my eternal home.

"Embracing Heaven's perspective transforms our trials into stepping stones toward greater joy."

FINDING JOY IN CHRIST

"I have told you this so that my joy may be in you and that your joy may be complete."
John 15:11

DEVOTIONAL

As we age, life often presents us with a slower pace and quieter moments. Mary, a retired schoolteacher, found herself feeling a bit aimless after leaving her classroom. One day, while cleaning out her attic, she stumbled across old letters from students. As she read their kind words and remembered the laughter and learning they shared, she felt a wave of joy washing over her. It was at that moment that she realized her impact on their lives didn't fade with her career; rather, it continued to bloom in the hearts of those she had taught. That day, Mary understood that joy is not just found in moments of great excitement but in the simple, heartfelt connections we cherish.

Embrace the joy that comes from reflecting on the blessings you've shared through the years, for they are treasures that can brighten your spirit.

DAILY REFLECTION

What brings you true joy in your daily life, and how can you seek a deeper connection with Christ to enhance that joy?

PRAYER

Dear Lord, thank You for the gift of each day and the endless opportunities to find joy in Your presence. As I navigate this season of my life, help me to recognize the beauty in the simple moments spent with You.

"Joy is not found in the circumstances of life, but in the steadfast love of Christ that embraces us through every season."

HOLDING SPACE FOR SILENCE

"The Lord will fight for you; you need only to be still."
Exodus 14:14

DEVOTIONAL

Marjorie had spent years caring for her family, nurturing friendships, and volunteering in her community. With each passing day of her retirement, she found herself surrounded by a quieter house and a slower pace of life. One morning, she decided to sit in her favorite sunlit corner with a steaming cup of tea, allowing herself to embrace the silence. As she listened to the whispers of the breeze outside and the gentle ticking of the clock, she felt a profound sense of peace wash over her. In that stillness, she realized that her heart was not just resting; it was also listening, reconnecting her with God's gentle presence.

In our fast-paced lives, even in retirement, we often overlook the importance of pausing to truly listen—to ourselves, to God, and to the world around us. Taking time to hold space for silence allows us to find clarity and reconnect with our true selves.

DAILY REFLECTION

What does silence mean to you in this season of your life, and how can you create more space for it each day?

PRAYER

Dear God, thank you for the gift of quiet moments that allow us to connect with You and ourselves. Help us to embrace the stillness and find peace in the silence that surrounds us.

"Silence is not the absence of sound, but the presence of peace."

REDISCOVERING PASSIONS

"Walk in obedience to all that the Lord your God has commanded you, so that you may live and prosper and prolong your days in the land that you will possess."
Deuteronomy 5:33

DEVOTIONAL

Ella, a 65-year-old retiree, had always dreamed of traveling the world. Yet, after leaving her job, she was hesitant to embark on new adventures, feeling that her age might hold her back. One day, while organizing her old photo albums, she stumbled upon pictures from her trip to Europe in her youth. The memories ignited a spark within her, reminding her that life is still full of possibilities. With a newfound determination, she began planning a solo journey to explore the beautiful sights she had always wished to see, embracing this chapter of self-discovery and joy.

Life, much like travel, is about the journeys we take—never too late to discover new paths or fulfill long-held dreams.

DAILY REFLECTION

What dreams and passions have remained unfulfilled in your life, and how can you take small steps to nurture them now?

PRAYER

Dear Lord, thank you for the rich tapestry of life you have woven for me. Help me to embrace this season with open arms, nurturing my dreams and passions as I trust in Your perfect timing.

"Every new season brings the chance to bloom in unexpected ways."

Near the End of Our Journey

You have spent many days reflecting through these devotionals.

If this book has supported your spiritual journey, sharing a short review on Amazon helps more women discover these pages of encouragement.

devo.anchoredgraces.com/retired

Your story may be the reason another woman finds hope.

CULTIVATING COMMUNITY

"Therefore, as God's chosen people, holy and dearly loved, clothe yourselves with compassion, kindness, humility, gentleness and patience." **Colossians 3:12**

DEVOTIONAL

Jean had always been the organized one in her family. Even in retirement, she found joy in coordinating gatherings and checking in on friends. One day, while visiting a local community center, she noticed a lonely woman sitting by herself. Feeling a nudge in her heart, Jean initiated a conversation that blossomed into a beautiful friendship. What started as a simple act of kindness turned into a weekly coffee date, and soon the once-lonely woman was laughing and sharing stories with Jean and her network of friends. This experience reminded Jean of the profound impact one person can have on another's life.

Embrace the opportunity to spread compassion and kindness, knowing that your actions can brighten someone's day.

DAILY REFLECTION

What are the unique treasures of wisdom and experience that you can share with those around you? How can embracing this season of life help you to touch the hearts of others?

PRAYER

Dear Lord, thank You for the rich tapestry of experiences You have woven into my life. Help me to recognize and share my wisdom with those around me, bringing joy and guidance to their journeys.

"With every wrinkle, a story; with every story, a gift."

THE HEART OF GENEROSITY

"Dear children, let us not love with words or speech but with actions and in truth."
1 John 3:18

DEVOTIONAL

Eleanor, a retired schoolteacher, found herself drawn to a local community center where she volunteered. Each week, she witnessed the joy in a young girl's face when Eleanor helped her read better. One day, as they sat together, the girl confided that her family was struggling and often skipped meals. With her heart stirred, Eleanor reached out to her church community and organized a food drive, rallying friends to fill baskets with love and nourishment. Watching the girl's eyes shine with gratitude reminded Eleanor that her time and compassion could nourish not just bodies but souls.

In this season of life, your heart of generosity can create ripples of joy and hope, showing that love in action is the most powerful gift we can share.

DAILY REFLECTION

What does generosity mean to you in this season of your life, and how can you embrace it in ways that bring joy to yourself and others?

PRAYER

Dear Lord, thank You for the gift of this new season filled with opportunities to give and share. Help me to open my heart wider and find joy in acts of kindness, no matter how small.

"Generosity is not just what we give but the love we share through each act."

THE GIFT OF TIME

"Teach us to number our days, that we may gain a heart of wisdom."
Psalm 90:12

DEVOTIONAL

In her cozy sunlit kitchen, Margaret found herself sifting through old photo albums, each picture a portal to cherished memories. She paused at a snapshot of her family gathered for a holiday feast, laughter and love radiating from their faces. In that moment, she realized how much those times meant, not only to her but to each of her loved ones. They were the gifts of time, the invisible threads weaving her family closer together. With a warm cup of tea in hand, she decided then and there to make new memories, embracing spontaneity and connection in the golden years ahead.

Every day is an opportunity to create moments that matter; cherish them and let love guide your time.

DAILY REFLECTION

What does the gift of time mean to you in this season of your life? How can you cherish these moments, and in what ways might you share your time with others?

PRAYER

Dear Lord, thank you for the precious gift of time and the opportunities it brings. Help me to embrace each moment and share my days with joy and purpose.

"Time is not measured by the ticking of a clock,
but by the warmth of relationships and the beauty of moments shared."

RESTING IN HIS GOODNESS

"Surely your goodness and love will follow me all the days of my life, and I will dwell in the house of the Lord forever." Psalm 23:6

DEVOTIONAL

Once, a retired woman named Martha sat on her porch, sipping tea as she watched the sun set over her garden. The soft whisper of the breeze carried memories of years spent raising her children and serving her community. Each petal in bloom reminded her of God's goodness that had accompanied her through every season of life. As she reflected on the past, she felt a profound sense of peace, realizing that even during difficult times, God had been weaving beauty into her story. With a heart full of gratitude, Martha embraced the quiet moments, knowing that His goodness would always be with her.

Remember, dear friend, that resting in the goodness of God allows us to see the beauty in every chapter of our lives.

DAILY REFLECTION

What does resting in God's goodness look like in your daily life, and how can you find moments to embrace His peace amidst your routine?

PRAYER

Dear Lord, thank you for your unwavering goodness and the peace that comes from resting in You. Help me to trust in Your loving presence and find joy in the simplicity of each day.

"Rest is not a reward for your work, but a gift from God,
allowing you to savor His goodness in every moment."

HE CAME FOR YOU

*"For God so loved the world that he gave his one and only Son, that whoever believes in him shall not perish but have eternal life." **John 3:16***

DEVOTIONAL

As a retired woman, perhaps you've experienced the solitude of quiet mornings, each cup of tea echoing the sound of your heart. One day, while tending to your garden, you noticed a small flower breaking through the soil, unassuming yet perfectly crafted. It reminded you that just as the flower emerges destined to bloom, you too were chosen for a purpose and a life designed by the Creator. In this season of your life, it's essential to remember that His love is ever-constant, and He came for you with grace that knows no bounds.

In the tapestry of your golden years, remember that you are cherished and called by His name, for He came for you, just as you are.

DAILY REFLECTION

What does it mean for you personally that Christ came into the world just for you, and how can that truth shape your daily life and interactions with others?

PRAYER

Dear Lord, thank You for coming into our lives with love and purpose. Help us to fully embrace the truth that You came for each of us and guide us to share that love with those around us.

"You are not forgotten; He came for you, personally, to fill your heart with His unending grace."

AWE AND ADORATION

*"Through the victories you gave, his glory is great; you have bestowed on him splendor and majesty." **Psalm 21:5***

DEVOTIONAL

A dear friend once shared how her morning coffee ritual turned into a sacred moment of awe. She would sit by her window, watching the sun rise, painting the sky with colors more brilliant than a canvas could capture. With each sip, she felt the warmth not just from her cup, but also from the presence of the Creator who designed such beauty. These quiet moments became a cherished time of adoration, where the simplicity of life stirred her heart to praise.

In life's later seasons, it's vital to find moments that inspire awe, inviting us into deeper adoration for the beauty that surrounds us.

DAILY REFLECTION

What moments in your life have filled you with awe, drawing you closer to the heart of God? Can you recall a time when you felt profound gratitude for His creation, love, or grace?

PRAYER

Dear God, help me to see the beauty in the ordinary and to recognize Your hand in every moment. Fill my heart with adoration for all that You are and all that You do in my life.

"True awe ignites a spirit of gratitude, revealing the divine within the daily."

GRACE FOR THE HOLIDAYS

*"The Lord is compassionate and gracious,
slow to anger, abounding in love."* **Psalm 103:8**

DEVOTIONAL

As the holidays approach, Martha reflects on the gatherings that used to bring her great joy. After losing her husband last year, she finds herself feeling overwhelmed and isolated. One day, while decorating her home with twinkling lights, she remembers the laughter and warmth shared with family and friends. Inspired by a message at her church about extending grace to herself, she decides to host a small gathering. Just a few friends come over, and together they share stories, laughter, and a few tears. Amidst this simplicity, Martha discovers that grace is not just about the grand celebrations but in the moments of connection with others.

This holiday season, you have the opportunity to embrace grace by allowing yourself to find joy in simple moments and sharing your love with those around you.

DAILY REFLECTION

What does grace mean to you in this season of joy and celebration, and how can you extend that grace to yourself and others during the holidays?

PRAYER

Dear God, thank You for the precious gift of grace that fills our hearts during this holiday season. Help us to embrace this grace in our lives and share it with those around us, fostering love and warmth in every encounter.

"Grace transforms our hearts, allowing us to find joy
in each moment and peace in every challenge."

WRAPPED IN HIS LOVE

"This is how God showed his love among us: He sent his one and only Son into the world that we might live through him. This is love: not that we loved God, but that he loved us and sent his Son as an atoning sacrifice for our sins." **1 John 4:9-10**

DEVOTIONAL

Not long ago, I sat with a dear friend at her kitchen table, sipping tea as the afternoon sun streamed through the window. She shared stories from her past, memories of laughter, heartache, and the sweet love of family. As she spoke, there was a glimmer in her eyes—a testament to the love she had received and given throughout her life. In that moment, I realized that just as she cherished those memories, God cherishes us in a deeper, more profound way. Wrapped in His love, we carry the essence of our experiences, woven together like a beautiful tapestry of grace and gratitude.

In this season of life, remember that your past, with all its beautiful and challenging moments, is held tenderly by the Lord, reminding you that you are forever wrapped in His love.

DAILY REFLECTION

What does it mean for you to feel wrapped in the love of God in this season of your life? How can you identify moments when His love has surrounded you?

PRAYER

Dear God, thank you for the comforting embrace of Your love. Help me to recognize and appreciate the ways You surround me each day with Your presence and care.

"Even in the quiet moments, His love wraps around you like a warm blanket."

A HOLY NIGHT

"On my bed I remember you; I think of you through the watches of the night. Because you are my help, I sing in the shadow of your wings." **Psalm 63:6-7**

DEVOTIONAL

As she settled into her favorite chair one chilly evening, Martha pulled a warm blanket around her shoulders and gazed out at the twinkling stars. The glow of the Christmas lights on her tree filled the room with a soft warmth, reminding her of the holy nights of her youth spent singing carols with her family. Through the years, she had seen many seasons come and go, but each December still brought back a flood of cherished memories. That night, reflecting on her life's journey, Martha felt enveloped in peace, knowing that every prayer spoken and every whispered hope had contributed to the unfolding story of her life. The gentle stillness of her home reminded her that these holy nights were not just about remembering the past, but also about embracing the present, bathed in the comforting light of faith.

Trusting in God's timing not only nurtures our patience but reveals the beauty of His perfect plans for our lives.

DAILY REFLECTION

What does the concept of a "holy night" mean to you in this season of your life, and how can you create moments of peace and joy amidst the everyday?

PRAYER

Dear God, thank you for the quiet moments you bring into our lives. Help us to embrace the holiness found in stillness and to see your light shining brightly in the night.

"In every stillness, God whispers."

JOY TO THE WORLD

"and those the Lord has rescued will return. They will enter Zion with singing; everlasting joy will crown their heads. Gladness and joy will overtake them, and sorrow and sighing will flee away." **Isaiah 35:10**

DEVOTIONAL

In her cozy living room, Margaret sat sipping her herbal tea, reminiscing about the joy-filled Christmases of her youth. The laughter of children, the warmth of family gathered around, and the twinkling lights that danced in the night filled her heart with gratitude. Now, with her children grown and moved away, she sometimes felt the weight of solitude. But one day, as she decorated her tree, she decided to invite neighbors over for a simple holiday gathering. That evening, her home overflowed with laughter and companionship, creating new memories and reminding her that joy can be shared no matter the season of life.

There is always an opportunity to find and share joy, even in the simplest moments of our lives.

DAILY REFLECTION

What brings you the deepest joy in your life today, and how can you share that joy with those around you?

PRAYER

Dear Lord, thank you for the abundant joy You bring into our lives. Help us to recognize and share that joy with others, becoming instruments of Your love and light in the world.

"Joy is a gift meant to be shared, illuminating the path for others as we walk in faith."

PEACE IN THE UNKNOWNS OF AGING

"Your beginnings will seem humble, so prosperous will your future be."
Job 8:7

DEVOTIONAL

Mary always dreamt of traveling the world, but life's responsibilities and raising her children kept her dreams on hold. Now, retired and with her heart still yearning for adventure, she decided to begin exploring her city's hidden gems first. Each week, she discovered a new cafe, park, or historical site, soaking in the beauty around her. Her explorations not only provided joy but also rekindled her passion for photography, allowing her to capture moments she had once overlooked. Surrounded by vibrant images and new experiences, Mary learned that adventure often begins right in our own backyard.

It's never too late to find joy and adventure in the everyday moments of life.

DAILY REFLECTION

What dreams or passions have you set aside, and how can you gently revisit them in this season of your life?

PRAYER

Dear Lord, thank You for this season of rest and renewal. Open my heart to the possibilities that lie ahead and help me embrace new opportunities with courage and joy.

In the quiet moments of life, we often discover the lost treasures of our heart.

LOOKING BACK WITH GRATITUDE

"And why do you worry about clothes? See how the flowers of the field grow. They do not labor or spin. Yet I tell you that not even Solomon in all his splendor was dressed like one of these. If that is how God clothes the grass of the field, which is here today and tomorrow is thrown into the fire, will he not much more clothe you—you of little faith?" **Matthew 6:28-30**

DEVOTIONAL

As Maria sits in her favorite chair, a gentle breeze flows through the open window, bringing with it the scent of blooming flowers from her garden. As she reflects on her life, memories flood her mind—moments of joy, challenges, triumphs, and the cherished faces of family and friends who have journeyed alongside her. She recalls the laughter of her children's childhood, her vibrant career, and the adventures taken with her late husband. Each memory feels like a precious jewel in her heart, as she realizes how each piece has shaped her into the woman she is today. Gratitude fills her spirit as she recognizes the abundance of blessings that have accompanied her through the years.

Life offers a tapestry of experiences; when we take the time to look back with gratitude, we discover the richness of our journey and the strength we have gained along the way.

DAILY REFLECTION

What are the moments from your past that fill your heart with gratitude, and how have they shaped the person you are today?

PRAYER

Dear God, thank you for the beautiful tapestry of life you've woven throughout the years. Help me to remember your blessings and to cherish each precious memory with a heart full of gratitude.

"Gratitude is the memory of the heart, capturing the beauty of our experiences."

PREPARING FOR THE NEW

"And no one pours new wine into old wineskins. Otherwise, the new wine will burst the skins; the wine will run out and the wineskins will be ruined. No, new wine must be poured into new wineskins." **Luke 5:37-38**

DEVOTIONAL

In her small garden, Elsie discovered a patch of soil that had lain dormant for years. After many seasons of nurturing, she decided it was time to clear out the weeds and debris. As she worked, she unearthed forgotten treasures—bulbs that had long been hidden and new seedlings sprouting forth. With her hands in the earth, she realized that just as her garden required attention and a willingness to embrace new growth, her heart and mind needed the same care. Each season brought not just change, but new beauty ready to flourish.

Embracing the new chapters in life can start as simply as tending to what has been left behind, unveiling fresh opportunities and experiences that await you.

DAILY REFLECTION

What new adventures or opportunities are you feeling called to explore in this season of your life?

PRAYER

Dear God, thank you for the gift of this new chapter in my life. Help me to embrace the changes ahead with courage and grace, trusting in Your guiding hand.

"Embrace the beauty of new beginnings, for they are gifts wrapped in the love of God."

GRATITUDE FOR THE LONG VIEW

"Love is patient, love is kind. It does not envy, it does not boast, it is not proud. It does not dishonor others, it is not self-seeking, it is not easily angered, it keeps no record of wrongs. Love does not delight in evil but rejoices with the truth. It always protects, always trusts, always hopes, always perseveres." **Corinthians 13:4-7**

DEVOTIONAL

There was a retired teacher named Helen who had spent decades nurturing young minds. As her students grew and flourished, she often sought to understand how her lessons shaped their lives. One sunny afternoon, she received an unexpected letter from a former student who had just graduated college and credited Helen's encouragement for pursuing a degree in education. Reading those heartfelt words, Helen felt a wave of gratitude wash over her. In that moment, she recognized how her long career, filled with challenges and triumphs, had created ripples of influence that she could only see now in the fullness of time.

Every moment spent nurturing others is an investment in a legacy that may unfold in beautiful ways long after you've stepped back.

DAILY REFLECTION

What are some moments in your life that, upon reflection, bring you a sense of gratitude despite any challenges you faced during those times? How have these experiences shaped your outlook today?

PRAYER

Dear God, thank you for the tapestry of life you have woven for us. Help us to see the beauty in each thread and to appreciate the long view of your faithfulness throughout our years.

"Every season of life has its gifts; may we learn to cherish each one."

GOD'S FAITHFULNESS NEVER ENDS

*Let us hold unswervingly to the hope we profess, for he who promised is faithful." **Hebrews 10:23***

DEVOTIONAL

Margaret had spent decades caring for her family, working hard, and serving her church. Now, in retirement, she sometimes wondered what her purpose was in this new season. One afternoon, as she sat on her porch watching the sun set, she remembered all the times God had provided—through health scares, family changes, and uncertain finances. Each memory was a gentle reminder that God's faithfulness had carried her through every chapter. Even now, as her days slowed, she felt His steady presence, guiding her with the same love and assurance as always.

No matter our age or stage, God's faithfulness continues to unfold in our lives, giving us hope and purpose each day.

DAILY REFLECTION

When you look back over the years, where have you seen God's faithfulness in your life, even in unexpected ways?

PRAYER

Lord, thank You for walking with me through every season. Help me to trust Your faithfulness today and always, knowing You never let me go.

God's faithfulness is the gentle thread weaving hope through every chapter of my story.

More Devotionals from Anchored Grace

If this devotional encouraged your heart, you may also enjoy these devotionals from Anchored Grace.

- 365 Day Devotional for Women
- 90 Day Devotional for Women Seeking Peace
- 90 Day Devotional for Women Facing Anxiety and Stress
- 90 Day Devotional for Women 50+
- Guided Prayer Journal for Women

Search **"Anchored Grace Devotional"** on Amazon to discover more devotionals designed to support your journey of faith.

Thank You
for Walking This Journey

Thank you for spending this devotional journey with Anchored Grace.

If this devotional encouraged your heart, strengthened your faith, or brought peace to your daily routine, would you consider leaving a short review on Amazon?

devo.anchoredgraces.com/retired

Reviews help other women discover devotionals that may support them through their own seasons of life.

Even a single sentence about your experience can make a difference.

We are grateful you chose Anchored Grace.